HERO

Rugby League's Greatest Award Winners

Graham Morris

VERTICAL EDITIONS

First published in the United Kingdom in 2005 by Vertical Editions, 7 Bell Busk, Skipton, North Yorkshire BD23 4DT

ISBN 1-904091-13-X

Cover design and typeset by HBA, York

Printed and bound by Cromwell Press, Trowbridge

CONTENTS

Front Cover Pictures, Background: Henry Paul – winner of the Lance Todd and Harry Sunderland Trophies – makes a determined attack for Bradford Bulls against Wigan Warriors in the 2001 Super League play-offs. Bottom left to right: Andrew Farrell of Wigan Warriors holding the coveted Man of Steel Award; Sean Long of St Helens celebrating Lance Todd Trophy success; Matt Diskin of Leeds Rhinos with the Harry Sunderland Trophy.

ACKNOWLEDGEMENTS

As usual, I have relied on the very generous help that exists amongst people who are either involved in Rugby League or support it. Firstly, I would like to offer my sincere gratitude to the following individuals who provided information and/or photographs: Ron Bailey, Tracy Barr, Nobby Clarke, Tony Collins, Jonathan Davies, Steve Donlan, John Edwards, Ray Fletcher, Mike Flynn, Ray French, Barbara Frost, Robert Gate, Graham Gerrard, Dave Hadfield, Derek Hallas, Andrew Hardcastle, Jim Hardicre, Phil Hodgson, Andrew Howard, Diane Howard, David Howes, Christine James, John Jenkins, Terry Jones, Sig Kasatkin, Michael Latham, John Lindley, Peter Lush, Keith Nutter, Ian Proctor, John Riding, Alex Service, Andrew Varley, Karl Waddicor, Dave Williams, Terry Williams and Dave Woods.

I would like to especially thank Mike Berry of MBA Broadcast Solutions for allowing me to access filmed interviews his company have conducted with many of the players who have won the Lance Todd Trophy. My appreciation also to the following organisations who provided (or gave permission to use) photographs: Bradford Bulls RLFC (thanks, in particular, to Stuart Duffy), Halifax Evening Courier, Lancashire Publications Ltd, Manchester Evening News and Yorkshire Post.

During the course of my research, I referred to the following Rugby League newspapers, periodicals and books: Open Rugby, Rugby League World, Rugby Leaguer, Rugby League Express, 100 Greats - Featherstone Rovers RLFC (Ron Bailey, 2002), 100 Great Rugby League Players (Ray French, 1989), Challenge for the Championship (John Lindley, 1968), The Encyclopaedia of Rugby League Players (Alan Whiticker and Glen Hudson, 1999), The Forbidden Game (Mike Rylance, 1999), The Kangaroos (Ian Heads, 1990), League Publications Limited Yearbooks, 1996 to 2004/05, Rothmans Rugby League Yearbooks, 1981/82 to 1999 (Ray Fletcher & David Howes), Rugby League Hall of Fame (Robert Gate, 2003) and the Rugby League Record Keepers' Club publications (Irvin Saxton). In addition, there are several other publications that receive due acknowledgement in the main body of the text, where appropriate.

My heartfelt thanks to many of the players (too numerous to list here) featured in this compilation, who so willingly provided information and details about themselves where required.

Lastly, although certainly not least, a big thank you to former Great Britain hooker Mike Stephenson of Sky Television fame – who also features in the pages that follow – for so readily and enthusiastically agreeing to provide the foreword.

Graham Morris
September 2005

FOREWORD

I, like many others, call Rugby League the 'Greatest Game of All', and who could argue when you witness the skills, passion, strength and athleticism that's displayed by the players of today.

Full time professionalism has lifted the fitness levels to bursting point and the excitement they offer for the fans is nothing short of superb but, those players from a past era also showed commitment, skills and toughness to thrill the crowds.

Rugby League first and foremost is a team game, a combination of differing styles, the rugged forwards and the silky skills of the three-quarter, the kicking game, and of course the crushing defence all rolled up into one unit, and when it all comes together it is a joy to watch. Yet sometimes it needs a touch of brilliance to get the well oiled machine working to its full potential, a man of vision, a player who can produce that touch of magic that breaks the will of the opposition. On the other side of the coin is the player who leads by example and puts his body on the line for the full eighty minutes and runs his blood to water. Either way it is this man we can claim to be the true hero of the day, the shining light that took himself and his team over the threshold of success. There are times of course when that hero of the hour falls short of basking in the glory of victory, where even his immense impact on the game is not enough to snare the trophy but, such was his effort on the field of play, he stood head and shoulders above them all, no lap of honour perhaps but, a feeling of pride and satisfaction he'd given his all.

It is times like this that make our game so great and I'm proud to think we still recognise such bravery and skills with Man of the Match or Man of the Season awards.

My mind goes back to when I was just a kid being dragged along by my dad to Wembley for the first time in 1960 to see Wakefield take on Hull in the Challenge Cup Final and that game changed my life. Despite Hull losing heavily to Trinity that day, I witnessed an almighty effort from the Hull hooker Tommy Harris, who ran and tackled like a demon, so much so it was no surprise he was carried off late in the game. It was nothing short of heroic and he fully deserved to win the Lance Todd Trophy but, it was his ability in the loose that impressed me for he was everywhere. I can remember telling my father as we walked away from the twin towers that one day I would play like Mr Harris and I have no shame to say I styled my entire playing career on the number nine from the Boulevard.

The true test of a League players character is when they enter the fray at Cup Final, Championship, Grand Final or International level, where the pressure is immense and, there is always a place for the man who throughout the entire season has produced the qualities needed to be classed as the best in the game that year, a player who week in and out stands tall and proud, truly a Man of Steel.

I hope you enjoy this tribute to those who have experienced winning such awards, and I feel proud to be included within these pages but I'm sure I can say on behalf of all the award winners that we couldn't have won anything without the help of our team mates.

Mike 'Stevo' Stephenson.
September 2005

INTRODUCTION

Rugby League is one of the toughest contact sports in the world, its protagonists requiring courage and the ability to co-ordinate their own skills and strengths with that of colleagues to the highest degree possible if their team is to prosper. It is a game where co-operation and good teamwork is paramount, success at the top level rarely occurring without the pre-match game-plan being strictly adhered to throughout the eighty minutes of play. As with most team sports, no individual player can single-handedly bring success to the club he plays for, although, it has to be acknowledged, that some stars shine brighter than others, commanding higher contracts and being acclaimed as potential 'match winners.'

Rugby League was probably Britain's first team sport to officially acknowledge the role of the individual in a team's performance. The awarding of the Lance Todd Trophy to the outstanding player in the Rugby League Challenge Cup Final saw the light of day way back in 1946, the first recipient being Wakefield Trinity captain Billy Stott. For years, it stood alone as the top individual honour in Rugby League until followed in 1965 by the instigation of the Harry Sunderland Trophy, given to the top man in the Championship Final, a contest that has evolved into today's emotional and atmospheric Super League Grand Final. It is a curious twist of fate that British Rugby League's premier 'Man of the Match' awards are dedicated to a New Zealander (Todd) and an Australian (Sunderland), although it has to be admitted the continuing development of the 13-a-side code in Britain for over a century is indebted to many players, coaches and officials originating from the Antipodes.

The plain fact is that both trophies were initiated primarily as a memorial to the two Australasian's they are named after rather than to glorify the prowess of the recipient. Over the years that emphasis has reversed and today the proud beneficiary is, rightly, feted by the media, whilst for many the names of Todd and Sunderland have become part of the mystique surrounding the two finals in which the awards are given. Indeed, very few people involved in the sport fully appreciate the influence that the two forward-thinking men exerted during their lifetimes.

In the age of the so-called celebrity, the role of the individual is now widely acknowledged at just about every team event that takes place, be it Rugby League, Rugby Union, Association Football or cricket with player awards for outstanding performances providing an ideal vehicle for sponsorship. In modern Rugby League, we have the media (television and press) and a myriad of businesses eager to promote their product through various awards, continuing a trend that picked up momentum during the 1970s. We see accolades for player of the month, top try scorer, top goal scorer - the list is almost endless.

Amongst the most popular events on the sporting calendar are the annual awards evenings, normally held at the end of a season. Soccer has long had the Footballer of the Year Award, first presented by the Football Writers' Association to the legendary Stanley Matthews in 1948. It is an occasion that has grown in stature, year on year, and has been replicated by many sports around the world since. In Rugby League, the stand-out annual ceremony is undoubtedly the Man of Steel Awards evening, which began in 1977. Unlike the Todd and Sunderland awards, the Man of Steel was created with unashamedly commercial motives, but for all the right reasons. It was introduced during a period of minor revolution by the, then, Rugby League hierarchy, who were anxious to lift the dwindling image of a sport that had been on a downward slide for over a decade. The Man of Steel ceremony, a glittering star-studded evening with attendees in dinner jackets and evening gowns, was an instant hit, quickly achieving its objective of gaining increased media coverage which in turn, raised the sports profile.

I believe that the Man of Steel Award, Lance Todd Trophy and Harry Sunderland Trophy have evolved into the three major individual awards in British Rugby League and I have attempted, in this compilation, to pay due homage to those who have won them. Some of the greatest players of the last sixty years have received one or the other – in some cases all three – whilst we also see less familiar names on the roll of honour, particularly for the latter two, as a previously unheralded performer emerges to play the game of his life in possibly the biggest match of his life. Whereas the Man of Steel Award will, by definition, put the icing on the season's cake for the worthy winner, the emotions connected to the Todd and Sunderland prize are less predictable.

On, thankfully few occasions, the Man of the Match announcement has raised a few eyebrows, usually a consequence of the press being required to deliver their verdict 10 minutes before the match ends rather than after its conclusion. Whilst I am sure there are good reasons for doing it this way, it is a situation that needs reviewing.

There have been some famous instances of the recipient being from the losing side, caring little for his achievement during the immediate aftermath of the fray. Time, as always, is a great healer and, when talking to those same players in later years, disappointment has often given way to pride at being a member of such an elite group. This perfectly illustrates the strength of the awards; a man may have lost at Wembley but the Lance Todd Trophy still earns pride of place in his trophy cabinet!

In the pages that follow, I have set out to explore and explain why these honours were bestowed, be it the Man of Steel Award, Lance Todd Trophy or Harry Sunderland Trophy. Regrettably, publication deadlines make it impossible to include the 2005 Man of Steel and Harry Sunderland winners, both being determined in mid-October. Hopefully, the reader will find some of the answers they seek as they become reacquainted with current and former heroes or, possibly, be introduced for the first time to others from the more distant past.

Graham Morris
September 2005

NOTES FOR GUIDANCE

Note on statistics:

The following should be noted where match summary details are given:
Drop-goals (now commonly referred to as field-goals – influenced by the terminology of our Australian cousins - since the late 1990s) are identified separately (instead of being included as 'goals') for matches from 1975, when their value was reduced from two points to one. The value of a try was increased from three points to four from the 1983/84 season.
Substitutes (introduced in 1964) are named only if they played.
All facts and figures are believed to be correct up to September 2005.

Note on Man of Steel venues:

Due to changes in ownership, etc., several venues have been renamed and the following should be noted:
The Wakefield Theatre Club and The Wakefield Pussycat is the same club.
The Golden Garter Theatre Club and Garter Theatre Club, based in Wythenshawe, is the same club.
The Holiday Inn Crowne Plaza Midland, the Crowne Plaza Midland and the Midland Hotel (its current name), based in Manchester, is the same hotel.
The Palace Hotel (its current name) and Le Meridian Palace Hotel, based in Manchester, is the same hotel.

THE LANCE TODD TROPHY

When Billy Stott received the inaugural Lance Todd award for his performance in the first Challenge Cup Final following the Second World War, held in 1946, there were no headlines acclaiming the feat. If anything, his achievement receives more reverence today as the first name on the trophy's immortalised list of recipients. Its ponderous beginning is reflected by the fact that it did not earn formal recognition in the Wembley final programme until 1962 when a full page was devoted, including the 'Distinguished List' of past winners. Previously, there had only been the occasional mention, usually contained within the 'pen picture' of one of the day's finalists. The 1948 programme was the first to admit its existence, albeit by implication, when it told the reader that Bradford Northern stand-off Willie Davies 'was awarded a special trophy for his brilliant individual performance at Wembley last year.' It was 1954 before the name of the man in whose memory it was presented was acknowledged when we were reminded that Warrington scrum-half Gerry Helme had 'earned the Lance Todd Trophy as the outstanding player in the 1950 Final.' Over a period of time, though, the award grew in stature, gaining more and more column inches in the press (who did the voting anyway), pre-match speculation on who the winner might be and post-match interviews with the eventual claimant becoming the norm. Today, due to its elevated status, together with the sponsorship it attracts, the lavishly produced magazine-style souvenir Challenge Cup Final programme rightly gives ample commentary on the trophy and its proud list of winners.

It was instituted following Todd's untimely death in a motor accident during November 1942, being the idea of British-based Australian journalist and former Kangaroos tour manager Harry Sunderland, the pair having become firm friends during the 1930s. They had appeared on radio together nine months before Todd's demise in a joint interview of the legendary Wigan full-back Jim Sullivan. This occurred during February 1942 in the 'Giants of Sport' series compered by the celebrated Manchester-based broadcaster of that period, Victor Smythe.

Sunderland organised a meeting in Manchester during February 1943 in which it was decided to establish what became known as The Lance Todd Memorial Trophy Fund, during which '£58 was subscribed towards the nucleus of £100.' Sunderland was supported in his desire to create a memorial to Todd by Warrington director Bob Anderton (who had jointly managed Great Britain's tours Down Under in 1932 and 1936), and well-known *Yorkshire Evening Post* sports editor John Bapty (who wrote under the name of 'Little John' during the 1930s).

Lance Todd, captured by the pen of 'Mac' in 1936.

With the three men acting as co-trustees, the interest generated by the fund afforded a prize to be awarded to the Challenge Cup Final's outstanding player although, despite the title of the fund, there was no actual trophy in the beginning. In 1946, Stott received a silver plated tankard, which appears to have been pre-determined although subsequent winners were invited to select a memento; usually a clock, watch, tankard or some other silverware, the chosen item being suitably inscribed. In 1953, for example, it was recorded that Huddersfield's Peter Ramsden received a £10 voucher from the fund with which he purchased a silver rose bowl. From 1957, the Red Devils Association provided a permanent trophy plus a replica for the winner to retain, officially presented at the Association's annual reunion a few days later, although the replica has been superseded by a glass sculpture for the past few years.

The formation of the Rugby League Writers' Association in 1960 allowed the responsibility of casting the votes to fall to its members, whereas previously it was determined by whichever sports journalists were present in the press gallery. In fact, the first vote in 1946 was, reportedly, carried out by a 'committee of old internationals and journalists', seven votes being cast on that occasion compared to the 30 or so registered now. The current practice is to collect and count the votes some ten minutes before the match ends, the result usually being announced whilst the match is still in progress. In the earlier years, the votes were not counted until the match had concluded and that was certainly still the case in 1953 and, presumably, in 1954 when the winner (Warrington's Gerry Helme) received his award for his showing in the replay at Odsal Stadium, Bradford, and not for the original drawn meeting with Halifax at Wembley.

Lance Todd (seated second right) with Salford players and officials at the Imperial Hotel in London reviewing the Sunday papers the morning after the clubs 1938 Challenge Cup Final win at Wembley.

Following that replay, the Red Devils Association decided, should there be a drawn final again, the Lance Todd Trophy would be awarded for the first match. Despite that decision, there was still confusion when the 1982 final between Hull and Widnes finished all-square, the Association confirming the following day that Widnes' Eddie Cunningham would,

indeed, receive the Lance Todd Trophy after polling most votes at Wembley, effectively ratifying their 1954 decision. It was still the case, up to the 2005 final, that no extra-time be allowed if scores are level after 80 minutes play, a replay being scheduled. From the 2003 final, the presentation to the winning player has taken place on the field of play following the final, a formal presentation still being held at the Red Devils reunion.

The Red Devils Association – presenters of the Lance Todd Trophy

The Red Devils Association was created in 1953 by former Salford stars Gus Risman, Barney Hudson, Emlyn Jenkins and Billy Williams, who had all played in Lance Todd's magnificent team of the 1930s, earning their famous title after the French dubbed them 'Les Diables Rouges de Salford' whilst touring their country in 1934. Initially, the Association was open to anyone who had played for the club during Todd's regime but, in 1958, with numbers dwindling due to Anno Domini, the scope was extended to include all former players, directors and members of staff of the Salford club. At the Associations annual meeting on 12 May 1956, it was proposed by ex-Salford player Jimmy Lindley that a donation of £25 be made to purchase a permanent trophy for presentation to the winner of the Lance Todd award, plus a replica to be retained by the player. The idea was carried, and it was decided to invite the recipient to the annual reunion to receive his trophy, an event that has been a focal point of the evening – usually held mid-week following the final – ever since. The first to receive the new trophy from the Association was Leeds scrum-half Jeff Stevenson in 1957, that year's event being at the Buile Hill Park Cafe in Salford. Buile Hill continued as the main venue until 1962, after which the Ellesmere Restaurant, situated on the East Lancashire Road, was host from 1963 to 1969, the evening being concluded with music and dance back at Buile Hill. (At that time wives and partners attended the reunion which has since reverted to a male-only evening.) From 1970, the reunion has been held at the Salford club's Willows Variety Centre.

The Rugby League Challenge Cup

The famous trophy – known as the Northern Union Challenge Cup until 1922 – was first competed for in 1897, Batley defeating St Helens 10-3 in the final at Headingley, Leeds. With crowds steadily rising (41,831 squeezed into Rochdale Hornets' ground in 1924 to witness the Oldham-Wigan decider), the final transferred to Wembley in 1929. It was a bold move for the essentially northern-based sport, but one that paid dividends, raising the profile of the competition nationally to the position of now being regarded as one of the highlights of the sporting calendar. With the exception of 1932 and the war-torn years of 1940 to 1945, Wembley continued as the venue until 1999, after which the former Empire Stadium was unavailable due to its redevelopment. Whilst awaiting a return to the 'new' Wembley, planned for 2006, subsequent finals have been held at the Rugby Union strongholds of Twickenham (once), Murrayfield (twice) and Cardiff's Millennium Stadium (three times). The Lance Todd Trophy made its debut in Wembley's first final after the Second World War, in 1946, although there had been three wartime finals – staged over two legs – since the decision had been taken, in 1943, to make the award.

Graham Morris

LANCE TODD

Lance Todd.

New Zealander Lancelot Beaumont Todd was a talented player who first made his name in England as a member of Wigan's illustrious three-quarter line that included Jimmy Leytham, Bert Jenkins and Joe Miller, the quartet terrorising opposing Northern Union defences in the pre-First World War years. But it was as the innovative and forward-thinking manager of Salford's outstanding 1930s team that he is celebrated. This second phase to his Rugby League/Northern Union career came unexpectedly when, like many things in life, fate took a hand.

After his playing career, he had drifted away from the game, having taken up an appointment as secretary to the Blackpool North Shore Golf Club in 1921 on an annual salary of £250 after beating off 486 other applications. During the late 1920s he was making plans to return to New Zealand but delayed because his wife, a Wigan girl that he married in 1911, was unwell. On 21 July 1928, an advertisement for secretary-manager to the Salford club appeared in the press, stating the applicant 'must have full knowledge of (the) game and secretarial duties'. Todd, having experienced both roles in the preceding twenty years was ideally suited and took up his duties on 1 August 1928. He was an instant success, taking Salford from 26th position in the League prior to his arrival, to fourth in his first season. From then, until the outbreak of the Second World War in 1939, 'Toddy's Toddler's' as the team became known, dominated British Rugby League. Unusually for a team manager, Todd was given a testimonial match during September 1938, acknowledging ten years service to the club. However, with the commencement of the Second World War in 1939, Todd's contract with Salford was not renewed when it expired on 9 November 1940, due to the uncertain situation.

His achievements with Salford earned Todd respect throughout the game, and he became a regular contributor in newspapers where he expressed so many of his innovative ideas designed to improve the image of the game, his most famous being his belief in summer Rugby League sixty years before it finally happened! He also became a familiar voice as a pioneering radio broadcaster on the sport for the BBC.

When the Second World War started, Todd joined the Salford Home Guard where he became a captain but, tragically, he was killed in a motoring accident on 14 November 1942, when the car he was travelling in hit an electric tram standard (reportedly he was returning from watching a Rugby League match). Todd was accompanied by his commanding officer, Lieutenant Colonel PR Sewell, who also died in the accident on Manchester Road, Oldham. Todd's daughter said, in later years, they had tried to avoid a boy who lost control of his bicycle.

Todd was born in Otahuhu, Auckland in 1884. He played Rugby Union at school and was scrum-half for the Otahuhu junior club at 13.

11

He joined the Suburbs (Auckland) club when he was 17, developing into a five-eighths (stand-off/inside centre). Standing five feet seven inches and weighing ten stone, he missed almost two seasons through twice breaking his collar-bone, making a successful comeback in 1904. Capable of spotting a gap in the tightest defence, he had the pace to exploit the opening and possessed an ability to read a game, an attribute that helped him dictate play. His transference to the City (Auckland) club in 1905 was followed, the following year, by a move to Parnell, another Auckland-based club. He was on the verge of having trials for the New Zealand All Blacks but decided, instead, to join the first professional New Zealand rugby tour in 1907, when the so-called 'All Gold's' visited England and Wales under Northern Union (later Rugby League) rules.

He impressed during the tour, Wigan officials signing him for £400 in the dressing rooms at Cheltenham following the final Test Match. Part of the deal was that Wigan agreed to support him in obtaining his tailoring diploma (a career he had been pursuing in Auckland). In 1909, Todd decided to return home for good but, having arrived, received an offer from Wigan to re-sign, setting sail for England again during November of the same year, having spent only two months in New Zealand. In January 1914, Todd was unexpectedly listed at £400, the outcome of him becoming increasingly unsettled following his non-selection in several matches. Dewsbury stepped in to sign him but he only played for them until the following April. When the First World War broke out later that year, he joined the armed forces, rising to the rank of captain.

Gus Risman, who became the Salford captain in 1935, wrote at length about Todd in his acclaimed biography 'Rugby Renegade' (1958) saying: 'Like all great leaders and great managers, Toddy was a strict disciplinarian. He had no favourites, and when he laid down a rule he assumed that everyone would obey it. No one ever disobeyed him twice! He wore glasses, and a visit to his office was a positive ordeal. He would peer at you over his glasses, weigh you up and then speak. And when Toddy spoke it was the voice of law! His crackling clear voice would rap out the orders and that was that. He never believed in sparing anyone's feelings, and his dressing room pep talks, were something that should have been recorded for posterity. Often I came into the dressing room after pulling my heart out and doing my very best, but it was not good enough for Toddy. He would immediately set to and run through every mistake I had made. For Lance Todd was a perfectionist and he couldn't really see why everyone else was not a perfectionist as well.' Albert Gear, who scored Salford's match-winning try at Wembley in 1938 revealed another side of Todd's personality saying: 'Todd looked after all the team like a father. If I had the 'flu he would come round with the medicine I needed.' Todd had two daughters, one of them recalling in a 2004 interview that 'He was a good father and always making jokes.'

Graham Morris

THE HARRY SUNDERLAND TROPHY

After Harry Sunderland passed away in 1964, the members of the Rugby League Writers' Association took the decision to commemorate an Australian who had established himself as a fellow journalist in England during the post-Second World War period. The Harry Sunderland Memorial Trophy, as it was originally known, was donated by the Association for presentation to the outstanding player in what was then the Championship Final, making its debut in 1965. The Championship Final has since gone through almost as many transformations as Doctor Who – launched on our television screens by the BBC eighteen months before the first Sunderland award – and, like the good doctor, has survived all obstacles, and grown in strength. The Harry Sunderland Trophy has remained a constant factor throughout many changes to the games end-of-season-finale, and stands today as a prominent feature of the Super League Grand Final. It is an occasion that now rivals the Challenge Cup decider, attracting an attendance of 65,547 in 2004, after showing increases each year since the Grand Final concept was launched in 1998.

Harry Sunderland, as caricatured in the Sydney Daily Telegraph, 1939.

It is a stark contrast to the uncertainty surrounding the traditional climax to the Rugby League campaign when the Sunderland award was first offered all those 40 years ago. Whilst Wembley hosted the classic Wigan-Hunslet encounter in 1965, as it continued to draw huge crowds for the Challenge Cup Final – often in excess of 90,000 – the Championship decider was losing its appeal. The 1965 event, reintroduced after a three-year gap (whilst two divisions was tried and rejected), attracted just 20,786, compared to 37,451 at the previous 1962 final, itself well below the record 83,190 that attended the Wakefield-Wigan clash at Odsal in 1960. By 1973, that figure – for what was destined to be the last Championship Final – was just 18,889, the lowest peacetime attendance at the event since 1936.

When two divisions were brought back for 1973/74, the Championship play-off was scrapped and replaced, successively, by a Club Championship (1974), Premiership Trophy (1975 to 1997) and Super League Grand Final (1998 to date), the Harry Sunderland Trophy being at stake for the decisive match of each. It was during the era of the Premiership Trophy that public interest reawakened to the idea of an end of season knock-out series, crowds being propelled dramatically upwards when the final was transferred to Manchester United's Old Trafford in 1987 (38,756 attended compared to 13,683 in 1986), increasing even more with the introduction of the Grand Final series.

There has been one replay during the life of the Harry Sunderland Trophy when, in 1967, Wakefield Trinity's Ray Owen received the award for his performance in their successful rematch with St Helens. During the Premiership era, from 1993, it was decided no further replays would take place, extra-time being added until a conclusion is reached. The current rule is to add two ten-minute periods of play, followed, if necessary, by a 'golden score', whereby the first team to trouble the scoreboard is declared champions although, to date, extra time has not been required.

The Rugby League Writers' Association – presenters of the Harry Sunderland Trophy

The Rugby League Writers' Association (RLWA) was founded in September 1960, chiefly through the efforts of Jack Bentley (*Daily Express*), Joe Humphreys (*Daily Mirror*), Tom Longworth

(*News Chronicle & Daily Dispatch*) and Harold Mather (*The Guardian*). Having already taken the responsibility of casting the votes for the Lance Todd Trophy at the Challenge Cup Final, they donated the Harry Sunderland Trophy to be awarded to the outstanding player at the, then, Championship Final, its members again determining the verdict. Although the winner receives his award after the game, a formal presentation takes place at the Associations annual dinner, which normally takes place in November, at venues including, in recent years, Leeds' Headingley headquarters and Lancashire Cricket Club at Old Trafford.

Grand Final and was originally awarded at the Second Division Premiership Final. The latter was for the leading performance in the pre-season Charity Match between the League Champions and Challenge Cup Winners, but last awarded in 1996 when the contest was shelved.

There is also the RLWA Player of the Year Award (inaugurated in 1996) and the Tom Keavney Trophy (which is actually a sword), celebrating the former British Amateur Rugby League Association (BARLA) secretary and presented to the man of the match in the BARLA National Cup Final.

Harry Sunderland (left) and Lance Todd relax at the Lancashire cricket ground, Old Trafford.

The Association makes several other presentations during the evening. Since 1982, the RLWA Merit Award has been given for services to the game linked, since 1985, with the name of Arthur Brooks in memory of the former *Daily Mirror* journalist. In 1987 two new awards were introduced; the Tom Bergin Trophy and Jack Bentley Trophy. The former, honouring the Associations ex-president, goes to the outstanding player in the National League

The Super League Grand Final

The seeds for the Super League Grand Final were sown in 1907 when the first Championship play-off took place, the authorities deciding an end-of-season knock-out involving the leading clubs was the only reasonable way to settle a League competition involving close to 30 clubs, making it impossible for every team to meet home and away during the season.

A top-four system was employed until 1962,

with large crowds being attracted to the final, particularly from the late 1930s, when the majority (excepting the period covered by the Second World War) were settled at Manchester City Football Club's Maine Road enclosure and Bradford Northern's Odsal Stadium. With interest in the Championship fading at the start of the 1960s, clubs were divided into two divisions for the 1962/63 and 1963/64 campaigns in an effort to stimulate interest for the mid-table clubs. Consequently, a Championship play-off was not required as all teams met each other within their own division. For 1964/65, however, with attendances still falling, an all-embracing League structure was reinstated, along with the Championship decider – coinciding with the introduction of the Harry Sunderland Trophy – the 1965 final being the climax of an extended top-16 play-off, a format retained until the last Championship elimination series in 1973.

Two divisions were reintroduced for the 1973/74 season, a divisional League system being retained ever since. Although the club that finished top of Division One was declared Champions, it was decided to retain the tradition of an end-of-season play-off through introducing a separate (and complex) Club Championship competition, replaced after one

year by the Premiership Trophy. The Club Championship – eventually won by Warrington - was contested by 25 clubs who 'qualified' through the allocation of so-called merit points, based on League position and knock-out cup competition results during the season. Qualification for the first Premiership Trophy competition, staged in 1975, was slightly easier to comprehend, being contested by 16 clubs; the top 12 in Division One and Top four in Division Two. From 1976 until 1995, just the leading eight clubs in Division One took part. Yet another change came about when it was condensed to a top four for the climax of the first summer season of Super League in 1996, being significantly increased once more to embrace all 12 Super League teams in what was destined to be the last Premiership Trophy competition in 1997.

In 1998, the Super League Grand Final play-off series was introduced, effectively replacing the 'first past the post' ideal that had endured since 1974, which had seen the League's top team crowned Champions. The new system involved the top five clubs (increased to six from 2002), which mirrored an elimination format developed in Australian Rugby League, the resultant Grand Final winner declared Super League Champions.

HARRY SUNDERLAND

Harry Sunderland.

Harry Sunderland was a visionary, an Australian journalist who travelled the world in his efforts to spread the game of Rugby League. He was a resolute man who held firm views and was noted for his, sometimes, abrasive nature. It was because of this that Sunderland – a short, stocky man – became known as 'The Little Dictator', but his self-belief and stubbornness also led to his many accomplishments.

Whilst there is no record of Sunderland having played the sport he loved, his passion for the 13-a-side code (inspired by seeing the first Northern Union tour to Australia in 1910) was evident when he became involved in administration duties with the Queensland Rugby League in 1913 whilst in his mid-20s, eventually becoming secretary. His stock-in-trade was journalism and he travelled to Britain in 1921 at his own expense, to cover that year's Australian tour, before moving to Melbourne in 1923 (following a fall-out with some of the

Brisbane-based Queensland clubs). There he took up journalistic duties whilst continuing his enthusiasm for his sport by helping to set up the Victorian Rugby League in an area dominated by Australian Rules football. In 1925, he was invited by the Queensland Rugby League to return and resume his position as secretary, to which he agreed, later joining the Australian Board of Control.

He was joint-manager of three Kangaroo tours to Britain (1929/30, 1933/34 and 1937). Following the first, which had concluded with a match against Wales at Wembley Stadium in January 1930 watched by 16,000, Sunderland offered to act on behalf of the English authorities in 1931 in attempting to establish the sport in London. He also included France in his ambitious plan (the French Rugby Union having been suspended from the Five Nations that year for alleged professionalism) and undertook four visits to Paris between 1929 and 1933 in pursuit of his dream. The English hierarchy rejected his proposals but, during the 1933/34 tour, he became a prime mover in helping to launch the game in France, an exhibition match taking place between England and Australia in the Stade Pershing in Paris. Played on 31 December 1933 (one day after the Australians had met Wales for a second time at Wembley), the Aussies won comfortably by 63-13 on a frozen pitch. Despite the lop-sided score and artic conditions, the game caught the imagination of French Rugby Union international Jean Gallia who had travelled a long distance to witness it. Within three months, Gallia organised a tour of England and the code quickly became established in France, the first club competition starting later that year.

Following their 1937 visit, the Kangaroos – again through Sunderland's influence – extended their tour by playing ten matches in France during January 1938, including the first ever Test meetings between the countries, an occurrence that must have brought quiet satisfaction to the pioneering Sunderland spirit. Returning home, he fell out with fellow-members of the Queensland Rugby League, causing him to quit as secretary in July 1938 and accept an offer (first made in December 1937) to become Wigan secretary-manager on £400 per year. He arrived at Wigan in September 1938 to take up his duties, but the agreement was mutually terminated a year later following the outbreak of the Second World War.

He remained in England, continuing as a journalist, in particular for the *Daily Mail* and *Sunday Dispatch* (on whose behalf he travelled to Australasia to cover Great Britain's 1946 and 1950 tours) and worked on radio as a commentator for the BBC. His quest to spread the game being undiminished, he arranged for Australia and New Zealand to play two propaganda matches in the United States on their way home from the inaugural 1954 World Cup in France, meeting twice in California during November, although it was not a success.

Born in Gympie in Toowoomba, Queensland in 1890, he passed away in Manchester on 15 January 1964, aged 74. Sunderland's name lives on in Australia through the Harry Sunderland Memorial Medal, first awarded in 1964. Initially presented to the outstanding Australian player in a home Test series, it was limited from the 1970s to Anglo-Australian Tests only. In 2004, however, the Aussies bestowed it on Anthony Minichiello as their leading player in the Tri-Nations series.

THE MAN OF STEEL AWARD

The Man of Steel Award is generally regarded as the biggest individual award in British Rugby League. Launched in 1977, it was the brainchild of the, then, Rugby League Public Relations Officer, David Howes, who had taken up office in October 1974 (as the sports first PRO) following the appointment of David Oxley as new Rugby Football League secretary three months earlier. The arrival of the pair at the former Chapeltown Road headquarters in Leeds signalled the dawning of a new era for Rugby League in Britain.

The first time that the title of Man of Steel appeared was during the second stage of the 1975 World Championship. In an ambitious departure from previous World Cups – normally held in one country over a short period – the 1975 competition was fought out on a global scale with early fixtures being held in Australia and New Zealand during June, the competition concluding in England, France and Wales during October and November. Howes wanted to set up a Man of the Match sponsorship, and Trumanns Steel, based in Walkden, near Manchester, came forward, the Man of Steel label being selected to reflect that company's business.

Believing that it was vital to promote the personalities in Rugby League as a means to raising the image and awareness of the sport, particularly in the media, Howes instigated an annual awards evening. This was to cover various categories, with a Personality of the Year prize offered as the main award to the person considered to have had most impact on the season. Howes said 'The scheme was taken to Trumanns for sponsorship backing to provide funds for prizes, free tickets, etc. They agreed

TRUMANNS-MEANS-STEEL

AT   COMPETITIVE PRICES

WITH   A FAST RELIABLE SERVICE

FOR   THE BUYER WHO COUNTS ON QUALITY

SPONSORS OF THE WORLD CHAMPIONSHIP £50 "MAN OF STEEL AWARD"

TRUMANNS (STEEL) LTD
MOSS LANE
WALKDEN   Tel No. 061 790 4821
MANCHESTER   Telex 667605

The original 'Man of Steel Award' went to the man of the match in the 1975 World Championship series as advertised here in one of the official programmes.

and because of their product, the title Man of Steel was introduced, thus coupling it with the Superman image.'

Compered by the well-known television and radio broadcaster Keith Macklin and with cabaret provided by the Barron Knights, the inaugural evening, which took place in 1977 at The Golden Garter, Manchester, was an instant hit with players, officials, media and supporters. It achieved its stated goal of raising the profile of the sport through its individuals, Oxley commenting at the time 'The Trumanns Man of Steel award scheme was very successful in its first season of operation, creating tremendous interest in every sector of the game.'

Howes explained 'The major marketing philosophy was that the event should be open to the Rugby League public. Thus it was decided to make the awards part of a cabaret format, hiring Wakefield Theatre Club one year and The Golden Garter, Wythenshawe, the next. Capacity in each was about 2,000, with people organising supporters' club outings and private bookings. The RFL would hire the club for the awards night and inherit the cabaret turn on that week; The Three Degrees, Ken Dodd, Danny La Rue, etc. The events were always sell-outs.'

The awards had five category winners; First Division Player of the Year, Second Division Player of the Year, Young Player of the Year (for players under 24 at the start of the season but reduced to under 21 from 1984 awards), Coach of the Year and Referee of the Year. The two divisional player awards were voted for by players in the respective divisions, clubs being issued with ballot slips in January and again in

David Howes (right), the prime mover in creating the Man of Steel concept, shares a joke with Rugby League broadcaster and journalist Keith Macklin (second left) who compered the first nine award ceremonies. They are seen here at a joint-testimonial evening for Salford players Colin Dixon (left) and Mike Coulman during 1979, on stage at The Willows Variety Centre, venue for the Man of Steel Awards from 1984 to 1989.

April, with the proviso that they could not nominate players from their own club. The mid-season poll was an inspired idea, the names of the front-runners being released to the press, thereby building up publicity in anticipation of the end-of-season ceremony. The referee award was determined from markings submitted by the clubs themselves whilst the remaining two categories were in the hands of a panel of judges (leading officials, journalists and statisticians). Howes added 'For all but the Personality of the Year (Man of Steel), there would be three nominees named in advance of the award ceremony, to further create publicity and comment.' At the first awards in 1977, it was decided that the Man of Steel would be bestowed by the judges on one of the five category winners at the climax of the evening, Young Player of the Year winner David Ward of Leeds being the first recipient but, thereafter, the Man of Steel was judged independently.

Initially, there was no actual Man of Steel trophy, the first awarded was in 1993 – the year in which it was broadcast live on Sky Television for the only time – Wigan's Andy Platt being the

recipient. Previously the winners, apart from collecting the sponsors cheque which rose steadily from £250 in 1977 (Ward also received £100 for his category award) to £4,000 by 1995, received mementos like a handsome silver champagne goblet (valued at around £300 plus). The Man of Steel also received a framed citation in the earlier years which, for example, told 1981 winner Ken Kelly of Warrington that he had been honoured 'for personal achievement on the domestic and international scene and for inspired leadership of his club.' In 1978, St Helens forward George Nicholls had the bonus of accepting an excellent portrait painting

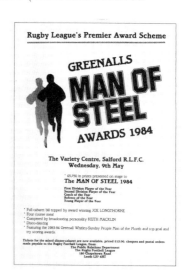

'Rugby League's Premier Award Scheme' as promoted in a 1984 edition of Open Rugby magazine.

of himself created by Wakefield artist Ron Jackson.

Excepting the brief introduction of a Third Division Player of the Year for 1992 and 1993 when the League was split into three divisions, the award categories remained unchanged up to 1995. The new era of Super League in 1996 led to several adjustments in format that included the introduction of new categories such as Top Try Scorer, Top Metre Maker, and Hit Man. From 1998 it became a Super League only ceremony, the awards for the lower divisions now taking place under the auspices of the National League clubs who celebrate their own awards evening.

Greenall Whitley took over the sponsorship from Trumanns in 1984, the first of several companies to support the award since, but the Man of Steel title was retained. Howes said 'Despite the change of sponsor from the original backers, steel company Trumanns, the Man of Steel has not changed to suit subsequent sponsors. This was a basic requisite during the early changes of backers to ensure that the title was consistent throughout its history rather than being changed to Personality of the Year, Top Man, etc.'

The award ceremony is now firmly entrenched in the media spotlight, the earlier cabaret club venues being superseded from 1990 by black tie functions at top ranking hotels of the calibre of the world famous Midland Hotel in Manchester.

STONES GOLD AWARDS

STONES GOLD AWARDS DINNER

AT
THE HOLIDAY INN
CROWNE PLAZA
MANCHESTER
ON
THURSDAY,
25TH SEPTEMBER 1997

Stones Gold Awards 1997

The menu card for the 1997 Man of Steel Awards evening, held at the prestigious Holiday Inn Crowne Plaza Midland Hotel in Manchester, its contents promising a 'Champagne Reception' prior to the distribution of dinner and prizes.

ALLAN AGAR (FEATHERSTONE ROVERS)
Man of Steel Award winner 1983

Allan Agar proved he had the Midas touch in the 1982/83 season after taking over as coach of a struggling Featherstone Rovers outfit in December 1982 and leading them to one of Wembley's biggest ever upsets. The Rovers – on the threshold of relegation with four wins in fifteen League fixtures when Agar arrived – went on an epic Challenge Cup run that saw

PROFILE

Allan Agar was an accomplished, dependable half-back, building his reputation at stand-off with Dewsbury and scrum-half with Hull Kingston Rovers. His debut was in 1964 with local club Featherstone Rovers, after impressing in their junior side, but, due to good half-back cover, made only a few appearances. He transferred to Dewsbury in 1969, playing for them in the 1972 Yorkshire Cup Final (which they lost) and the sensational 1973 Championship Final victory over Leeds. He joined Division Two side New Hunslet in 1975, his career hitting another high through moving to Hull Kingston Rovers the following year. With the Robins he won the Championship (1978/79) and Challenge Cup (1980 – his last appearance for the club). He spent 1980/81 at Wakefield Trinity, joining newcomers Carlisle as player-coach for 1981/82, taking them to promotion as Division Two runners-up in the club's first term. Reportedly 'disillusioned', he quit his Carlisle posting during the 1982 close-season, subsequently being invited to rejoin first club, Featherstone as coach, taking over in December 1982. Within five months he led them to their famous Wembley win over Hull, remaining in charge until 1985 before taking similar roles with Bramley (1985-87 – he came back for five appearances during 1986), Rochdale Hornets (1989-91) and Featherstone again (1991-92).

them cause a mighty upset in winning 11-10 at St Helens in the quarter-final, eliminate Bradford Northern 11-6 at the semi-final stage and defy all pre-match odds in beating Hull 14-12 in the final. Without making any changes to his squad, he also ensured the club retained its First Division status.

It all added up to Agar receiving the Man of Steel Award at The Wakefield Pussycat club just two days after master-minding the Wembley triumph. Although Hull's Arthur Bunting took

the Coach of the Year award that evening, Agar was rightly considered by the judges to have made the biggest impact on the season as a whole.

The second coach to win the award, he could claim to be the only one to do so entirely from the sidelines, predecessor Doug Laughton having been player-coach of Widnes when honoured in 1979. Twelve months earlier, whilst in charge of Carlisle, Agar's assistant coach Mick Morgan took the accolade, although, on that occasion, Morgan received it primarily for his on-field contribution.

Trumanns Man of Steel Awards 1983
Monday 9 May at The Wakefield Pussycat
Compered by Keith Macklin
Man of Steel: Allan Agar (Featherstone Rovers).
First Division Player of the Year: Keith Mumby (Bradford Northern).
Second Division Player of the Year: Steve Nash (Salford).
Young Player of the Year: Brian Noble (Bradford Northern).
Coach of the Year: Arthur Bunting (Hull).
Referee of the Year: Robin Whitfield (Widnes).

Allan Agar poses with his Man of Steel awards and winners' cheque.

RAY ASHBY (WIGAN)
Lance Todd Trophy winner 1965

Wigan full-back Ray Ashby shares with Hunslet's Brian Gabbitas the distinction of being the only joint winner of the Lance Todd Trophy, an event that happened following the classic 1965 Challenge Cup Final when they received the same number of votes from the journalists present. Ashby recalled: 'My first impression was; typical me – doing things by half!' adding 'In the heat of it all I didn't even know I'd won the Trophy until someone from the BBC came and picked me out and asked me would I do an interview.'

Ashby played his part in keeping Hunslet at bay, whilst his link up on attack provided a constant source of danger to the Yorkshire side. It was his attacking flair, whilst combining with loose-forward Laurie Gilfedder, that created space for Keith Holden to score the opening try after 16 minutes, Wigan leading 12-9 at half-time. With almost an hour played, Ashby was the creator of one of Wembley's most spectacular tries as, from inside the Wigan 25, he manoeuvred his way past three defenders to race 30 yards towards the left flank, transferring

> ### PROFILE
>
> *Ray Ashby originated from St Helens and played for the Blackbrook amateur club prior to joining Liverpool City in 1956. Initially he played in the centre but moved to full-back in 1958, his attacking flair and ability to link up on offence bringing him to the fore. Wigan signed him for £3,500 in 1964 and he appeared for them in the Challenge Cup Finals of 1965 and 1966, winning the former, and was in the team that captured the 1966 Lancashire Cup. His last Wigan match was in 1967, turning out later for Blackpool Borough (1968-70), an ankle injury forcing his retirement. He played twice for Great Britain (1964 and 1965) and once for Lancashire (1963).*

to Trevor Lake on halfway, the Rhodesian speedster diving over in the corner for his second try of the match. With the score at 20-9 it gave Wigan breathing space, although Hunslet, to their great credit, came back strongly losing by only 20-16.

Ashby, who was in his first full season with Wigan after moving from Liverpool City 14 months earlier, and the first full-back to receive the Lance Todd Trophy, said afterwards: 'I never dreamed I'd be here so soon after joining Wigan. It was a great game to play in. They had us stretched several times but their handling let them down.'

Rugby League Challenge Cup Final 1965
Saturday 8 May at Wembley Stadium, London
Wigan 20
Ashby, Boston, Ashton (captain, goal), Holden (try), Lake (2 tries), C Hill, Parr, Gardiner, Clarke, McTigue, T Stephens, Evans, Gilfedder (try, 3 goals).
Hunslet 16
Langton (5 goals), Griffiths (try), Shelton (try), Preece, Lee, Gabbitas, Marchant, Hartley, Prior, Eyre, Ramsey, Gunney, Ward (captain).
Half-time: 12-9. Referee: J Manley (Warrington).
Attendance: 89,016.

Ray Ashby breaks into open space at Wembley during the 1965 Challenge Cup Final.

BILL ASHURST (WIGAN)
Harry Sunderland Trophy winner 1971

Bill Ashurst became the first player to win the Harry Sunderland Trophy in defeat, although when the votes were being cast towards the end of the 1971 Championship Final, it must have

respected *Manchester Evening News* writer Jack McNamara saying he gave 'one of the finest all round displays of back-row forward work seen for many a match.'

The 1971 Wigan side with Bill Ashurst on the back row, extreme left.

Bill Ashurst looks for an opening in a 1971 clash with Hull at Central Park.

looked for all the world as though his Wigan side was about to claim victory over old enemy St Helens. In the final four minutes, a 12-man St Helens scored two tries – the second of which was claimed by Wigan to come from an off-side position – turning a six-point deficit into a shock 16-12 triumph. Despite the late horror show, Ashurst fully deserved his accolade, the

Ashurst was an integral part of an influential Wigan back row – the others being Dave Robinson and skipper Doug Laughton – that had swept the Cherry and Whites into the final having lost just four League fixtures during the campaign. It was the gifted Ashurst with a perfectly timed pass that carved open the Saints defence in the 8th minute for Robinson to score the only try of the first half, although St Helens held the half-time lead 6-3 thanks to three goals from the boot of their captain Kel Coslett.

Supported by a strong wind, Wigan, who had been on top for much of the first period, turned their authority into points after the interval, the non-stop Ashurst diving underneath the posts for a touchdown two minutes after the resumption. His conversion, to which he later added two excellent opportunist drop-goals, put

Bill Ashurst joined Wigan as a centre from the local Rose Bridge amateur club in 1968. It was following his move to the second-row, however, in late 1969 that his career really took off, his handling skills, power and awareness – allied to a supreme tactical kicking game – bringing him to the fore. He suffered the disappointment of defeat with Wigan in the Challenge Cup (1970) and Championship (1971) Finals, but was successful in the 1969 BBC2 Floodlit Trophy and 1971 Lancashire Cup Final. He joined the Australian club Penrith Panthers in July 1973 for A$27,700 (approximately £15,000) returning to Wigan in 1977 for £6,250. His return was brief, transferring to Wakefield Trinity for a British record of £18,000 in 1978. He returned to Wembley with Trinity in 1979, although losing once more, a knee injury eventually forcing his retirement in 1982. He became Trinity coach (1981-82) and then assisted Alex Murphy at Wigan (1982-83). He reappeared as Runcorn Highfield coach (1987-89), making one appearance at the aged of 40 in 1988, when his side was short-handed due to a players' strike. Due to his time spent in Australia and problems with injuries, he was limited to just three appearances for Great Britain (1971-72) and two for Lancashire (1971-72).

Wigan 12-6 in front. With the St Helens numbers depleted after Welsh second-row forward John Mantle was sent off for allegedly kicking Ashurst, Wigan, with six points to spare and seven minutes remaining, looked safe until the Saints barn-storming finish.

Northern Rugby League Championship Final 1971
Saturday 22 May at Station Road, Swinton
St Helens 16
Pimblett, Jones, Benyon (try), Walsh, Blackwood (try), Whittle, Heaton, Stephens, Karalius, Rees, Mantle, E Chisnall, Coslett (captain, 5 goals).
Substitutes: Kelly, Wanbon.
Wigan 12
Tyrer (goal), Kevin O'Loughlin, Francis, Rowe, Wright, D Hill, Ayres, Hogan, Clarke, Fletcher, Ashurst (try, 2 goals), Robinson (try), Laughton (captain). Substitute: Cunningham.
Half-time: 6-3. Referee: E Lawrinson (Warrington).
Attendance: 21,745

This spectacular second half try from Bill Ashurst looked as though it would turn the 1971 Championship Final in Wigan's favour, but St Helens staged a 'grandstand' finish.

Graham Morris

MAL ASPEY (WIDNES)
Harry Sunderland Trophy winner 1980

Mal Aspey won the Harry Sunderland Trophy in 1980 in the Premiership Trophy Final win over Bradford Northern at Station Road, Swinton, after giving what the *Yorkshire Post* described as 'a class centre performance throughout.' Bradford, strongly fancied to claim their third piece of silverware that season, were knocked off course by a stylish Widnes display on a hot, sunny afternoon, the left wing partnership of experienced centre Aspey and young up-and-coming wing Keith Bentley, providing a potent attacking mix.

Mal Aspey.

Each grabbed a try as Widnes ran out comfortable 19-5 victors, the three-pointer created by Aspey for Bentley being described by Brian Smith in the *Bradford Telegraph & Argus* as 'a glorious try which will be treasured for years.' It came two minutes before the interval when Bradford were laying siege on the Widnes line only to lose the ball, scrum-half Reg Bowden eagerly scooping it up and passing to Aspey. Running in 'a wide arc' down the flank, Aspey then executed a dummy scissors movement with Bentley, Aspey seemingly offering the ball with one hand but racing clear of a confused Bradford defence to reach halfway before being checked by full-back Keith Mumby. As he succumbed to the tackle, Aspey somehow managed to boot the ball, sending his perfectly judged kick towards the Bradford try line, the speedy Bentley outpacing two defenders for the try of the match. Crucially, it pushed Widnes 9-5 ahead at the interval, building on the earlier efforts of hooker Keith Elwell who had chased his own 16th minute kick for a touchdown, goaled by Mick Burke, and coolly added a drop-goal 12 minutes later. Northern, in one of their few worthwhile moves of an otherwise error strewn display, had taken a 5-0 lead through a third minute converted try from David Redfearn.

Widnes continued the momentum in the second half, scoring three more touchdowns through Stuart Wright, Aspey (sealing his man of the match credentials) and Les Gorley, Burke failing to augment any in an unusual off-day with the boot in which he landed just one of five attempts, David Eckersley contributing a drop-goal following Aspey's score.

The 1980 Widnes squad. Mal Aspey is standing, third from right.

Whilst Bradford suffered their second successive defeat in the Premiership Trophy Final, it was Widnes' first win in the competition and Aspey became the first three-quarter to claim the Harry Sunderland Trophy.

Premiership Trophy Final 1980
Saturday 17 May at Station Road, Swinton
Widnes 19
Burke (goal), Wright (try), George, Aspey (try),
Bentley (try), Eckersley (drop-goal), Bowden
(captain), Shaw, Elwell (try, drop-goal), M O'Neill,
Gorley (try), Hull, Adams. Substitute: Hogan.
Bradford Northern 5
Mumby (goal), MacLean, D Redfearn (try), Parker,
Gant, Stephenson, A Redfearn, Thompson (captain),
Bridges, Forsyth, Clarkson, Grayshon, Hale.
Substitutes: Ferres, van Bellen.
Half-time: 9-5. Referee: WH Thompson
(Huddersfield). Attendance: 10,215.

A publicity picture of Mal Aspey, taken in 1976.

MARK ASTON (SHEFFIELD EAGLES)
Lance Todd Trophy winner 1998

=== PROFILE ===

Mark Aston, born in Allerton-Bywater, has probably been associated with Sheffield Eagles longer than anyone, signing from the Selby-based Gaffers club and making his debut in 1986, just two years after the Eagles were founded. A quick-thinking scrum-half and supreme on-field organiser, he previously played at amateur level for Stanley Rangers (Wakefield), Oulton (near Rothwell), Lock Lane (Castleford) and Castleford under-17s. In 1988, he was loaned to Bramley for a couple of matches, quickly establishing his credentials on his return to the Eagles, taking the Tom Bergin Trophy as the outstanding player in the club's 1989 Division Two Premiership Final win over Swinton at Old Trafford. Aston – and Sheffield – repeated that success in 1992 against Oldham, climaxing a season in which they also won the Division Two Championship. In 1992, the club reached the Yorkshire Cup for the only time in its history, Aston earning a runners-up medal against Wakefield Trinity. He transferred to Featherstone Rovers in 1994 but was back with Sheffield the following year, taking part in the club's greatest triumph in winning the 1998 Challenge Cup Final at Wembley. Aston played his final match for the old Eagles set-up in 1999, the club amalgamating with Huddersfield to create the ill-fated Huddersfield-Sheffield Giants in 2000. Aston transferred his allegiance to become a central figure in the newly constituted Sheffield Eagles club as player-coach, commencing operations in 2000. Led by Aston, the club won the National League Two Championship in 2003 but missed promotion in the play-offs. Aston now concentrates on coaching duties at Sheffield, his last match as a player being in 2004. He made one appearance for Great Britain in 1991.

Sheffield Eagles, founded in 1984, caused one of the biggest upsets in Rugby League Challenge Cup history in defeating favourites Wigan 17-8 in the 1998 final. For Mark Aston, who had been with the club for most of its existence – much of it spent in the Second Division – it was an extra-special experience, winning the Lance Todd Trophy after edging out colleagues Dave Watson and skipper Paul Broadbent in the voting.

Aston's massive influence on the outcome of the final was felt in the fourth minute when his towering cross-field kick was seized in mid-air over the Wigan try line by speedy winger Nick

Pinkney in the right corner. Aston missed the difficult touch-line conversion but atoned with his next attempt after Matt Crowther got a second try, Sheffield holding a shock 10-0 lead after 28 minutes. Andrew Farrell pulled two points back for Wigan with a penalty, Aston sending his Sheffield team mates into the dressing rooms with an 11-2 lead through a calmly taken drop-goal from in front of the posts just a minute before the break.

Mark Aston.

Whilst many anticipated a Wigan fight-back, it was Sheffield that struck first, twelve minutes after the restart, Aston converting the Eagles third try for a 17-2 lead. The touchdown had come from Darren Turner, who, from acting half-back under the posts, managed to stretch out his ball carrying arm through a melee of defenders to place the ball on the line. It was after Mark Bell scored Wigan's only try, Farrell adding the goal to cut the deficit to nine points, that Aston confirmed his right to be man of the match. Farrell crossed the line for what looked a certain Wigan try in the 64th minute, but Aston scrambled to get his hand underneath the ball

preventing the grounding. Video replays showed it was a correct call although Wigan players disputed the decision, being subsequently penalised, Sheffield surviving to complete a famous win.

Aston later recalled an unusual telephone conversation with his mother on the eve of the final, saying: 'My mother phoned me on the Friday night and said she'd been to see a clairvoyant who said we were going to win and I was going to get the Lance Todd Trophy! I thought "The pictures been painted fully here and I hope it comes off!" Whether it was destiny, or whatever it was, it certainly sticks in my mind. Somebody up there was looking down and blessing us!'

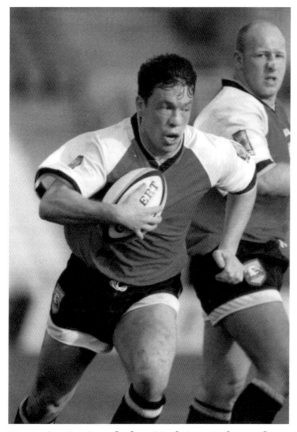

Determination is etched on Mark Aston's face as he attempts to break.

Rugby League Challenge Cup Final 1998
Saturday 2 May at Wembley Stadium, London
Sheffield Eagles 17
Sovatabua, Pinkney (try), Taewa, Senior, Crowther (try), Watson, Aston (2 goals, drop-goal), Broadbent (captain), Lawless, Laughton, Carr, Shaw, Doyle. Substitutes: Jackson, Turner (try), Wood.
Wigan Warriors 8
Radlinski, M Bell (try), Moore, Connolly, Robinson, Paul, Smith, Holgate, McCormack, Mestrov, Betts, Haughton, Farrell (captain, 2 goals). Substitutes: Gilmore, Cowie, Cassidy, O'Connor.
Half-time: 11-2. Referee: S Cummings (Widnes). Attendance: 60,669.

BOB BEARDMORE (CASTLEFORD)
Lance Todd Trophy winner 1986

Bob Beardmore became the third Castleford player to capture the Lance Todd Trophy, having directed play in a tightly contested 1986 Challenge Cup Final with Hull Kingston Rovers, scoring a try and drop-goal. The scrum-half made his first contribution to the scoreboard in the 32nd minute when twin brother Kevin fed the ball back from acting half-back in a planned move, resulting in a neat drop-goal ten yards out. It edged Castleford 7-2 ahead, Tony Marchant having scored the afternoon's first try midway through the half. The good work was almost undone when Rovers' centre Gary Prohm scooted over for an unconverted try against the run of play, following an Andy Kelly interception, Castleford leading 7-6 at the break

A delighted Bob Beardmore clutches the Challenge Cup

Beardmore restored the five-point advantage three minutes after the resumption. From a play-the-ball a few yards in from the right touchline just inside the Rovers 25, acting half-back Kevin Beardmore turned the ball inside to his brother, who hacked a speculative kick through a group of defenders towards the

> ### PROFILE
>
> *Bob Beardmore signed for his local Castleford team in 1978, a move that reunited him with twin brother Kevin who arrived at Wheldon Road the previous year, the pair having played together at Fryston. Initially he played for the Castleford Colts side, gaining representative honours at that level for Great Britain and Yorkshire, his senior Castleford debut being in 1979. Developing into a classy workmanlike scrum-half, he won the Yorkshire Cup with Castleford (1981 and 1986), achieving the pinnacle of his career in winning the 1986 Challenge Cup. In 1989 he moved across the Pennines to join Leigh, staying at Hilton Park until 1991, followed by one appearance for the short-lived Scarborough Pirates during September 1991.*

corner, racing after it through a static looking Rovers defence, Prohm in particular being slow to react. Beardmore dived on the ball at his feet registering an unconverted try, a further touchdown by Jamie Sandy pushing Castleford 15-6 ahead. Two more Rovers tries created a grandstand finish, John Dorahy missing both goals, the latter – a difficult touchline attempt in the dying minutes – causing Castleford players to leap in the air in celebration as the projectile sailed wide.

Elated at winning the Lance Todd Trophy, Beardmore said afterwards: 'I was thrilled to bits at winning the award. Coach Malcolm Reilly, who received the award in 1969, told me a few weeks ago I was capable of emulating his feat and I worked hard to this end.'

Rugby League Challenge Cup Final 1986
Saturday 3 May at Wembley Stadium, London
Castleford 15
Lord, Plange, Marchant (try), Hyde, Sandy (try), Joyner (captain), B Beardmore (try, drop-goal), Ward, K Beardmore, Johnson, England, Ketteridge (goal), French. Substitutes: Roockley, Horton.
Hull Kingston Rovers 14
Fairbairn, Clark, M Smith, Prohm (2 tries), Laws, Dorahy (goal), Harkin, Johnston, Watkinson (captain), Ema, Kelly, Harrison, Miller. Substitutes: G Smith, Lydiat (try).
Half-time: 7-6. Referee: R Whitfield (Widnes).
Attendance: 82,134.

DEAN BELL (WIGAN)
Man of Steel Award winner 1992
Lance Todd Trophy winner 1993

Wigan centre Dean Bell is the only New Zealander, to date, to have won the coveted Man of Steel Award, bestowed upon him at the end of what had been a dream 1991/92 season, both for player and club. In brilliant form throughout the campaign, he also proved an outstanding club captain – a role he had previously fulfilled at international level – taking over that responsibility during October. With Bell at the helm, Wigan dominated the final months of the season, achieving a first ever treble of Championship (eight points clear of runners-up St Helens), Challenge Cup (beating Castleford 28-12 at Wembley following a mammoth 71-10 semi-final mauling of Bradford Northern) and Premiership Trophy (vanquishing St Helens 48-16 at Old Trafford and annihilating Leeds 74-6 in the semi-final). A highly competitive player, he proved himself as a fine ambassador for his adopted country when leading Wigan to a magnificent win in the 24-team World Sevens competition held in Sydney, Australia, during February, Brisbane Broncos being beaten 18-6 in the final. Commenting recently on his Man of Steel Award, Bell said: 'Even though it is a very difficult honour to achieve, not least because of the extremely talented players in my own team, it was a goal that I always set out to achieve each year as there is no higher recognition.'

Bell was again Wigan's Wembley captain in 1993 – on the way to equalling Ellery Hanley's record of being presented with the trophy in three successive Challenge Cup Finals – when he was also a clear winner of the Lance Todd Trophy. Opponents Widnes provided stiff opposition and Wigan trailed 12-6 when Bell – playing in the less familiar position of loose

Applauding the fans – Dean Bell celebrates another Wigan victory.

forward – crossed for a try in the 23rd minute. Offiah had provided him with a basketball pass over a defenders head after scooping the ball up on the left touchline when Widnes winger John Devereux (who had retrieved a Shaun Edwards kick) lost the ball 15 yards from the line. Botica's conversion and subsequent penalty put Wigan 14-12 in front at the interval.

The second half – which saw Widnes forward Richard Eyres become the second player to be dismissed in a Wembley final – was as keenly fought as the first. Bell, restored to his normal centre position ten minutes before the break, pulled the trigger for the opening shot two minutes after the resumption, bursting through an attempted two-man tackle near the posts to put substitute Sam Panapa through. Botica's goal was to be Wigan's final points, Jonathan Davies, with a penalty, providing the only remaining score.

Bell fully justified his Lance Todd achievement, having given exemplary leadership in what was the most competitive final of Wigan's eight consecutive Wembley wins whilst giving a typically full-blooded performance himself. He later said: 'It is without doubt the highest individual man of the match honour in the game and it feels so privileged to have my name on it.'

Dean Bell, accompanied by Ken Allen (national sales manager of sponsors ESAB), shows off the Lance Todd Trophy in 1993.

PROFILE

New Zealand international centre Dean Bell was born in Otara, Auckland, and played for Manukau. He came to England in 1982, appearing in the colours of Carlisle during 1982/83, during which time he represented Cumbria against the 1982 Kangaroos. He returned the following season with the New Zealand Maoris touring side that played several matches against amateur opposition, seeing out the season with Leeds during which time he was a winner in the John Player Trophy Final. After a brief spell back home with Manukau, he transferred to Eastern Suburbs in Sydney where he spent the 1985 and 1986 Australian seasons (he returned there on loan during 1988).

Wigan secured his services in September 1986, the talented, visionary centre earning the name 'Mean Dean' through his reputation as a tough, uncompromising opponent. With Wigan, he won the Challenge Cup seven times (1988 to 1994 - captain in the latter three), Championship six (1986/87 and 1989/90 to 1993/94), Premiership Trophy twice (1987, 1992), John Player Trophy twice (1986/87, 1988/89), Regal Trophy twice (1989/90, 1992/93), and Lancashire Cup four times (1986, 1987, 1988 and 1992). He stood down from the 1987 and 1991 World Club Challenge victories through injury but was captain in 1992, losing to Brisbane Broncos at Central Park. He left Wigan at the end of the 1993/94 campaign, to take over as skipper of Auckland Warriors in their 1995 debut year, after which he retired as a player. Back in England once more, he became Leeds coach in September 1995, stepping down in October 1997 to take over their youth development. He moved to Wigan in a similar capacity during November 1999 and, at the time of writing, still fulfils that role. He made 26 New Zealand Test appearances (1983-89), being captain in four. A Kiwi tourist three times, including captaincy of the 1987 party to Australia and Papua New Guinea, he was the subject of televisions 'This is Your Life' in 1993. His father Cameron Bell coached Carlisle, Auckland and the New Zealand Maoris.

Stones Bitter Man of Steel Awards 1992
Thursday 14 May at the Holiday Inn Crowne Plaza
Midland, Manchester
Compered by Eddie Hemmings
Man of Steel: Dean Bell (Wigan).
First Division Player of the Year: Graham Steadman
(Castleford).
Second Division Player of the Year: Iva Ropati
(Oldham).
Third Division Player of the Year: Wally Gibson
(Huddersfield).
Young Player of the Year: Garry Connolly (St
Helens).
Coach of the Year: John Monie (Wigan).
Referee of the Year: Robin Whitfield (Widnes).

Rugby League Challenge Cup Final 1993
Saturday 1 May at Wembley Stadium, London
Wigan 20
Hampson, Robinson, Lydon, Farrar, Offiah, Botica (4
goals), Edwards, Skerrett (try), Dermott, Platt, Betts,
Clarke, Bell (captain, try). Substitutes: Panapa (try),
Farrell.
Widnes 14
Spruce, Devereux, Currier, Wright, Myers, Davies (3
goals), Goulding, Sorenson (try), P Hulme (captain),
Howard, R Eyres (try), Faimalo, D Hulme.
Substitutes: J O'Neill, McCurrie.
Half-time: 14-12. Referee: R Smith (Castleford).
Attendance: 77,684.

Dean Bell with the Challenge Cup at Wembley in
1993.

DENIS BETTS (WIGAN)
Lance Todd Trophy winner 1991
Man of Steel Award winner 1995

Graham Morris

Denis Betts.

Wigan second-row forward Denis Betts signed off in style when he concluded his first period with Wigan in 1995 (he returned in 1998) winning the Man of Steel Award after a trophy-laden season. He was about to further his career in New Zealand with newly founded Auckland Warriors who were to compete in the Australian Premiership, joining Wigan's departing coach John Monie and Central Park colleagues Dean Bell, Frano Botica and Andy Platt in the venture.

He had stood out in the Wigan side all season, the speedy back-row man contributing 20 tries in his 37 appearances as he helped the Cherry and Whites sweep the board as far as domestic honours were concerned. The Championship and Challenge Cup double was achieved for an incredible sixth consecutive season, a clean sweep being completed through adding the Premiership Trophy and Regal Trophy. Betts also raised his Test match count to

25 during the campaign, playing his part in the three match series against the 1994 Kangaroos, staged at Wembley, Old Trafford (Manchester) and Elland Road (Leeds), although only the former was won against the powerful Australian outfit.

PROFILE

Denis Betts was a quick, skilful, exciting second-row forward who joined Wigan in 1986 from Leigh Rangers amateur club, making his debut the following year. At Wigan his trophy haul included six Championship wins (1989/90 to 1994/95), seven Challenge Cup successes (1989 to 1995), plus victories in the World Club Challenge (1991, 1994), Premiership Trophy (1992, 1994, 1995), John Player Trophy (1988/89), Regal Trophy (1989/90, 1992/93, 1994/95) and Lancashire Cup (1988, 1992). The Salford-born player joined New Zealand club Auckland Warriors (1995 to 1997), returning to Wigan in 1998 and appearing in that years Challenge Cup Final loss to Sheffield Eagles, but missing the Super League Grand Final win over Leeds through injury. He subsequently appeared in the Grand Final defeats of 2000 and 2001 (his last match as a player). He then joined the Wigan coaching staff, being head coach during 2004, assisting the incoming Ian Millward from 2005. He played in 32 Test Matches for Great Britain (including the 1992 World Cup when he took part in the final against Australia at Wembley), and toured three times (1990, 1992, 1996). He made four appearances for England (all in the 1995 World Cup when captain for the final against Australia at Wembley) and represented Lancashire once (1991).

Betts had previously been Young Player of the Year at the 1991 Man of Steel ceremony 12 days after capturing his other major individual honour; the Lance Todd Trophy. He won it on another record making Wembley occasion for Wigan as they became the first club to appear in front of the twin towers in four consecutive Challenge Cup Finals, and – through Betts – the first to provide four successive Lance Todd winners. The match itself, a 13-8 victory over St Helens was a disappointing affair. Victims of their own success, Wigan had been forced to complete their League programme with eight matches in 19 days and, although they miraculously retained the title, it left the side battle weary and injury scarred for their Wembley date. It was probably as a result of the reduced energy levels that Wigan inflicted most

Denis Betts searches for an opening.

damage early on, racing into a 12 point lead in as many minutes with tries from David Myers and Frano Botica, with two goals from the boot of Botica, a 5th minute penalty that opened the scoring, and the conversion of his own try. It was 21-year-old Betts, who provided most of the zip in Wigan's first half performance, that put Botica in for his touchdown. The initial break came from Dean Bell who, having received the ball 20 yards inside the Wigan half, evaded the

despairing tackle of Jonathan Griffiths, to go on a brilliant run into the heart of the Saints defence. Betts – alert to the situation – quickly came up in support on Bell's left side, accepting a pass on the halfway line to go racing some 40 yards deep inside the Saints 25 before delivering a perfect pass for Botica to go haring over the line.

Andy Gregory increased Wigan's lead to 13-0 with a crucial killer drop-goal seven minutes after half-time, the tiring Central Park outfit clinging on to win 13-8. Betts – who made three telling breaks during the final – still recalls the match: 'I remember it, basically, because we'd had a very tough year. The team was falling to pieces and a number of players shouldn't have really played. Andy Goodway put his arm around me at the end, when we were celebrating, and said "You've won the Lance Todd." I think the great thing about this trophy is that your name goes on it. Somebody wins it every year but you're on there forever.'

Rugby League Challenge Cup Final 1991
Saturday 27 April at Wembley Stadium, London
Wigan 13
Hampson, Myers (try), K Iro, Bell, Botica (try, 2 goals), Edwards, Gregory (drop-goal), Lucas, Dermott, Platt, Betts, Clarke, Hanley (captain). Substitutes: Goulding, Goodway.
St Helens 8
Veivers, Hunte (try), Ropati, Loughlin, Quirk, Griffiths, Bishop (2 goals), Neill, Dwyer, Ward, Harrison, Mann, Cooper (captain). Substitutes: Connolly, Groves.
Half-time: 12-0. Referee: J Smith (Halifax).
Attendance: 75,532.

Stones Bitter Man of Steel Awards 1995
Tuesday 16 May at the Holiday Inn Crowne Plaza Midland, Manchester
Compered by Eddie Hemmings
Man of Steel: Denis Betts (Wigan).
First Division Player of the Year: Bobbie Goulding (St Helens).
Second Division Player of the Year: Nick Pinkney (Keighley Cougars).
Young Player of the Year: Andrew Farrell (Wigan).
Coach of the Year: Graeme West (Wigan).
Referee of the Year: Russell Smith (Castleford).

LES BOYD (WARRINGTON)
Harry Sunderland Trophy winner 1986

Warrington's Australian powerhouse prop, Les Boyd, became the second overseas player to win the Harry Sunderland Trophy after a textbook display of forceful and intimidating front-row play against luckless Halifax in the 1986 Premiership Trophy Final. The Warrington skipper's inspirational performance was fully supported by a rampant pack that overwhelmed the 'Fax forwards after the interval when 28 points were notched without reply.

PROFILE

Australian prop or second-row forward Les Boyd arrived at Warrington in 1985 having acquired a 'bad boy' image in his homeland following suspensions of 12 months and 18 months. As team captain at Wilderspool he put all that behind him, channelling his explosive, fierce running style into inspirational performances that took Warrington to a convincing 1986 Premiership Trophy Final win over Halifax. Born in Nyngan, in the New South Wales country, he was brought up in Cootamundra where he played for the local team until snapped up by Sydney club Western Suburbs in 1976. He remained with them until 1979, subsequently playing for Manly-Warringah (1980-84). He toured Great Britain with the Kangaroos in 1978 and 1982, his career covering 17 Test appearances (1978-82) and seven matches for New South Wales (1979-83). He played his last match for Warrington in 1989, following which he returned to Cootamundra as captain-coach.

Fittingly, Boyd scored the first and last tries of the afternoon as Warrington ran up the biggest score so far in a Premiership Final. He crossed the whitewash after only two minutes, crashing over after being put through by hooker Kevin Tamati, but newly crowned League Champions Halifax stayed in contention, the lead changing hands several times, the outcome looking finely balanced at half-time 10-10.

The stage was set for the second half when Tamati and prop forward Bob Jackson registered a converted try each as Warrington shot ahead 22-10 within five minutes of the restart as Halifax – hindered by the 29th minute loss of second-row forward Neil James with a dislocated shoulder – began to wilt. Boyd completed Warrington's quintet of second half touchdowns by dummying his way into space to charge over from 20 yards in the final minutes for a 38-10 win.

Although producing record receipts of £50,879, the Elland Road encounter was the last Premiership Trophy Final held before the successful switch to Old Trafford in 1987.

Premiership Trophy Final 1986
Sunday 18 May at Elland Road, Leeds
Warrington 38
Ford, Forster (try), Cullen, R Duane, Carbert, Bishop (try, 5 goals), A Gregory, Boyd (captain, 2 tries), Tamati (try), Jackson (try), Sanderson, Roberts, M Gregory. Substitutes: Johnson (try), McGinty.
Halifax 10
Whitfield (3 goals), Riddlesden, T Anderson, C Anderson (captain, try), Wilson, Crossley, Stephens, Robinson, McCallion, Scott, Juliff, James, Dixon. Substitutes: Smith, Bond.
Half-time: 10-10. Referee: GF Lindop (Wakefield). Attendance: 13,683.

Les Boyd.

MICK BURKE (WIDNES)

Lance Todd Trophy winner 1981
Harry Sunderland Trophy winner 1982

Mick Burke.

It did not take eventual Lance Todd Trophy winner Mick Burke long to stamp his authority on the 1981 Challenge Cup Final. His side Widnes took a quick tap-penalty in the 4th minute after holders Hull Kingston Rovers had been penalised for offside, Burke running wide to receive an Eric Hughes pass on Rovers 25 propelling a short kick towards the try-line whereupon he raced passed three defenders, gathering a perfect bounce to dive over in the corner. Rovers seemed shaken by Burke's early strike, making unforced errors in their play despite dominating the scrums. After 22 minutes, Burke kicked a penalty following a foul by hooker David Watkinson on Brian Lockwood – Lance Todd Trophy winner with Rovers 12 months earlier – and, four minutes later, he linked with the attack again. Accepting a typical Lockwood defence splitting pass, he drew the remaining cover, releasing the ball to Mick George who flew over, Burke also adding the goal.

Leading 11-4 at the break, Widnes extended their lead to 18-4 within five minutes of the restart, Burke converting a brilliant solo try from

teenage prodigy Andy Gregory and adding a penalty three minutes later when Gregory was flattened by Rovers skipper Len Casey. Rovers scored a converted try ten minutes later which, with the score at 18-9, provided some hope of a comeback, but it was to be the last points of the day. Burke was a deserving winner of the Lance Todd award, just edging out Gregory in the voting, although his time would come!

The following year, Burke became the third player to complete a Todd-Sunderland 'double', receiving all bar one of the votes to take the Harry Sunderland Trophy for his outstanding contribution to the 1982 Premiership Trophy Final, Widnes defeating Hull at Headingley, Leeds. Having only played a few games in the previous four months due to a painful back injury, he returned to the spotlight with a powerful display. The architect of his team's opening two tries, he crossed the line himself twelve minutes from time for a score that virtually guaranteed victory, the *Widnes Weekly News* correspondent describing his performance as 'real Roy of the Rovers stuff!'

PROFILE

St Helens-born Mick Burke joined Widnes in 1978 from Liverpool-based Waterloo Rugby Union club. An excellent goal-kicker – he still holds the Widnes record of 140 for a season from 1978/79 – he settled at full-back having been tried in several back positions including stand-off, wing and centre. Noted for his 'chunky' appearance, he could still show a fair turn of speed and was a reliable, steady defender, a fact noted in the selection of representative sides. He played for Great Britain in 15 Test Matches (1980-86) including the 1984 tour, played once for England (1984), and five times for Lancashire (1979-85). He club honours with Widnes included the Challenge Cup (1979, 1981 and 1984 – he also appeared at Wembley in the 1982 drawn final), Premiership Trophy (1980, 1982 and 1983), John Player Trophy (1978/79), Lancashire Cup (1978 and 1979) and BBC2 Floodlit Trophy (1978). Following his Widnes finale in 1986, he played for Oldham (1987-88), enjoying a Division Two Championship and Premiership double in the 1987/88 campaign.

Burke had put his side two points up with a 4th minute penalty but a one-man rearguard action by Hull second-rower Lee Crooks (with a try, conversion and drop-goal) saw the Humbersiders lead 6-2 six minutes before the interval. Three minutes later, though, an inspired Burke burst through the middle, transferring the ball to left wing John Basnett who evaded two defenders for a try. Burke missed the goal but Widnes returned to the dressing room with renewed belief, trailing by one point.

In the opening exchanges of the second half, Burke stood firm in heroic style as Hull bombarded the Widnes defence, before turning the tide in the 48th minute when he again broke through. This time he attacked on the right hand side, delivering a perfectly placed pass to Stuart Wright who, from 10 yards out, made his way to the line, diving over in spectacular fashion to place the ball, Burke converting for a 10-6 lead. Hull pulled two points back with a Crooks penalty but, in the 65th minute, Widnes stand-off Eric Hughes went on a great solo run, covering 40 yards before crossing the whitewash, Burke missing the goal (13-8). Three minutes later, executing a set-piece move from a scrum, Hughes accepted Gregory's pass before delivering a short ball to the irrepressible Burke who raced up from the back to crash through three defenders for the killer score, adding the goal. With two minutes remaining Mick Adams emphasised Widnes' supremacy with a fifth try, Burke obliging with the goal for a 23-8 victory.

Rugby League Challenge Cup Final 1981
Saturday 2 May at Wembley Stadium, London
Widnes 18
Burke (try, 4 goals), Wright, George (try), Cunningham, Bentley, Hughes, Gregory (try), M O'Neill, Elwell, Lockwood, Gorley, Prescott, Adams (captain, drop-goal). Substitutes: Myler, Shaw.
Hull Kingston Rovers 9
Hall, Hubbard (3 goals), Smith, Hogan, Muscroft, Hartley, Harkin, Holdstock, Watkinson, Crooks, Lowe, Burton (try), Casey (captain). Substitutes: Proctor, Millington.
Half-time: 11-4. Referee: DG Kershaw (York). Attendance: 92,496.

Premiership Trophy Final 1982
Saturday 15 May at Headingley, Leeds
Widnes 23
Burke (try, 4 goals), Wright (try), O'Loughlin, Cunningham, Basnett (try), Hughes (try), Gregory, M O'Neill, Elwell, Lockwood, Gorley, Prescott, Adams (captain, try). Substitutes: Myler, Whitfield.
Hull 8
Kemble, O'Hara, Leuluai, Evans, Prendiville, Topliss (captain), Harkin, Tindall, Wileman, Stone, Skerrett, Crooks (try, 2 goals, drop-goal), Norton. Substitutes: Day, Lloyd.
Half-time: 5-6. Referee: S Wall (Leigh). Attendance: 12,100.

With just twelve minutes remaining in the 1982 Premiership Trophy Final, Mick Burke seals a great personal performance with a try near the posts.

LEN CASEY (HULL KINGSTON ROVERS)
Harry Sunderland Trophy winner 1981

=== PROFILE ===

Hull-born loose forward Len Casey starred for both his city's senior clubs during a near 18-year career. He joined Hull from amateurs Beverley in 1968, his debut coming two years later, joining Hull Kingston Rovers for £6,000 in 1975. A good ball-player and tough competitor, his career took off with Rovers, being a member of Great Britain's 1977 World Cup squad in Australasia, appearing in the side beaten by Australia in the final. He returned Down Under with the 1979 tourists, missing the 1984 tour through suspension. He appeared in 14 Tests (1977-83 – three as captain), played five times for England (1978-81) and once for Yorkshire (1978).

A high profile £25,000 move to Bradford Northern came in 1979 but he returned to Rovers the following year for a Rugby League record £38,000. His second spell ended when he joined Wakefield Trinity as player-coach in 1985, playing his final match that year but continuing as coach until 1986. He was in charge at Hull (1986-88) and Scarborough Pirates (1991), later returning to Beverley as coach. With Hull Kingston Rovers he contributed to two Championships (1978/79 – leaving mid-season to join Bradford – and 1983/84), winning the Challenge Cup (1980 – runner-up in 1981), Premiership Trophy (1981) and BBC2 Floodlit Trophy (1977). At Bradford he won the John Player Trophy (1979/80) receiving the man of the match award.

Woods – with 15 minutes remaining, making for a tense finish as Rovers held on to win 11-7.

Although the voting was close – team-mate Phil Lowe and Hull's Tony Dean and Steve Norton were also in the running – Casey deserved the recognition for his determined defence and organisation, lifting and driving the Rovers pack towards winning the confrontation with a formidable Hull six, thereby engineering space for their faster backs to operate in.

Premiership Trophy Final 1981
Saturday 16 May at Headingley, Leeds
Hull Kingston Rovers 11
Proctor, Hubbard (goal), M Smith (try), Hogan (try), Muscroft, Hartley (try), Harkin, Holdstock, Watkinson, Millington, Lowe, Casey (captain), Hall. Substitute: Burton.
Hull 7
Woods (2 goals), Peacham, Elliott, Wilby, Prendiville, Banks, Dean, Tindall, Wileman, Stone (captain), Skerrett, Crane (try), Norton. Substitute: Madley.
Half-time: 8-2. Referee: J Holdsworth (Kippax). Attendance: 29,448.

Hull Kingston Rovers skipper Len Casey played a real captain's role in leading his side to their first Premiership Trophy victory in 1981, the press electing him Harry Sunderland Trophy winner. Played against his former club Hull, the clash of Humberside's giants caught the imagination, producing a record crowd (29,448) and receipts (£47,529) for the competition.

Rovers held a comfortable 8-2 half-time lead, a penalty two minutes before the break from Hull's Paul Woods, reducing the deficit created by tries from Phil Hogan (13th minute) and Steve Hartley (35th minute – a spectacular 65 yard race to the line), Steve Hubbard converting the former. Rovers took a firmer grip when Mike Smith got a third, eleven minutes after the teams returned to the field, making it 11-2. Hull, however, proved they were not spent and came back strongly, a try from Mick Crane – goaled by

Len Casey.

Graham Morris

TERRY CLAWSON (LEEDS)
Harry Sunderland Trophy winner 1972

Leeds prop Terry Clawson was transformed from villain to hero in the space of a week when he was voted man of the match in the 1972 Championship Final win over St Helens at Station Road, Swinton. Seven days earlier, he

Born in Normanton, Terry Clawson signed for Featherstone Rovers in 1957 having progressed through the club's junior side. It began a career that saw him play for nine different senior clubs in England, his initial stint at Featherstone Rovers (from 1957 until 1965) proving to be the longest. His rugby journey took him to Bradford Northern (1965-68 and 1976-77), Hull Kingston Rovers (1968-71), Leeds (1971-73), Oldham (1973-74), York (1974-75), Featherstone Rovers (returning to his first professional club in 1978 when he was also appointed player-coach), Wakefield Trinity (1978-79), Huddersfield (1979) and Hull (1980). He topped that up by playing in Australia for New South Wales country club, South Newcastle during three consecutive British close-season breaks (1975, 1976 and 1977).

Clawson – a tough, hard working forward who could play effectively at prop and second-row – had his first experience of antipodean rugby as a member of Great Britain's 1974 touring side. He made 14 Test appearances (1962-74) during his career including the 1972 World Cup, held in France, when he was a member of Britain's victorious team, scoring two goals in the final. He also played 10 times for Yorkshire (1960-72). His club honours included wins in five major finals; the Championship (with Leeds in 1971/72), Player's No.6 Trophy (Leeds 1972/73) and Yorkshire Cup (Featherstone Rovers 1959, Bradford Northern 1965, Leeds 1972). Clawson scored vital goals in all five matches, contributing to a career total of 1,177 that covered a phenomenal 640 matches.

Terry Clawson.

had blamed his poor goal-kicking form for his team's Wembley defeat by Saints but this time his kicking boots were in much better working order. Favourites St Helens led 3-2 at half-time against a Leeds side that lacked four key players from their previous weeks line-up, Clawson's straight forward penalty goal, which had put Leeds in front after ten minutes, being the only challenge to an 18th minute St Helens try from their hooker Les Greenall.

It was during the final 40 minutes that Clawson's match winning qualities shone through with two superb coolly taken touchline goal kicks when adding a second penalty and converting John Atkinson's try in the corner to put Leeds 9-3 ahead. John Walsh reduced the gap through an excellent long distance drop-goal but it was not enough, Leeds gaining revenge for their Challenge Cup Final defeat in capturing their second Championship title in three years, winning 9-5.

A delighted and relieved Clawson, who also did a lot of the hard work in defence, said of his Harry Sunderland Trophy accolade in a post-match interview: 'It's fantastic! I wish it could

Terry Clawson, back row, second from left, with the Leeds team in 1972.

have been last week, but this more than helps me forget that nightmare. It was hell kicking that first goal, but once I saw it go over I felt much better and could settle down to my normal game.'

Northern Rugby League Championship Final 1972
Saturday 20 May at Station Road, Swinton
Leeds 9
Holmes, A Smith, Langley, Dyl, Atkinson (try),
Hardisty (captain), Barham, Clawson (3 goals),
Ward, Fisher, Cookson, Eccles, Batten. Substitutes:
Pickup, Hick.
St Helens 5
Pimblett, Jones, Benyon, Walsh (goal), Wilson, Kelly,
Heaton, Rees, Greenall (try), Stephens, Mantle, E
Chisnall, Coslett (captain). Substitute: Whittle.
Half-time: 2-3. Referee: S Shepherd (Oldham).
Attendance: 24,055.

Terry Clawson, bottom right, shares the dressing room celebration after Leeds had beaten Salford in the 1973 Player's No.6 Trophy Final at Huddersfield.

FRANK COLLIER (WIDNES)
Lance Todd Trophy winner 1964

Widnes' burly six feet one inch, 16 stone prop Frank Collier enjoyed his most memorable Rugby League day when he deservedly walked off the field as the winner of the Lance Todd Trophy following the 1964 Challenge Cup Final victory over pre-match favourites Hull Kingston Rovers. The oldest player in the final at 31, Collier – and Widnes – certainly had a shock in store for the Humberside outfit who, although making their Wembley debut, were expected to be too fast for the forward-dominated Chemics side.

Frank Collier.

Widnes' pack, thanks to a plentiful supply of scrum possession from hooker George Kemel, controlled the first half with Collier and ex-St Helens loose-forward Vince Karalius, leading the way. The only points of the half were from a magnificent long-range penalty by Widnes full-back Bob Randall five minutes before the break. Having subdued Rovers pack, Widnes opened out in spectacular fashion during the second period, Collier making all the running in the 52nd minute for Karalius to send a perfect pass to centre Alan Briers, who evaded three would-be tacklers for the first touchdown of the final. Four minutes later Frank Myler got a second, Randall's conversion making it 10-0.

Rovers managed to compose themselves, bringing the score back to 10-5, before Widnes came on strong again at the finish, Collier capping a great performance by forcing his way

over the try line two minutes from the final whistle after Kemel had made the opening with a dummy pass. Collier – lauded by skipper Karalius as 'easily the best forward of the game' – received two-thirds of the votes given by the journalists present.

Rugby League Challenge Cup Final 1964
Saturday 9 May at Wembley Stadium, London
Widnes 13
Randall (2 goals), Chisnall, Briers (try), Myler (try), Thompson, Lowe, Owen, Hurstfield, Kemel, Collier (try), Measures, Hughes, Karalius (captain).
Hull Kingston Rovers 5
Kellett (goal), Paul, Major, Elliott, Blackmore, Burwell (try), Bunting, Tyson, Flanagan, Mennell, Palmer, Clark, Poole (captain).
Half-time: 2-0. Referee: RL Thomas (Oldham).
Attendance: 84,488.

Widnes 1964. Frank Collier is standing, extreme right.

GARY CONNOLLY (LEEDS RHINOS)
Lance Todd Trophy winner 2003

Having appeared in seven Challenge Cup Finals over a 14-year period for three different clubs, the maturity and experience of Gary Connolly shone through in the 2003 decider for Leeds Rhinos when awarded the Lance Todd Trophy. Unfortunately for Connolly, his outstanding performance under the closed roof of Cardiff's Millennium Stadium could not save his side from losing a closely fought encounter with Bradford Bulls 22-20.

It was Connolly that rallied Leeds after Bradford threatened to run away with the game at the start, taking an early 6-0 lead through a 6th minute Robbie Paul try. Recovering the ball in his own in-goal area just three minutes later, he saved Leeds from a testing goal line drop-out by diving forward to place the ball on the right side of the whitewash with Jamie Peacock clinging on to his legs. A

Gary Connolly leads the way for Leeds Rhinos in the 2003 Challenge Cup Final at Cardiff's Millennium Stadium.

minute later, Connolly showed initiative some 15 yards from the Bradford line, when from acting half-back he dummied his way through four defenders on a 30 yard diagonal run that took him across the face of goal to slide over on the left side with two defenders clinging on. A

PROFILE

Centre or full-back Gary Connolly has enjoyed a long high profile career in professional Rugby League since his signing with hometown St Helens from the Blackbrook amateur club in 1988, making his debut in January 1989. Connolly won the Premiership Trophy (1993) and Lancashire Cup (1991) and was a runner-up at Wembley twice (1989 – when he was aged 17 – and 1991) whilst with St Helens. He transferred to Wigan in 1993 for £250,000, where, playing mostly in the centre, he enjoyed tremendous success. A speedy, courageous player, he found himself on the winning side in the Championship (1993/94, 1994/95 and 1995/96), Super League Grand Final (1998), Rugby League Challenge Cup (1994, 1995 and 2002), Premiership Trophy (1994, 1995, 1996 and 1997), Regal Trophy (1994/95 and 1995/96) and World Club Challenge (1994). Connolly signed for Leeds following the 2002 season, after creating a big impression in the Test series against New Zealand in the autumn of 2002 when he was a late inclusion. His stay with the Rhinos (which included an appearance in the 2003 Challenge Cup Final) lasted until the opening months of the 2004 term, when, released by Leeds, he rejoined Wigan until the end of that season, subsequently moving to Widnes for 2005. A tourist in 1992, Connolly made 31 Test appearances for Great Britain (1991-2003) including the 1992 World Cup Final against Australia at Wembley, played four times for England (1992-1996) including the 1995 World Cup, when he again met Australia in the final at Wembley, once for Ireland (1998 – through the parent/grandparent rule) and twice for Lancashire (2001 and 2003). He had a loan spell in Australia with Canterbury in 1993 and with Harlequins Rugby Union club during the 1996/97 winter break.

suspected double movement was ruled out, the video referee judging Connolly's momentum had taken him over. Kevin Sinfield's goal tied the scores at 6-6, a further converted try and penalty to each side tying the contest 14-14 at the interval.

Again, when Bradford took a 22-14 second half lead, no one worked harder to bring the Challenge Cup back to Headingley than Connolly, Leeds coming within two points after a Dave Furner try midway through the half. The crucial decision of the match came six minutes from the end when Sinfield passed up a kickable penalty chance that would have levelled the scores, electing to run the ball against a Bradford side that was back-pedalling at that point, but the anticipated try did not come.

For the first time in its history, the Lance Todd Trophy was presented after the match, immediately before the Challenge Cup was given to the jubilant Bradford team. Performed on the pitch itself, it was a ceremony Connolly clearly did not enjoy during his moment of despair, leaving the scene, head bowed, the trophy dangling from his right hand like a child would carry a rag doll. For all players who win the award in defeat, it is something treasured

after the pain of losing eases and he was in a happier mood several days later when attending the Red Devils reunion for the formal presentation. Connolly was given the verdict after one of the closest polls ever, receiving 12 of the 25 votes cast, one ahead of Peacock. Having come to terms with the disappointment of defeat, Connolly later said: 'I knew I was going to go out there and give it my all. It's probably the best stadium I've ever played at for atmosphere especially with the roof closed. The noise was deafening. It was one of the best days ever even though we did lose.'

Rugby League Challenge Cup Final 2003
Saturday 26 April at The Millennium Stadium, Cardiff
Bradford Bulls 22
R Paul (captain, try), Vaikona, Naylor, Hape, Vainikolo (try), Pryce, Deacon (5 goals), Vagana, Lowes, Gartner, Radford, Peacock (try), Forshaw. Substitutes: Anderson, Gilmour, Parker, Pratt.
Leeds Rhinos 20
Connolly (try), Calderwood, McKenna (try), Senior, Cummins, Sinfield (captain, 4 goals), Dunemann, Bailey, Diskin, McDermott, Walker, Adamson, Furner (try). Substitutes: Ward, McDonald, Burrow, Poching.
Half-time: 14-14. Referee: R Smith (Castleford). Attendance: 71,212.

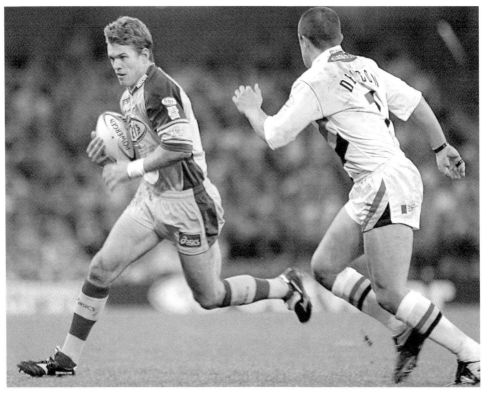

Paul Deacon of Bradford Bulls attempts to close down Gary Connolly during the 2003 Challenge Cup Final.

43

GARY COOPER (WAKEFIELD TRINITY)
Harry Sunderland Trophy winner 1968

Wakefield Trinity retained their Championship in 1968, beating Hull Kingston Rovers 17-10 in an exciting, tense final where, for seventy minutes, the outcome was in doubt. Trinity full-back Gary Cooper's perceived superiority over opposite number David Wainwright was described as a key factor in the win, Cooper continually linking up to provide the vital extra man in attack. His alertness in the 20th minute led to the opening try, combining with second-row pair Bob Haigh and Matt McLeod to send Ray Owen racing over near the posts. Neil Fox added the extras, although the determined Rovers drew level 5-5 by the interval.

Gary Cooper.

Wakefield, with wind advantage in the second half, increased their lead through a bulldozing run from prop David Jeanes, carrying three defenders over as he scored, Neil Fox adding the goal. Never-say-die Rovers responded, placing Cooper and company under siege for some 15 minutes, Trinity holding out against intense pressure, conceding only a drop-goal by Roger Millward (10-7). With time running short Neil Fox got Trinity's third

touchdown, brother Don augmenting, skipper Harold Poynton adding a drop-goal, opening an eight point lead before Rovers grabbed a late consolation try.

Apart from Cooper's spectacular running from full-back, Trinity supporters owed much to their hard-working pack in which Haigh stood out. The *Yorkshire Post* said: 'Cooper won the Harry Sunderland Trophy for the outstanding individual performance but a more reliable guide to the way Trinity played is that at least four other players were nominated for the award – and deserved to be.' Success was bitter-sweet for Neil Fox, aggravating a groin injury which cost his Wembley place the following week and the upcoming World Cup, as Great Britain captain, in Australia and New Zealand.

Northern Rugby League Championship Final 1968
Saturday 4 May at Headingley, Leeds
Wakefield Trinity 17
G Cooper, Coetzer, Brooke, N Fox (try, 2 goals), Batty, Poynton (captain, goal), Owen (try), Jeanes (try), Shepherd, D Fox (goal), Haigh, McLeod, Hawley.
Hull Kingston Rovers 10
Wainwright, Young, Moore (try), Burwell, Longstaff (try), Millward (2 goals), C Cooper, L Foster, Flanagan, Mennell, Lowe, Major, F Foster (captain).
Half-time: 5-5. Referee: DS Brown (Preston).
Attendance: 22,586.

Graham Morris

KEL COSLETT (ST HELENS)
Lance Todd Trophy winner 1972

A proud Kel Coslett with the Challenge Cup at Wembley in 1972.

In a season where he had been booting over goals for St Helens with monotonous regularity – finishing the campaign with a club record 214 – it was entirely predictable that the Welsh loose forward would be just as deadly on his big day at Wembley stadium in the 1972 Challenge Cup Final. It was through his ability to remain calm whilst attempting his goal kicks, and his usual thorough all-round display in leading Saints to victory over Leeds, that earned him the Lance Todd Trophy.

The match began sensationally when St Helens' Welsh prop Graham Rees scored Wembley's quickest try after 35 seconds having charged down and recovered a clearance kick by Leeds' Keith Hepworth, Coslett adding the first of his goals. After sixteen minutes, Les Jones scored St Helens second – and last – try in the right hand corner. Coslett narrowly missed the difficult conversion by inches, but added two penalties, the first of which, after 22 minutes, was a super effort from inside his own half,

giving St Helens a 12-6 lead at the interval. A minute after the restart, Phil Cookson scored an unconverted Leeds try, but Coslett continued to give the Saints that vital edge with his immaculate goal-kicking adding another magnificent penalty after 47 minutes, followed by a 35-yard drop-goal on 61 minutes, two Leeds penalties making the final score 16-13.

PROFILE

Kel Coslett was a big-name signing when he arrived at St Helens from Aberavon Rugby Union club in 1962 having already represented Wales three times that year. Formerly with Bynea (his place of birth) and Llanelli, he was an outstanding goal-kicker who established St Helens club records of 214 goals and 452 points in a season (1971/72) and 1,639 goals and 3,413 points in a career. He played his last match for the Saints in 1976, having set a further club record with 519 career appearances (plus 12 as substitute), a remarkable feat when it is realised Coslett was plagued by injuries for a two year period in the mid-1960s following a leg fracture. His absences caused him to miss the club's Challenge Cup and Championship Final wins of 1966, although playing sufficient League matches to qualify for a medal in the latter. Having arrived at Knowsley Road as a full-back, he resurrected his career with dramatic effect when he became the regular choice at loose forward in 1967. At six feet tall and weighing just over 14 stone, he was perfectly built for the role, excelling in the extra work where his ability to time a pass was put to good use by his speedier forwards. His calm, collected approach made him an ideal captain, being Saints skipper from 1971 onward. At St Helens he won further Championships (1969/70, 1970/71 and 1974/75), plus wins in the Challenge Cup (1972 and 1976), Premiership Trophy (1976), Western Division Championship (1963/64), Lancashire Cup (1962, 1963, 1967 and 1968) and BBC2 Floodlit Trophy (1971 and 1975). He played 12 times for Wales (1968-75, including the 1975 World Cup) and once for Other Nationalities (1974) at county level. He was later player-coach at Rochdale Hornets (1976-79), and coach at Wigan (1979-80) and St Helens (1980-82) as well as Wales (1977-82).

Coslett has fond memories of his Lance Todd award, saying: 'It meant a lot at the time but it gets better as the years go on. I won it in 1972 and it's still remembered!' Referring to St

Helens injury worries in the week beforehand, Coslett added: 'I hadn't gone into the game thinking of being man of the match. We'd had a few problems going into the game so I was thankful of being there because it had taken me ten years to get to Wembley. In the tunnel we were interviewed afterwards by Frank Bough – the BBC man then – who said I'd won the Lance Todd Trophy, and it was a tremendous feeling.'

Whilst St Helens celebrated, it was another disappointing day for Leeds, losing at Wembley for the second successive year after being favourites both times. Whilst Coslett had been on the mark, prop forward Terry Clawson had a poor day for Leeds in trying to master Wembley's swirling winds. Although he matched Coslett's tally of five, he missed another four, including three in front of the posts, lamenting later: 'They won't say it, but I'm responsible for

us losing.' Clawson's moment came the following week when he received the Harry Sunderland Trophy.

For Coslett, who enjoyed Challenge Cup success again in 1976, his Wembley day was a particularly rewarding experience after missing the clubs 1966 victory over Wigan through injury.

Rugby League Challenge Cup Final 1972
Saturday 13 May at Wembley Stadium, London
St Helens 16
Pimblett, Jones (try), Benyon, Walsh, Wilson, Kelly, Heaton, Rees (try), Greenall, Stephens, Mantle, E Chisnall, Coslett (captain, 5 goals).
Leeds 13
Holmes, A Smith, Hynes, Dyl, Atkinson, Hardisty (captain), Hepworth, Clawson (5 goals), Fisher, Ramsey, Cookson (try), Haigh, Batten. Substitute: Langley.
Half-time: 12-6. Referee: E Lawrinson (Warrington).
Attendance: 89,495.

St Helens 1972. Skipper Kel Coslett is seated, centre, behind the ball.

EDDIE CUNNINGHAM (WIDNES)
Lance Todd Trophy winner 1982

Eddie Cunningham was a tough competitor who could run and tackle with devastating effect whether picked for a centre or second-row berth. A native of St Helens, he was one of the many players to emerge through the town's Pilkington Recs amateur club, signing with Wigan in 1969. His only success whilst at Central Park was in winning the Lancashire Cup in 1973, although he was a runner-up in the 1971 Championship Final. In 1975, he returned to his home town after signing for St Helens, arriving mid-season and helping them secure the 1974/75 Championship title. He played twice at Wembley with the Saints (winning in 1976, losing in 1978) and was a winner in the 1977 Premiership Trophy Final. He transferred to Leeds for £25,000 in 1979, moving on to Widnes the following year for a £20,000 fee. He played for the Chemics – as they were previously known – until 1983, making two more appearances in the Challenge Cup Final (victory in 1981 being followed by defeat in the 1982 replay) and winning the Premiership Trophy in 1982. Cunningham made one Great Britain appearance (the opening Test against the 1978 Kangaroo tourists) and played twice for Lancashire (1971 and 1978). He also elected to play for Wales (via the parent/grandparent rule), appearing in eight matches between 1975 and 1978, including the 1975 World Cup when he made his debut playing against England in Brisbane, Australia.

If the selection of Lance Todd Trophy hero Eddie Cunningham by Widnes for Wembley in 1982 was a shock, his gutsy performance that produced two critical tries in the 14-14 Challenge Cup Final draw with Hull was even more astounding. The centre-cum-second row forward had not played in the first team since the previous February, due to a neck injury and, having failed in a comeback attempt with the reserves two weeks earlier, he had been widely written off for the season. Even his coach Doug Laughton had stated he would not have played with such an injury. If anyone thought Cunningham would take a cautious approach, they were soon convinced otherwise as he charged over for a try in the corner after only ten minutes play, having been put through by Les Gorley as the Cumbrian forward succumbed to a tackle. Mick Burke's touchline conversion plus an earlier drop-goal from Keith Elwell propelled Widnes into an early 6-0 lead. However, three penalties from Hull's Sammy Lloyd squared matters at 6-6 by half-time.

Widnes regained the upper hand in the

Eddie Cunningham completes his 1982 Wembley brace in the 51st minute.

second half, Cunningham again causing the damage when, eleven minutes after the restart, he outmanoeuvred three defenders from acting halfback for a brilliant opportunistic try. A further touchdown from Stuart Wright after a length of the field dash following an interception put Widnes 14-6 ahead but all their good work – and Cunningham's – was undone when Hull staged a late rally to force a replay.

Despite the Humbersiders winning the rematch 18-9 at Elland Road, Leeds, 18 days later, Cunningham – one of five rugby playing brothers, four of whom turned professional including Keiron Cunningham who rose to prominence with St Helens in the 1990s – had the consolation of twice being a Wembley winner with St Helens (1976) and Widnes (1981). He looks back on his achievement of winning the Lance Todd Trophy with pride saying: 'What you've got to remember is your name goes in the programme every year and they'll still be doing it after you're not here. It's there for your kids. It's there for your grand-kids. It's there for your great grand-kids.'

Rugby League Challenge Cup Final 1982
Saturday 1 May at Wembley Stadium, London
Hull 14
Kemble, O'Hara (try), Day, Evans, Prendiville, Topliss (captain), Harkin, Skerrett, Wileman, Stone, Crane, Lloyd (4 goals), Norton (try). Substitute: Crooks.
Widnes 14
Burke (goal), Wright (try), O'Loughlin, Cunningham (2 tries), Basnett, Hughes, Gregory (goal), M O'Neill, Elwell (drop-goal), Lockwood, Gorley, Prescott, Adams (captain). Substitutes: Myler, S O'Neill.
Half-time: 6-6. Referee: GF Lindop (Wakefield).
Attendance: 92,147.

Disbelief for Eddie Cunningham, right, as Dane O'Hara earns Hull a replay.

JONATHAN DAVIES (WARRINGTON)
Man of Steel Award winner 1994

Jonathan Davies.

His fine form earned him a place in the Great Britain line-up for the three Test Matches against the New Zealand tourists. Chosen, surprisingly, at full-back, he proved a match-winner as Britain won the lot, scoring a try, 10 goals and a drop-goal. Davies completed his international campaign as captain of Wales, demonstrating his versatility by playing stand-off against New Zealand in Swansea during October (scoring five goals in a 24-19 defeat) and centre versus France in Cardiff during March (four goals and a drop-goal in a 13-12 win).

In receiving the Man of Steel Award, Davies became the first and, to date, only Welshman to receive the honour (excepting the claim of 1998 winner, Oldham-born Iestyn Harris who

All out action from Warrington's Jonathan Davies as he breaks the Sheffield Eagles line.

Former Welsh Rugby Union star Jonathan Davies took the 1994 Man of Steel Award after a brilliant debut season with Warrington. His much publicised pre-season arrival from local rivals Widnes helped steer the club from mid-table to third, only scoring difference separating them from the leading pair – Wigan and Bradford Northern – after the trio had finished level on points in the closest three-way finish ever recorded for the League title. Playing in the centre, he scored 293 points (21 tries, 99 goals, 11 drop-goals) in 30 appearances. Davies recalled: 'Wigan and Bradford had some great players, but Warrington had some tremendous hard workers', adding modestly 'I got a free transfer to Warrington and was able to score some tries and kick some goals.'

represented the Principality at both codes through Welsh ancestry). Davies himself claims his First Division Player of the Year Award at the 1991 Man of Steel Awards evening (a feat he repeated in 1994) whilst with Widnes gave him most satisfaction, saying: 'Winning the Player of the Year gave me a lot of credibility. Having come into the game and having a very tough time at first it gives you the greatest pleasure because it's voted for by your peers. With all the tough players that are in Rugby League, people still don't believe I won the Man of Steel!'

PROFILE

The dazzling play and exciting breaks of Jonathan Davies turned him into Welsh Rugby Union's most prized possession during the 1980s making 27 appearances for his country from 1985 to 1988. Born in Trimsaran, near Llanelli, the former Neath fly-half signed for Widnes from Llanelli Rugby Union club on a reported £150,000 contract in January 1989 surrounded by a blaze of publicity. Davies proved himself equally adept at 13-a-side rugby as a full-back, centre or stand-off, whilst continuing to demonstrate his skill as an outstanding marksman, both with place and drop-kicks, setting a Widnes club record for a season of 342 points in 1990/91 (30 tries, 110 goals, 2 drop-goals). In 1993, he appeared for Widnes at Wembley in his only Challenge Cup Final, although losing to Wigan. He did enjoy plenty of success, however, winning the Championship (1988/89), Premiership Trophy (1989 and 1990), Regal Trophy (1991/92) and Lancashire Cup (1990). His biggest triumph with Widnes was the World Club Challenge win over Canberra Raiders at Old Trafford in 1989.

In 1993, he joined Warrington on a free transfer – his new club taking over his contract – where, although not adding to his club honours, he continued to entertain the crowds with his inspirational performances. He played his final match for Warrington in 1995 whereupon he returned to Rugby Union with Cardiff, following that codes decision to go professional, playing five more times for Wales (1996-97). His representative honours in Rugby League covered 13 Test Matches for Great Britain (1990-94, including the 1990 tour) and nine appearances for Wales (1991-95, including the 1995 World Cup when he was captain). He also had two spells with Australian clubs, playing for Canterbury-Bankstown in 1991 and North Queensland Cowboys in 1995. Awarded the MBE in 1995, he is now a regular commentator on both codes of rugby for BBC television.

Stones Bitter Man of Steel Awards 1994
Tuesday 17 May at the Holiday Inn, Leeds
Compered by Eddie Hemmings.
Man of Steel: Jonathan Davies (Warrington).
First Division Player of the Year: Jonathan Davies (Warrington).
Second Division Player of the Year: Martin Oglanby (Workington Town).
Young Player of the Year: Andrew Farrell (Wigan).
Coach of the Year: John Joyner (Castleford).
Referee of the Year: John Connolly (Wigan).

Jonathan Davies attempts a goal for Great Britain

WILLIE DAVIES (BRADFORD NORTHERN)
Lance Todd Trophy winner 1947

=== PROFILE ===

Former Swansea Rugby Union player Willie Davies was born in Penclawdd and played six times for Wales Rugby Union (1936 to 1939) – making his debut when he was 19 years old – before eventually moving to Yorkshire in 1939 to take up a teaching post. A graduate of Swansea University, he joined the Headingley Rugby Union club but was then tempted to change codes, joining Bradford Northern later that year. Developing into a brilliant, attacking stand-off, capable of turning a match with his incisive breaks, he was a Great Britain tourist in 1946, represented Britain three times in internationals (1946-47) and Wales nine (1939-48). With Bradford, he won the Championship (1939/40 and 1944/45), Rugby League Challenge Cup (1944, 1947 and 1949), and Yorkshire Cup (1941, 1943, 1948 and 1949). He retired in 1950 to accept a new teaching position.

The brilliance of Bradford Northern's Welsh stand-off half Willie Davies stood out in the disappointing all-Yorkshire Challenge Cup Final between Northern and Leeds at Wembley in 1947. The match-up of two of the White Rose county's most prominent clubs had attracted 77,605 – easily beating the previous best of 55,435 that were at the stadium for the Halifax-Salford final in 1939 – but many must have wondered if their long journey was worthwhile to witness a match littered with collapsed scrums and untidy play-the-ball's. Leeds led 2-0 at the break, the second half providing some modicum of entertainment as things settled down more after an untidy first 40 minutes. Davies came to the fore during the second period, his supreme handling and distribution skill bringing his centres Jack Kitchen and Ernest Ward into the game more. With Davies involved in seemingly everything, Bradford – through winger Emlyn Walters and second-row forward Trevor Foster – scored the only two tries of the match, Ernest Ward contributing a drop-goal in the low-scoring 8-4 win.

The *Yorkshire Post's* Alf Drewry commented: 'Northern's backs always handled more smoothly and their running carried more punch than the Leeds set. To lay all the credit for this state of affairs at the door of Bill (Willie) Davies would be unfair to Kitching and Ernest Ward who also played well, but it was Davies' pace over the first five yards, his excellent passing, and his unerring judgement in kicking that accounted more than anything for Northern's clear-cut superiority behind the scrum.'

Davies, aged 30 and making the first of three consecutive Wembley appearances with Bradford, was the first Welshman to win the Lance Todd award, the *Yorkshire Post* advising that 'Davies received an overwhelming majority

Willie Davies.

51

of votes from the panel of judges.' It was a match that involved 13 Welsh-born players, a record for a Challenge Cup Final at Wembley, eight of them turning out for Leeds, including their up-and-coming 22-year-old Dickie Williams who played opposite Davies but had to settle for second-best on this occasion.

Rugby League Challenge Cup Final 1947
Saturday 3 May at Wembley Stadium, London
Bradford Northern 8
Carmichael, Batten, Kitching, E Ward (captain, goal), Walters (try), Davies, D Ward, Whitcombe, Darlison, Smith, Tyler, Foster (try), Evans.
Leeds 4
Cook (2 goals), Cornelius, Price, L Williams, Whitehead, D Williams, Jenkins, Brereton, Murphy, Prosser, Watson, Clues, Owens (captain).
Half-time: 0-2. Referee: P Cowell (Warrington).
Attendance: 77,605.

Willie Davies, third from the far end of the line, awaits his pre-match introduction to His Royal Highness The Duke of Gloucester at Wembley in 1947.

Bradford Northern stand-off Willie Davies, on ground, is tackled by opposite number Dickie Williams of Leeds during the 1947 Challenge Cup Final.

PAUL DEACON (BRADFORD BULLS)
Harry Sunderland Trophy winner 2002

Paul Deacon's Harry Sunderland Trophy win of 2002 followed Bradford Bulls' 19-18 defeat to St Helens in the closest, most exciting Super League Grand Final to date. Deacon did not deserve to be a loser, having put his heart and soul into a match that went to the wire. It was his prompting and cajoling that put Bradford's pack in the ascendancy from the kick-off, sweeping to an early 8-0 lead, Deacon converting a 3rd minute Scott Naylor try and kicking a 45-yard penalty 18 minutes later. The margin could have been greater had the video referee not ruled out his 10th minute 'try' under the posts, match referee Russell Smith also ignoring his

Paul Deacon makes a break during the 2002 Super League Grand Final at Old Trafford.

PROFILE

Wigan-born former Hindley amateur Paul Deacon signed with Oldham Bears in 1997, joining Bradford Bulls later that year. A superb organiser, the quick-witted scrum half also excels with the boot, whether kicking for goal, field position or putting pressure on the opposition in-goal area. To date with the Bulls he has appeared in five Super League Grand Finals, winning in 2001 and 2003, and two Challenge Cup Finals, tasting victory in 2003. He played in the 2002 World Club Challenge success over Newcastle Knights (missing the 2004 win over Penrith through injury). So far, he has represented Great Britain eight times (2001-03), England seven (1999-01 including the 2000 World Cup), and Lancashire four (2001-03).

obstruction plea whilst chasing a Robbie Paul kick just before the interval. Instead, St Helens fought back magnificently to lead 12-8 at half-time.

The Bulls, with Deacon again pulling the strings, were quickly out of the blocks after the break, his inside pass sending Paul Anderson on a charge resulting in Brian McDermott sending Paul over for Bradford's second try. Deacon's goal restored their advantage. Three minutes later, Deacon was again to the fore, his pass sending Naylor scything through on the left, Withers being on hand to score in the corner to lead 18-12. St Helens again came back, to level at 18-18, setting up a flurry of late drop-goals.

Deacon attempted two, one from halfway, Sean Long, with his third effort, pulling victory out of the hat for St Helens in the final minute. The dying seconds provided controversy when St Helens skipper Chris Joynt appeared to deliberately fall at the feet of two Bulls' defenders amid claims of a voluntary tackle. Referee Smith dismissed appeals that would have given Deacon a difficult, but kickable, chance to claim victory.

Super League Grand Final 2002
Saturday 19 October at Old Trafford, Manchester
St Helens 19
Wellens, Albert, Gleeson (try), Newlove, Stewart, Sculthorpe, Long (try, 3 goals, drop-goal), Britt, Cunningham, Ward, Bennett (try), Jonkers, Joynt (captain). Substitutes: Hoppe, Shiels, Stankevitch, Higham.
Bradford Bulls 18
Withers (try), Vaikona, Naylor (try), Costin, Vainikolo, R Paul (captain, try), Deacon (3 goals), Vagana, Lowes, Fielden, Gartner, Peacock, Forshaw. Substitutes: Gilmour, Anderson, McDermott, Pryce.
Half-time: 8-12. Referee: R Smith (Castleford).
Attendance: 61,138.

KEVIN DICK (LEEDS)
Harry Sunderland Trophy winner 1979

The fifth Premiership Trophy Final in 1979 was the first held east of the Pennines, Huddersfield's ex-Fartown home being host for the only time, drawing the, then, biggest crowd of 19,486. The all-Yorkshire affair produced a disappointingly one-sided contest as Leeds defeated Bradford Northern 24-2, their half-back duo of Harry Sunderland Trophy winner Kevin Dick, at stand-off despite wearing number '7' on his back, and John 'Sammy' Sanderson continually forcing Bradford's vaunted pack back with a great display of tactical kicking.

Despite Leeds possessing the extra edge Bradford were still in the hunt after almost an hour until Dick's timely 59th minute interception sent David Smith racing away. Although tackled, his quick play-the-ball resulted in acting-half Alan Smith going over to open a 15-2 advantage, Leeds becoming totally dominant from that point as they sensed victory.

Bradford had scored first through a Steve Ferres penalty, Leeds not going in front until the 32nd minute when David Smith registered the only first half try, Dick adding a fabulous

touchline effort, followed by a penalty goal for a 7-2 interval lead. Dick continued to keep the scoreboard operator busy after the restart adding two more penalties and a drop-goal prior to Alan Smith's crucial second try. During the final ten minutes Dick confirmed his man of the match performance by registering three further goals – two penalties and the conversion of David Ward's last minute try – for a personal contribution of fifteen points.

Premiership Trophy Final 1979
Sunday 27 May at Fartown, Huddersfield
Leeds 24
Hague, A Smith (try), D Smith (try), Dyl, Atkinson, Dick (7 goals, drop-goal), Sanderson, Harrison, Ward (captain, try), Pitchford, Joyce, Eccles, Cookson. Substitutes: Fletcher, Adams.
Bradford Northern 2
Mumby, Parker, Okulicz, Gant, Spencer, Ferres (goal), A Redfearn, Thompson (captain), Bridges, Forsyth, Trotter, Grayshon, Casey. Substitutes: Mordue, van Bellen.
Half-time: 7-2. Referee: WH Thompson (Huddersfield). Attendance: 19,486.

Kevin Dick.

MATT DISKIN (LEEDS RHINOS)
Harry Sunderland Trophy winner 2004

=== PROFILE ===

Dewsbury-born hooker Matt Diskin signed with Leeds Rhinos from his local side Dewsbury Moor in 1998, although it was not until 2001 that he made his senior debut, having just passed his 19th birthday, his thirst for work and keen defence established him as a Rhinos regular by 2002. Apart from winning the Super League Grand Final in 2004, he was a runner-up in the 2003 and 2005 Challenge Cup Finals. His representative honours, to date, include one appearance for Great Britain in the 2004 Tri-Nations (when he sustained a knee injury causing him to miss most of the 2005 season) and three for Yorkshire (2002-03).

Matt Diskin.

Matt Diskin became the first hooker since Mick Stephenson in 1973 – both of them being born in Dewsbury – to lift the Harry Sunderland Trophy after collecting 15 of the 28 votes delivered by the press, nine ahead of second-placed Leeds Rhinos colleague Richard Mathers. He gave such a committed, non-stop performance in the 2004 Grand Final victory over Bradford Bulls that he eventually ran himself to a standstill, coach Tony Smith finally taking him off the field after 67 minutes play. Despite that absence, he had done more than enough to convince the majority of journalists present that he was the game-star.

He was the spur to Leeds' pack getting on top of their Bulls counterparts in a tense first half during which both teams scored one try each. Lesley Vainikolo's 7th minute touchdown put Bradford ahead 4-2 before Diskin responded with a brilliant piece of individualism eight minutes later. Taking the ball from acting half-back about 20 yards from the try line, his angled run and dummy-pass took him between two defenders to touch down for a crucial go-ahead try to the left of the posts. Kevin Sinfield

converted, Leeds going on to lead 10-4 at the break.

Shontayne Hape gave Bradford hope with a try three minutes into the second-half reducing their arrears to two points, the match remaining on a knife-edge until a spectacular Danny McGuire effort five minutes from full-time – Sinfield adding his fourth goal – sealed Leeds' first 'championship' since 1972 with a 16-8 win.

Super League Grand Final 2004
Saturday 16 October at Old Trafford, Manchester
Leeds Rhinos 16
Mathers, Calderwood, Walker, Senior, Bai, Sinfield (captain, 4 goals), McGuire (try), Ward, Diskin (try), Bailey, McKenna, Lauitiiti, Furner. Substitutes: Poching, McDermott, Burrow, Jones-Buchanan.
Bradford Bulls 8
Withers, Reardon, Johnson, Hape (try), Vainikolo (try), Harris, Deacon, Vagana, R Paul (captain), Fielden, Peacock, Swann, Radford. Substitutes: Anderson, Pratt, Parker, Langley.
Half-time: 10-4. Referee: S Ganson (St Helens).
Attendance: 65,547.

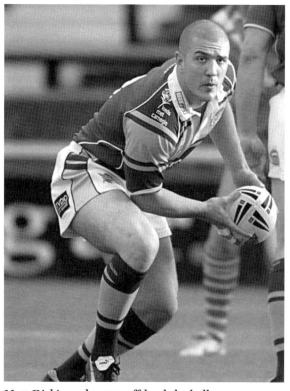

Matt Diskin – about to off-load the ball.

CARL DOOLER (FEATHERSTONE ROVERS)
Lance Todd Trophy winner 1967

BBC television sports commentator David Coleman interviews Lance Todd winner Carl Dooler following the 1967 Challenge Cup Final at Wembley.

Featherstone Rovers finally got their hands on the Challenge Cup in 1967, Carl Dooler deservedly winning the Lance Todd Trophy after a good all-round team performance. Although both combatants were surprise finalists (Barrow finished 15th in the League,

---

PROFILE

Carl Dooler was – like fellow Lance Todd Trophy winners Don and Neil Fox – from Sharlston, joining Featherstone Rovers in 1960. A clever, hard working scrum-half, whose telling breaks often turned the course of a match, he was a British Lions tourist in 1966 (although destined not to appear in any Tests), and selected five times for Yorkshire (1962-67). He played for Featherstone until 1968, winning the Challenge Cup in 1967, transferring to Hull Kingston Rovers for £6,500 in 1969, but forced to retire at the end of that year due to a back injury. He created a surprise in making a comeback with York in 1973, moving to Batley and playing a handful of games for them in 1974.

Featherstone 20th), they served up an entertaining match in front of Her Majesty Queen Elizabeth II, attending her second Challenge Cup Final.

Barrow got on top early and led 7-2 with almost a half-hour played. Dooler, with Featherstone's heavyweight pack gaining the ascendancy, then turned the match around. Second-row forward Jim Thompson, having been tackled following a surging run that took him close to the Barrow try line, rose quickly to play the ball to the waiting Dooler, whose sharp, crisp pass sent 18 stone prop Arnold Morgan crashing through a gap to go under the posts, Tom Smales' goal levelling the scores. Two minutes later, Dooler struck again with a 35-yard drop-goal putting his side two points ahead, a lead they would not lose.

A dominant Featherstone extended their lead to 14-7 in the second-half, the busy Dooler (who had just failed with another drop-goal attempt) virtually sealing the match in the 64th minute when he broke away from a play-the-ball to race past two Barrow defenders before turning the ball inside for Smales to score an unconverted try. Barrow gained a deserved consolation try and goal in the final minutes. Tom Ashcroft, writing in the *Rugby Leaguer*, said: 'Dooler first fulfilled the scrum-half's main function by keeping the back line on the move. He had his flashes of inspiration with the drop-goal and the making of a try and when his side was in control he turned to the unorthodox with some clever back-flip passes.'

Rugby League Challenge Cup Final 1967
Saturday 13 May at Wembley Stadium, London
Featherstone Rovers 17
Wrigglesworth, Thomas (try), Cotton, Jordan, Greatorex, M Smith, Dooler (goal), Tonks, Harris, Dixon (captain), Morgan (try), Thompson, Smales (try, 3 goals).
Barrow 12
Tees (goal), Burgess, Challinor (captain), Hughes, Murray, Brophy (try), G Smith, Kelland, Redhead, Hopwood, Sanderson, Delooze (2 goals), Watson (try).
Half-time: 9-7. Referee: E Clay (Leeds). Attendance: 76,290.

JOHN DORAHY (HULL KINGSTON ROVERS)
Harry Sunderland Trophy winner 1984

PROFILE

John Dorahy is a native of Sydney, Australia, beginning his career as a member of the Wollongong Wests club. He visited England as an 18-year-old in 1973 with brother Tony, appearing five times for Leigh. Returning to Australia, he played for Western Suburbs (1974-79), building his reputation as a classy back, be it at full-back, centre or stand-off, and became renown for his kick and chase. An outstanding goal-scorer, he earned the nickname 'Joe Cool' for his calm looking approach to place kicking.

His career in Australia continued with Manly-Warringah (1980-81), Illawarra Steelers (1982-85) and North Sydney (1987-89). He interrupted his Illawarra commitment to play for Hull Kingston Rovers throughout most of the 1983/84 British season, winning the Championship and Premiership Trophy. On completing his contract with Illawarra, he returned to the Rovers (1985-87), winning the Yorkshire Cup (1985) but losing the 1986 Challenge Cup Final. After North Sydney, he went back to England, concluding his career with Halifax during the 1989/90 term, taking over as coach (1989-90). Further coaching appointments followed at Wigan (1993-94) and Warrington (1996-97). Returning to Australia, he has worked on the coaching staff at several leading clubs. He played twice each for Australia (1978, missing that year's Kangaroo tour through injury) and New South Wales (1979).

Australian stand-off John Dorahy became the first overseas player to capture the Harry Sunderland Trophy, taking the 1984 award as Hull Kingston Rovers eventually subdued Castleford to win an entertaining Premiership Trophy Final 18-10. Castleford excelled during the first half to lead 8-0, Rovers coach Roger Millward making several pack changes during the interval, including Mike Smith's relocation from centre to loose-forward. Even Millward could not have anticipated his team's thrilling four-try revival, Castleford's only response being a penalty goal.

Dorahy, a unanimous press choice as outstanding player, excelled after the break, his deft handling and positive running being pivotal to Rovers comeback. A minute into the half, he carved out an opening to send Gary Prohm racing over. Dorahy was central to everything as the Robins tore Castleford apart, Smith grabbing the go-ahead try in the 54th minute. Dorahy got the next, haring across the whitewash three minutes later, David Laws adding the final touchdown with three minutes to go.

All four tries came near the left corner flag, providing Dorahy with a quartet of difficult conversion attempts, only the first – a magnificent effort nonetheless - finding the mark. He also failed with three drop-goal attempts but it could not detract from his eye-catching display as Rovers won their second Premiership Trophy in four years, whilst being the first to claim a Championship and Premiership double.

John Dorahy.

Premiership Trophy Final 1984
Saturday 12 May at Headingley, Leeds
Hull Kingston Rovers 18
Fairbairn, Clark, M Smith (try), Prohm (try), Laws (try), Dorahy (try, goal), Harkin, Holdstock, Rudd, Millington, Burton, Broadhurst, Hall (captain).
Substitutes: Lydiat, Robinson.
Castleford 10
Rookley, Coen, Marchant, Hyde, Kear (try), Robinson, B Beardmore (captain, 3 goals), Ward, Horton, Connell, Crampton, Atkins, Joyner.
Half-time: 0-8. Referee: R Campbell (Widnes).
Attendance: 12,515.

RAY DUTTON (WIDNES)
Lance Todd Trophy winner 1975

For the third consecutive Challenge Cup Final it was the goal-kicking prowess of the winning full-back that played a significant part in determining the destination of the much prized trophy, the trusty boot of Widnes' Ray Dutton dominating in 1975. As with Warrington's Derek Whitehead the previous year, Dutton's composure and accuracy was rewarded with receipt of the Lance Todd Trophy.

Ray Dutton.

Whitehead – present again on the big occasion as Warrington defended their guardianship of the cup – was the first of the two marksmen to place the ball between the uprights, converting John Bevan's fifth minute try as his team dominated the early stages. It was Dutton who brought some order to the Widnes camp when, after just missing with a 40-yard penalty attempt, he made amends with another

effort from almost the same position after 16 minutes play. Suddenly, with points on the board, confidence surged through the Widnes ranks and both Eric Hughes and Mick Adams almost found their way over the whitewash for tries. In the latter attempt, however, Whitehead, in his desperation to foil the score, tripped Adams, allowing Dutton to notch his second. Now one point in arrears, the Chemics went all out for that vital try, and Mal Aspey (twice) and John Foran went close, before mighty prop Jim Mills raced over almost unopposed on 33 minutes. Dutton added the goal and, on the stroke of half-time, was again on target with an easy penalty following a scrum infringement, and Widnes were looking good for their 11-5 interval lead.

A Whitehead penalty narrowed the gap to 11-7 just three minutes after the resumption, but it was Dutton who restored Widnes' grip with two goals in a critical three minute spell. The first, after 50 minutes play, occurred when he calmly struck home Wembley's first one point drop-goal from 30 yards out, quickly followed by his fourth

The 1975 Widnes line-up including Ray Dutton, back row, third from left.

successful penalty from just 10 yards. Although 25 minutes remained on the clock, it completed the scoring at 14-7 to Widnes, the prospect of having to score twice proving too big a hurdle for the deflated Warrington outfit.

Rugby League Challenge Cup Final 1975
Saturday 10 May at Wembley Stadium, London
Widnes 14
Dutton (5 goals, drop-goal), Prescott, George, Aspey,
Anderson, Hughes, Bowden, Mills (try), Elwell,
Sheridan, Foran, Adams, Laughton (captain).
Warrington 7
Whitehead (2 goals), M Philbin, Noonan, Reynolds,
Bevan (try), Whittle, Gordon, D Chisnall (captain),
Ashcroft, Wanbon, Conroy, Martyn, B Philbin.
Substitutes: Briggs, Nicholas.
Half-time: 11-5. Referee: P Geraghty (York).
Attendance: 85,098.

A perfect follow through from goal kicking ace Ray Dutton.

GRAHAM EADIE (HALIFAX)
Lance Todd Trophy winner 1987

Halifax full-back Graham Eadie became the second Australian recipient of the Lance Todd Trophy following a thrilling Challenge Cup Final that saw the Yorkshire side just pip St Helens 19-18. The 33-year-old, known as 'Wombat', embellished a powerful personal performance when shrugging off two would-be tacklers to charge behind the posts for a crucial 50th minute try, after loose forward John Pendlebury broke away to the right of a scrum near St Helens line to accept Gary Stephens' pass. With Colin Whitfield's extra points, the 18-8 score-line gave Halifax breathing space, St Helens having reduced their 12-2 half-time lead by six points following a Mark Elia try 35 seconds into the second period after sprinting 75 yards.

Graham Eadie battles through the St Helens defence at Wembley in 1987.

PROFILE

Graham Eadie carved out a second career after joining Halifax in 1986. Despite almost three years of 'retirement', he helped the club reach the Challenge Cup Final at Wembley in 1987 and 1988. He became player-coach in 1988 but left after four months in the role, Halifax, reportedly, wishing to create room on their overseas quota. He later worked on the coaching staff at several lower-grade Australian clubs.
Born in Sydney, he was a product of the Woy Woy club, based in the New South Wales Central Coast region, signing for Manly-Warringah in 1971 and winning four Grand Finals (1972, 1973, 1976 and 1978). A quality, attacking full-back, he retired following the 1983 season as the, then, highest ever point scorer in the Australian competition. He represented Australia in 12 Tests (1973-79), covering the 1973 and 1978 Kangaroo tours and successful 1975 and 1977 World Cup campaigns. He played 12 times for New South Wales (1974-80).

minutes (dramatically losing the ball in a Pendlebury tackle as he dived over the line and then for a forward pass). Having been doubtful for the final with a hamstring injury, Eadie, who won his award ahead of colleagues Stephens and Pendlebury, said: 'Hearing that final hooter had to be the greatest. It was just a fantastic feeling to know that we had won. It will be something I will savour for the rest of my life.'

Eadie had already proved a hero in defence during the opening 23 minutes of the match producing three try saving tackles – on Kevin McCormack (twice) and Brett Clark – when St Helens were looking to take control. In the final analysis, it was Pendlebury's 64th minute drop-goal that made the difference, St Helens storming back with two further tries with Elia having two others disallowed in the final seven

Rugby League Challenge Cup Final 1987
Saturday 2 May at Wembley Stadium, London
Halifax 19
Eadie (try), Wilson, Whitfield (3 goals), Rix, George (try), C Anderson (captain), Stephens, Beevers, McCallion (try), Neller, Dixon, Scott, Pendlebury (drop-goal). Substitutes: Juliff, James.
St Helens 18
Vievers, Ledger, Loughlin (try, 3 goals), Elia (try), McCormack, Clark, Holding, Burke, Liptrot, Fieldhouse, Platt, Haggerty, Arkwright (captain). Substitute: Round (try).
Half-time: 12-2. Referee: J Holdsworth (Kippax). Attendance: 91,267.

SHAUN EDWARDS (WIGAN)
Man of Steel Award winner 1990

The glittering honour laden career of Wigan's Shaun Edwards reached its zenith in 1990 with his well-deserved Man of Steel Award. In truth, Edwards would have been a worthy contender for the honour in most of his fourteen seasons at Central Park. No stranger to the awards ceremony, he had picked up the Young Player of the Year accolade in three consecutive years from 1986.

His award was cited as being 'for courage above and beyond the call of duty', a reference to his spirited contribution to Wigan's record-making third successive Challenge Cup win at Wembley. Having taken a pre-match pain-killing injection to nullify the effect of a broken hand, he suffered a facial injury in only the 10th minute – later diagnosed as a double-fracture of the eye socket and a depressed cheekbone. The

Danger always threatened when Shaun Edwards had possession.

injury eliminated him from the forthcoming tour of New Zealand and Papua New Guinea after he had been selected as tour captain.

He had enjoyed a splendid 1989/90 season at international level, being selected as Great Britain captain for the second of the two match series with France during March and April and playing his part in the earlier 2-1 Test series win over the touring New Zealanders played during the autumn. His contribution against the Kiwis led to him being acclaimed as Britain's Man of the Series, to which he added the Ernest Ward Memorial Trophy as his country's player of the year.

Shaun Edwards.

61

PROFILE

Shaun Edwards spent the majority of his honour-strewn career with Wigan, who he joined – amidst much publicity – at midnight on his seventeenth birthday during October 1983. Previously with Wigan St Patrick's and the son of former Warrington half-back Jackie Edwards, his reported £35,000 payment was believed the highest paid for an amateur Rugby League player until then. Edwards developed into one of Britain's greatest ever half-backs, a committed, influential player who scored 274 tries (including a club record-equalling 10 in a match) for Wigan, many of them due to his alertness when supporting breaks. He created Wembley records as the youngest Challenge Cup Finalist in 1984 (17 years, 202 days) and youngest captain in 1988 (21 years, 195 days) being victorious in nine Challenge Cup Finals for Wigan (1985 and 1988 to 1995), losing in just two; his first (1984) and last (1999 – when he was with London Broncos).

He earned medals for a record eight Championship successes (1986/87 and 1989/90 to 1995/96), other team honours including victory in the World Club Challenge (1987, 1991 and 1994), Premiership Trophy (1987, 1992, 1994, 1995 and 1996), John Player Trophy (1985/86, 1986/87 and 1988/89), Regal Trophy (1989/90, 1992/93, 1994/95 and 1995/96) and Lancashire Cup (1985, 1986, 1987, 1988 and 1992). He was a tourist in 1988 and 1992, and represented Great Britain in 36 Test Matches (1985-94), England three times (1995-96, being captain of the 1995 World Cup squad where illness restricted him to one game), Ireland once (1998 – qualifying through the parent/grandparent rule) and Lancashire four times (1985-91). He joined London Broncos for £60,000 during 1997, moving to Bradford Bulls later that year for £40,000, rejoining the Broncos in 1998, with whom he concluded his playing days in 2000. During 1989, he played for Australian club Balmain Tigers, appearing in their Grand Final defeat of that year. He later joined the coaching staff at London Wasps Rugby Union club where he became head coach. He received the OBE in 1996.

In addition to the 36-14 Challenge Cup Final victory over Warrington, he helped Wigan regain the Championship after a three-year gap and to win the Regal (previously John Player) Trophy for the fourth time in five seasons. During the campaign he scored 25 tries and 10 goals for Wigan in 33 appearances.

Stones Bitter Man of Steel Awards 1990
Thursday 10 May at the Holiday Inn Crowne Plaza Midland, Manchester
Compered by Harry Gration
Man of Steel: Shaun Edwards (Wigan).
First Division Player of the Year: Andy Goodway (Wigan).
Second Division Player of the Year: John Woods (Rochdale Hornets).
Young Player of the Year: Bobbie Goulding (Wigan).
Coach of the Year: John Monie (Wigan).
Referee of the Year: Robin Whitfield (Widnes).

GEORGE FAIRBAIRN (WIGAN)
Man of Steel Award winner 1980

George Fairbairn.

George Fairbairn became the first non-English Man of Steel Award winner and only Scot to date, when honoured at the 1980 ceremony. It followed a season where he showed character during adversity at club level, Wigan eventually being relegated to Division Two. Referring to Wigan's poor campaign, *Open Rugby* magazine commented: 'Through it all, George Fairbairn has stood like a rock, carrying on the club's traditions of providing international quality players.' His dedication and determination was recognised by Wigan in appointing him their player-coach at only 25 years old, during April as the season drew to a close.

He commenced the domestic season late, missing the opening six matches due to being on Great Britain's 1979 tour of Australia and New Zealand. His continuing fine form at club level on his return was recognised by inclusion in the England team, helping them win the European Championship title, registering a personal tally of 15 points (a try and six goals) in the 26-9

victory over Wales at Craven Park, Hull, during February.

As well as accepting his Man of Steel winners' cheque and silver goblet, Fairbairn – one of three nominees for the First Division Player of the Year Award – received a framed citation stating his recognition was for 'talent, leadership, loyalty and commitment at both club and international level.'

Trumanns Man of Steel Awards 1980
Wednesday 21 May at the Wakefield Theatre Club
Compered by Keith Macklin
Man of Steel: George Fairbairn (Wigan).
First Division Player of the Year: Mick Adams (Widnes).
Second Division Player of the Year: Steve Quinn (Featherstone Rovers).
Young Player of the Year: Roy Holdstock (Hull Kingston Rovers).
Coach of the Year: Peter Fox (Bradford Northern).
Referee of the Year: GF (Fred) Lindop (Wakefield).

PROFILE

Scottish full-back George Fairbairn joined Wigan in 1974 from Kelso Rugby Union club for a reported £8,000. Born in Peebles, he was a brave defender with an exciting attacking style, and an accomplished goal-kicker. He impressed the Great Britain selectors, being included in the squad for the 1977 World Cup – staged in Australia and New Zealand – playing in the final against Australia in Sydney and taking part in the 1979 tour to the Southern Hemisphere, his final Test count reaching 17 (1977-82). His Scots ancestry was overlooked with 15 appearances for England (1975-81) including the 1975 World Cup, and two for Lancashire (1977 and 1978). Playing for Wigan during an unusually barren time for the club, his only medal was through being a runner-up in the 1980 Lancashire Cup Final. Having spent his final season at Central Park as player-coach, he transferred to Hull Kingston Rovers in 1981 for a then Rugby League record £72,500. The move paid off for Fairbairn, winning three Championships (1983/84, 1984/85 and 1989/90), the Premiership Trophy (1984), John Player Trophy (1984/85) and Yorkshire Cup (1985) and appearing in the 1986 Challenge Cup Final at Wembley, although losing. He played his final match for the club in 1990, becoming their coach (1991-94), followed by similar assignments with Huddersfield (1994-95) and Scotland (1996-97).

ANDREW FARRELL (WIGAN/WIGAN WARRIORS)

Man of Steel Award winner 1996 and 2004
Harry Sunderland Trophy winner 1996 and 1997

Andrew Farrell won the Man of Steel Award in 2004 for the second time after a heroic season for Wigan and Great Britain. Having waited eight years since the first, in 1996, he told the audience: 'This is unbelievable. Since I won it the first time it has been a goal of mine to come back and win another award.'

His 2004 honour was widely predicted. Having missed the opening matches recovering from a knee operation, he proved his versatility during an injury-hit Wigan campaign with ten games in the unaccustomed role of

Andrew Farrell

prop, twelve in the second-row and seven at loose forward. To most observers, Farrell gave the impression he had spent a career in the demanding front row position, rather than months. It was all the more creditable when it is remembered he moved there after a torrid spell in which he suffered a broken nose against Leeds during June (returning for the second half wearing a protective face mask), complicated by a further painful facial injury at Widnes a few weeks later.

Farrell, voted the Super League Players' Player of the Year at the same ceremony, was unable to convert his inspirational performances into team success, beaten in the Challenge Cup Final by in-form St Helens and the Final Eliminator at Leeds during the Super League play-offs, a match that would be Farrell's last for the club. He subsequently led Great Britain to

the Tri-Nations Final, where Australia's 44-4 victory could not detract from Britain's excellent form in the earlier games.

He received his first Man of Steel award when he was 21, at the climax of the first Super League season in 1996. It followed a glorious term for the rising star, voted Young Player of the Year in 1994 and 1995, being appointed captain of all he surveyed; Wigan (in mid-season), England (winning that year's European Championship), and Great Britain (the youngest-ever tour captain for the post-season trip to the Southern Hemisphere). Although Wigan relinquished their eight-year stranglehold on the Challenge Cup, they subsequently won the Premiership Trophy Final at Old Trafford.

It was in that 1996 Premiership Trophy Final, a few days after his Man of Steel success, that Farrell endorsed the judges choice by taking the Harry Sunderland award after defeating St Helens 44-14. It was a match in which Wigan, facing their first trophy-less season since 1983/84, exploded with a 26-point burst in the final 30 minutes with five superb tries. Young skipper Farrell had a fine match, his constant link-up with scrum-half Shaun Edwards proving influential, having a direct hand in four of the Cherry and Whites nine tries. The pair combined in putting hat-trick hero Danny Ellison over for his first – and Wigan's third – in

PROFILE

Andrew Farrell is one of Great Britain's outstanding players of recent years, the powerful, ball-playing second-row or loose forward proving an inspirational captain for club and country. He first appeared for Wigan in 1991, being signed from local amateurs Orrell St James, his subsequent achievements in the famous cherry and white jersey making impressive reading. In 1993, he became the youngest player at 17 years, 11 months, to appear in a Challenge Cup winning side at Wembley, appearing as a substitute in the win over Widnes, subsequently being appointed club captain in 1996 when only 21. His club honours include wins in the Championship (1993/94, 1994/95 and 1995/96), Super League Grand Final (1998), Rugby League Challenge Cup (1993, 1994, 1995 and 2002), World Club Challenge (1994) and Premiership Trophy (1994, 1995, 1996 and 1997). He was a runner-up twice in Challenge Cup deciders (1998 and 2004) and in three Super League Grand Finals (2000, 2001 and 2003). Farrell took over the goal-kicking duties in 1995 following the departure of Frano Botica, surprising everyone with his assured marksmanship. His total haul of 1,355 goals (and 3,135 points) for Wigan is second only to the legendary Jim Sullivan. His 183 goals (including five drop-goals), plus 17 tries, set up a new seasonal club record of 429 points in 2001.

Farrell became Great Britain's youngest Test forward (18 years 5 months) when making his debut against New Zealand in November 1993, appearing in every Test Match for the remainder of his Rugby League career, a record run of 34 consecutive appearances that ended with the Tri-Nations Final in November 2004. In 1996, he became Britain's youngest tour captain, retaining the role for the remainder of his Test career; another record breaking run of 29 matches. His international career included eleven matches for England (1995-2001) including the World Cups of 1995 (when he played in the final against Australia at Wembley) and 2000. He also appeared three times for Lancashire (2001-03). He was awarded the OBE in the 2005 New Years Honours, followed by the surprise announcement of his move to Rugby Union, signing for Saracens in March 2005, his final Wigan appearance, therefore, being in October 2004.

influencing Wigan's next two touchdowns by Simon Haughton (Farrell providing a perfect scoring pass) and Henry Paul (Farrell breaking from a scrum as Edwards again provided the link). Amid criticism during the campaign that they were past their best, the comprehensive manner of Wigan's win gave notice that they were still a potent force.

In 1997, the renamed Wigan Warriors won their fourth consecutive Premiership Trophy Final, St Helens again the victims in a repeat of the 1996 showdown. Another replicated item was Farrell's name on the Harry Sunderland roll of honour, receiving an overwhelming 26 of the 28 votes cast. Wigan led 14-8 at the break, both of their first half tries the result of Farrell's prowess with the boot, Andy Johnson latching on to a high kick in the corner (4th minute) and Robinson diving onto a ball dribbled through by his skipper (31st minute).

In a repeat of the 1992 and 1996 finals against St Helens, Wigan pulled away in the second half, although the final 33-20 score was closer on this occasion. Wigan's three second half tries came in a 12-minutes blitz, Farrell, Radlinski and Haughton combining for each of them and, appropriately, grabbing one apiece. Farrell's, in the 59th minute, climaxed a thrilling

the 26th minute. His second concluded the first half scoring ten minutes later, being the most spectacular of the final, Kris Radlinski breaking from well inside the Wigan half, the move continued in mesmerising fashion by Farrell, Jason Robinson and Edwards before Ellison flew over in the corner.

Wigan's 18-8 lead at the turnaround looked precarious eight minutes after the restart when St Helens reduced it to four points through a converted Tommy Martyn try. Within 15 minutes, though, Farrell restored order,

Andrew Farrell hands off Widnes winger John Devereux during the 1993 Challenge Cup Final when, still only 17, he became Wembley's youngest winner.

Weighing up the options – Andrew Farrell.

Stones Gold Awards Dinner 1996
Tuesday 3 September at the Holiday Inn Crowne Plaza Midland, Manchester
Compered by Eddie Hemmings and Mike Stephenson
Man of Steel: Andrew Farrell (Wigan).
Super League Player of the Year: Robbie Paul (Bradford Bulls).
First Division Player of the Year: Nathan McAvoy (Salford Reds).
Second Division Player of the Year: Stanley Gene (Hull Kingston Rovers).
Super League Young Player of the Year: Keiron Cunningham (St Helens).
Super League Coach of the Year: Shaun McRae (St Helens).
Referee of the Year: Stuart Cummings (Widnes).

Tetley's Super League Man of Steel Awards 2004
Tuesday 12 October at the Midland Hotel, Manchester
Compered by Eddie Hemmings and Mike Stephenson
Man of Steel: Andrew Farrell (Wigan Warriors).
Super League Players' Player of the Year: Andrew Farrell (Wigan Warriors).
Super League Young Player of the Year: Shaun Briscoe (Hull).
Super League Coach of the Year: Shane McNally (Wakefield Trinity).
Super League Referee of the Year: Steve Ganson (St Helens).

Premiership Trophy Final 1996
Sunday 8 September at Old Trafford, Manchester
Wigan 44
Radlinski, Ellison (3 tries), Connolly (try), Tuigamala, Robinson (try), Paul (try), Edwards (try), Skerrett, Hall, O'Connor, Haughton (try), Cassidy, Farrell (captain, 4 goals). Substitutes: Cowie, Barrow, A Johnson, Murdock (try).
St Helens 14
Prescott, Hayes, Hunte, Newlove (try), Sullivan, Martyn (try), Goulding (captain, 3 goals), Perelini, Cunningham, Fogerty, McVey, Morley, Hammond. Substitutes: Pickavance, Arnold, Haigh, Booth.
Half-time: 18-8. Referee: D Campbell (Widnes).
Attendance: 35,013.

Premiership Trophy Final 1997
Sunday 28 September at Old Trafford, Manchester
Wigan Warriors 33
Robinson (try), Ellison, Connolly, Radlinski (try), A Johnson (try), Paul, Smith, Cowie, J Clarke, Hansen, Haughton (try), Cassidy, Farrell (captain, try, 6 goals). Substitutes: Wright (drop-goal), O'Connor, Holgate, Tallec.
St Helens 20
Arnold, Stewart, Hunte, Newlove (try), Sullivan, Hammond (try), Long (2 goals), Leathem, Cunningham, O'Neill, McVey (try), Perelini, Joynt (captain). Substitutes: Booth, Pickavance, Morley, Anderson (try).
Half-time: 14-8. Referee: S Cummings (Widnes).
Attendance: 33,389.

length-of-field move he instigated himself, their efforts putting Wigan ahead 33-10, Saints rallying with two late tries. As well as scoring his try, Farrell enjoyed a far more satisfying time with his goal-kicking than the previous year (when he uncharacteristically converted just four of Wigan's nine tries) scoring six through three conversions and three penalties.

Farrell's Man of Steel and Harry Sunderland doubles make him the only player to have won more than one of the awards featured in this compilation a second time.

Graham Morris

TERRY FOGERTY (HALIFAX)
Harry Sunderland Trophy winner 1965

PROFILE

Glossop-born Terry Fogerty was signed by Halifax from the Saddleworth Rangers amateur club in 1960, making his senior debut the following year when he was 16 years, 9 months old. The speedy, ball-playing back-row forward quickly established himself in the Halifax pack and was in their winning line-up for the finals of the Yorkshire Cup (1963), Eastern Division Championship (1963/64) and Rugby League Championship (1964/65 – being a runner-up in 1965/66). He transferred to Wigan in 1966 for £7,500, where he helped win the BBC2 Floodlit Trophy in 1968/69. Returning to Halifax in 1969 for £5,500, he was in the team that won the inaugural Player's No.6 Trophy competition of 1971/72, moving once again, in 1973, to join Rochdale Hornets for £7,000. He continued to play for the Hornets until 1976, helping them reach the 1973/74 Player's No.6 Trophy Final, where they lost to Warrington. A tourist in 1966, he played in three Test Matches with Great Britain (1966-74) and made four appearances for Lancashire (1965-68). He was coach at Rochdale during 1981/82.

Halifax's 20-year-old second-row forward Terry Fogerty became the first winner of the Harry Sunderland Trophy following his side's unexpected victory over St Helens in the 1965 Championship Final. St Helens – who won their opening 17 League fixtures – had led the table all season, Halifax reaching the final at Station Road, Swinton, from seventh position, after working their way through the expanded top sixteen play-off. St Helens' dominance was based around their fearsome pack which usually subdued the opposition in the first quarter before involving their talented back division. Against Halifax – whose strength also lay with the forwards – they met their match on the day, although the loss of Cumbrian ball-playing prop John Tembey, due to a twisted ankle after 28 minutes, was a major blow to the Lancashire side.

Fogerty instigated the opening try just two minutes before Tembey left the scene when, having almost got over in the corner, his pass – knocked down by a Saints defender – was

retrieved by Paul Daley. The live-wire Halifax scrum-half – who also had a big influence on the outcome – sent centre and captain John Burnett racing over through the tiniest gap for the first of his two touchdowns, full-back Ronnie James converting. Two penalties from Len Killeen closed the margin to 5-4 at half-time.

Saints expected second-half onslaught was kept in check by the rampant Halifax pack, Fogerty in particular breaking their line as he exploited gaps created by the battering charges of props Ken Roberts and Jack Scroby. Whilst St Helens looked increasingly nervy and over-anxious, spilling possession at vital moments,

Terry Fogerty

Halifax showed ruthless efficiency, extending their lead to 10-4 in the 61st minute as Fogerty again found an opening, handing on to the supporting Scroby who put Burnett in for his second, James again adding the two points. Killeen gave St Helens some hope six minutes later with a try, but it was Fogerty who delivered the decisive blow four minutes from time when he broke through Saints fragile looking defence yet again. He pulled out of three attempted tackles before half-backs Daley and Barry Robinson took over to send winger Duncan Jackson racing in behind the posts. James' goal made the final score 15-7 as Halifax celebrated its first Championship success since 1906/07.

Fogerty – who finished two votes ahead of second-row colleague Colin Dixon in the Harry Sunderland poll – said: 'I didn't think I played as well as I did in the semi-final.' Whether or not that was true – and Fogerty certainly stood out in scoring two tries in the 26-18 semi-final win over Castleford – he clearly impressed in the final. Garrett Cotter of *The Observer* echoed the views of several scribes, saying: 'Many of the breaks were made by Fogerty, who deservedly became the first man to win the trophy.' The *St Helens Reporter* journalist heaped praise on Halifax's second-row pair claiming: 'Both Fogerty and Dixon made hay in Saints ranks as no forward had done since the time of Billy Ivison. Both were quick off the mark and able to beat an opponent by skill and not by dash.'

Northern Rugby League Championship Final 1965
Saturday 22 May at Station Road, Swinton
Halifax 15
James (3 goals), Jackson (try), Burnett (captain, 2 tries), Kellett, Freeman, Robinson, Daley, Roberts, Harrison, Scroby, Fogerty, Dixon, Renilson.
St Helens 7
F Barrow, Harvey, van Vollenhoven, Northey, Killeen (try, 2 goals), Murphy, Smith, Tembey, Dagnall, Watson, French, Mantle, Laughton. Substitute: Warlow.
Half-time: 5-4. Referee: DS Brown (Dewsbury).
Attendance: 20,776.

Terry Fogerty – one of the best ball-distributors of his era.

DON FOX (WAKEFIELD TRINITY)
Lance Todd Trophy winner 1968

> **PROFILE**
>
> *Born in Sharlston, Don Fox signed for Featherstone Rovers in 1953 having played at junior level for Streethouse Intermediates and Featherstone Intermediates. A talented scrum-half with an ability to motivate others, he was also good with the boot, whether attempting goals from a placed or dropped kick or gaining vital yardage with a deft aim into the corner. He was a tourist in 1962, played twice for Great Britain (1956 and 1963), once for England (1956) and three times for Yorkshire (1956-58). He won the Yorkshire Cup with Featherstone in 1959, relocating to loose-forward in 1963 following the emergence of another talented scrum-half in Carl Dooler (also destined to win the Lance Todd Trophy). In 1965, he joined his brother Neil at Wakefield Trinity in a £3,000 deal, making a further positional change when moving to prop midway through the 1967/68 season. With Wakefield, he won the Championship in 1966/67 and 1967/68 and was a runner-up at Wembley in the 1968 Challenge Cup Final. He joined Batley in 1970, his final match being in 1971, after which he was Batley coach from 1972 to 1974.*

Wakefield Trinity's Don Fox was a clear and deserving winner of the Lance Todd Trophy in 1968, giving a performance that defied the most bizarre conditions imaginable in that year's Challenge Cup Final against Leeds. In the time since, much has been made over his goal miss from in front of the posts during the dying seconds that resulted in defeat rather than victory, but to dwell on that incident alone distorts what was otherwise a near-faultless and heroic display. Had the match not been such a showpiece occasion it is doubtful it would have started as the pitch was

Don Fox.

already saturated through rain and, at the very least, would have been abandoned before half-time. The playing area, soaked by a heavy rainfall the day before and considered potentially dangerous even then, was even worse on the big day. A huge downpour occurred an hour before the start and, although the sun optimistically showed by kick-off, the heavens opened again during the first-half and it came down in torrents, complete with thunder and lightening, even hailstones. The ground looked more like a lake than a rugby field, with players sliding all over the pitch, barely able to handle the bar of soap that was doubling up as a rugby ball. It was an occasion remembered in Rugby League folklore as the 'Watersplash Final'.

The plain facts of the match are that Leeds won 11-10, Wakefield scoring two tries and Leeds one. Wakefield led 7-4 at the interval, thanks to a beautifully struck Fox penalty after six minutes – a 35-yard effort from in front of the posts – and a Ken Hirst try on 15 minutes. In scoring, Hirst had dribbled the ball over the try line after Leeds' John Atkinson unwittingly kept the ball in play whilst losing his footing as he tried to cover a finely judged Fox kick towards the right corner, aimed from ten yards inside his own half. Fox, deputising as kicker for brother Neil, who missed out due to a groin injury, added a magnificent conversion, ten yards in from the touchline. Fox, in fact, constantly pushed the ball deep into Leeds territory throughout the final, quickly realising it was the best way to gain yardage in such appalling conditions. It was a tactic that, through the difficult handling conditions, presented a better than even chance of quick ball turnover in an advantageous field position.

There were no further points until the final ten minutes when Leeds turned the game on its head with a seven point burst to lead 11-7, courtesy of a disputed obstruction try which was converted by Bev Risman who subsequently added his third penalty with a minute remaining. The Leeds players were already celebrating victory when, from the restart, drama struck. Wakefield's Ray Owen had already placed the ball on the centre spot but, as he was about to kick to his forwards gathered on the left, Fox – almost impulsively – ran up and grubber kicked to the opposite, more spacious right side of the field instead. An alert Hirst read the situation perfectly to reach the ball first, twice kicking towards the Leeds posts, defenders sliding in different directions in a vain attempt to reach the ball which settled behind the uprights, Hirst diving on it to leave Wakefield trailing by only one point. In the days before kicking tees were used, Fox had the task of placing the ball on a mound of mud but slipped on the rain soaked pitch at the vital moment, the ball squirting to the right of the posts.

Despite that heartbreaking end, Fox had done more than enough to be acclaimed man of the match through his tactical kicking, control around the play-the-ball area, and determined tackling, and had had a major hand in both of Wakefield's tries. As Wakefield Trinity historian John Lindley wrote in his history of the club, '100 Years of Rugby' (1973): 'His considerable contribution to that freakish game easily won him the Lance Todd Trophy.'

Rugby League Challenge Cup Final 1968
Saturday 11 May at Wembley Stadium, London
Leeds 11
Risman (4 goals), A Smith, Hynes, Watson, Atkinson (try), Shoebottom, Seabourne, Clark (captain), Crosby, K Eyre, Ramsey, A Eyre, Batten.
Wakefield Trinity 10
Cooper, Hirst (2 tries), Brooke, Coetzer, Batty, Poynton (captain), Owen, Jeanes, Shepherd, D Fox (2 goals), Haigh, McLeod, Hawley.
Half-time: 4-7. Referee: JP Hebblethwaite (York).
Attendance: 87,100.

The atrocious conditions at Wembley in 1968 are clearly illustrated in this unusual picture. Wakefield Trinity players (in the light jerseys) appear to be drowning their Leeds opponent!

NEIL FOX (WAKEFIELD TRINITY)
Lance Todd Trophy winner 1962

Neil Fox's relentless appetite for scoring points was encapsulated with his contribution to Wakefield Trinity's 12-6 Challenge Cup Final win over Huddersfield in 1962, a match that was as dull as the overcast sky that hung over Wembley that afternoon. He had previously

Neil Fox – caricatured in 1962 by the pen of Ken Adams.

PROFILE

Neil Fox is the most prolific point scorer in Rugby League history, having amassed 6,220 in a career spanning over 23 years. A tall, well-built centre, he always threatened danger, making powerful bursts through the defensive line or drawing opponents in before creating openings for others. He was a deadly tackler and an accomplished marksman, his left boot producing a career 2,575, second only to Wigan legend of the 1920s and 1930s Jim Sullivan. Born at Sharlston, near Wakefield, he joined the Featherstone Rovers junior set-up from school, creating a surprise by signing for Wakefield Trinity in 1955, rather than emulate elder brothers Peter (who later made his name as an outstanding coach) and Don, and their father Tom (who played in the back-row during the early 1930s) in signing professionally for the Rovers. At Trinity, he went on to collect winners' medals for the Championship (1966/67 and 1967/68), Challenge Cup (1960, 1962 and 1963) and Yorkshire Cup (1960, 1961 and 1964). In 1969, he transferred to Bradford Northern for £6,000 where he eventually became player-coach, returning to Wakefield Trinity in a similar role in 1970. He remained at Wakefield until 1974, following which he played for Hull Kingston Rovers (1974 to 1975 – winning the Yorkshire Cup in 1974 and moving into the second-row), York (1976), Bramley (1976 to 1977), Huddersfield (1977 to 1978 when he was also coach), rejoining Bradford Northern (1978 to 1979, winning the Premiership Trophy and Yorkshire Cup, both in 1978). He also spent time as player-coach of Wellington in New Zealand during 1975. He was a tourist in 1962, represented Great Britain in 29 Tests (1959-69), England once (1962) and Yorkshire 17 times (1958-68). He received the MBE during 1983 and was voted into the Rugby League Hall of Fame in 1989.

---

scored 20 points in the annihilation of Hull in the 1960 showpiece and was destined to add ten more to his Wembley tally when beating Wigan in 1963. What was unique about his 1962 haul was that his trio of goals were all from drop-kicks

– a Wembley record – each being struck at key moments in a tight, tense match. The 22-year-old centre also scored the opening try on the way to earning personal glory as winner of the Lance Todd Trophy.

With both sides scoring two tries, the match was settled in Wakefield's favour during two crucial periods. The first began in the 17th minute when Fox opened the scoring with his first drop attempt, adding his try three minutes later after linking up with winger Ken Hirst, putting his side 5-0 up. The first half scoring was completed when Huddersfield scrum half and captain Tommy Smales grabbed an unconverted try on the half-hour to make it 5-3 at the interval. The second vital spell came on 63 minutes, another Fox drop effort being followed a minute later by a try from Hirst, who outwitted four defenders before scoring, putting Wakefield 10-3 ahead.

Neil Fox aims for the posts during the 1960 Challenge Cup Final, in which he scored a Wembley record 20 points in Wakefield Trinity's thrashing of Hull.

Peter Ramsden, their 1953 Lance Todd hero, gave Huddersfield hope with a try three minutes from time before Fox struck once more with his third drop goal in the final moments. After the dust had settled on the match, it was revealed that Fox's drop-goal efforts had been pre-planned to counter the correctly anticipated doggedness of the Huddersfield defence. Huddersfield gained revenge the following week when they defeated Trinity 14-5 in the Championship decider, thus denying them their fourth major trophy of the season.

Rugby League Challenge Cup Final 1962
Saturday 12 May at Wembley Stadium, London
Wakefield Trinity 12
Round, Smith, Skene, Fox (try, 3 goals), Hirst (try), Poynton, Holliday, Wilkinson, Oakes, Firth, Briggs, Williamson, Turner (captain).
Huddersfield 6
Dyson, Breen, Booth, Haywood, Wicks, Deighton, Smales (captain, try), Slevin, Close, Noble, Clark, Bowman, Ramsden (try).
Half-time: 5-3. Referee: DTH Davies (Manchester).
Attendance: 81,263.

An all-star Wakefield Trinity line-up from 1963. Neil Fox is standing, third from left.

BRIAN GABBITAS (HUNSLET)
Lance Todd Trophy winner 1965

PROFILE

Brian Gabbitas signed for his local club Hunslet in 1951, having emerged through the club's nursery system. He was a brilliant, creative stand-off half who gave the south Leeds club 14 years of loyal service. In addition to being a runner-up in the 1965 Challenge Cup Final, he won the Second Division Championship (1962/63) and Yorkshire Cup (1962) with Hunslet. He played for Great Britain once (1959) and Yorkshire three times (1958-61). During his National Service, he represented the Royal Signals and the Army at Rugby Union.

Hunslet's talented stand-off Brian Gabbitas shared the Lance Todd Trophy in 1965, with Wigan's Ray Ashby, after playing a major role in one of the most exciting Challenge Cup Finals seen at Wembley, being the third player honoured from a losing side. Alf Drewry of the *Yorkshire Post* commented 'Gabbitas has never played better in all his long and distinguished career with Hunslet, every time he got the ball he was a menace to the Wigan defence.'

Twice in the first half Gabbitas had provided excellent passes to send winger John Griffiths away, a move that would have produced tries against a winger with less pace than Wigan's flying Rhodesian Trevor Lake. Two minutes before half-time, Wigan saw their comfortable 12-4 lead reduced by five points with Gabbitas' beautifully timed off-load to Geoff Shelton who sidestepped his way over the try line, close to the posts. It set Hunslet up for a determined second-half siege but territorial advantage was nullified by poor handling when a try-scoring pass seemed on the cards. Wigan took advantage and with their extra pace scored two more touchdowns, extending the lead to 20-9. It was in the final 20 minutes that Hunslet, spurred on by Gabbitas, really got on top and almost stole the match and the Challenge Cup from under Wigan's noses, Griffiths charging over the line for a try following a well delivered pass from Dennis Hartley. Langton's conversion and subsequent penalty brought Hunslet agonisingly close but, in the tense minutes that remained they were unable to reduce the four-point gap any further.

Harold Mather, writing in *The Guardian* said of Gabbitas: 'Wigan never really knew where he was going to pop up next or, if they did, what he would do with the ball. His, indeed, was a brilliant performance.'

Brian Gabbitas.

Rugby League Challenge Cup Final 1965
Saturday 8 May at Wembley Stadium, London
Wigan 20
Ashby, Boston, Ashton (captain, goal), Holden (try),
Lake (2 tries), C Hill, Parr, Gardiner, Clarke,
McTigue, T Stephens, Evans, Gilfedder (try, 3 goals).
Hunslet 16
Langton (5 goals), Griffiths (try), Shelton (try),
Preece, Lee, Gabbitas, Marchant, Hartley, Prior,
Eyre, Ramsey, Gunney, Ward (captain).
Half-time: 12-9. Referee: J Manley (Warrington).
Attendance: 89,016.

ANDY GREGORY (WIGAN)
Lance Todd Trophy winner 1988 and 1990

Wigan scrum-half Andy Gregory capitalised on his Wembley big match know-how to become the second player (after Gerry Helme) to capture the Lance Todd Trophy twice, winning it in 1988 and 1990 – his fourth and sixth Challenge Cup Final, respectively. Having appeared in three previous finals for Widnes, he produced a dominant, masterly display in the former as the Cherry and Whites set off on their epic run of eight consecutive victories.

It was not until 13 minutes before the interval that Wigan scored the first of their four tries of the opening half against

Andy Gregory.

cup holders Halifax. Gregory created the gap for half-back partner Shaun Edwards to sprint half the length of the field before being held a few yards short of the try-line. From the play-the-ball, powerful centre Kevin Iro forced his way over the whitewash between two opponents. Gregory again opened up Halifax's defence for the second effort, four minutes later, scored in the corner by Henderson Gill, Dean Bell providing the final pass. Following another try from Kevin Iro, Gregory once more prised Halifax open two minutes before half-time, setting up a brilliant move involving Gill, Bell and Edwards, Joe Lydon finishing off by touching down near the posts. Without a recognised kicker none of the tries were converted (one attempt by Gregory hitting the

post), Wigan returning to the changing room 16-0 to the good.

Six minutes after the break Tony Iro – brother of Kevin – scored in the right corner, fed, almost inevitably by a perfect long pass from Gregory, who continued to boss the show. Lydon then caught the ball from the restart, racing 70 yards before sending Ellery Hanley under the posts for a great try. Gregory adding the extra two points, giving Wigan a comfortable 26-0 lead. Halifax gained small consolation by scoring two converted tries, sandwiching Wigan's final try which was yet again scored after Gregory opened the defence, Bell registering the touchdown and Lydon adding the goal. Lance Todd Trophy winner Gregory said after the game: 'I was thrilled at being part of Widnes' Wembley success, but I'm a Wigan lad and today is the greatest moment in my life.'

His second Lance Todd win, against Warrington in 1990, pushed both himself and Wigan into the record books. Gregory could claim to be the first player to win the Lance Todd award twice at Wembley – Helme having completed his double in the 1954 Odsal replay – whilst Wigan, in emulating Bradford Northern and Widnes by reaching three consecutive Wembley finals, were the first to win three on the run at the venue.

Gregory showed his true character in holding his side together in a hesitant opening half that was out of character with their two previous visits, his astute passing and probing helping to gradually raise the team's performance level. Wigan led at half-time 16-8, scoring two tries to one, both the result of poor Warrington kicks. The first came after 22 minutes when Edwards charged down David Lyon's attempted clearance ten yards in front of his own posts, Denis Betts pouncing on the loose ball to score, and the second, 12 minutes later, when Mark Preston sprinted 75 yards before touching down after intercepting a wayward chip kick from Gary Mercer.

The second half was a different matter with Wigan taking total command to run in four more tries, including a brilliant 64th minute effort by Ellery Hanley after Gregory had outwitted three defenders before sending his skipper an over-the-shoulder pass to score. Gregory recalled the moment saying 'I just passed over my shoulder because I knew Ellery was somewhere about and he caught it and went under the posts. It was probably a great try to watch, but it was individual skill what set the try up, and that possibly turned it for me to get the Lance Todd Trophy.' Kevin Iro also claimed two tries making it three years running that the New Zealander had scored a brace at Wembley, earning him runner-up slot in the Lance Todd vote, a repeat of the previous year. Gregory's achievement meant that Wigan had provided the winner of the coveted award three years in succession, thereby emulating Bradford Northern's feat of the 1940s.

Rugby League Challenge Cup Final 1988
Saturday 30 April at Wembley Stadium, London
Wigan 32
Lydon (try, goal), T Iro (try), K Iro (2 tries), Bell (try), Gill (try), Edwards (captain), Gregory (goal), Case, Kiss, Shelford, Goodway, Potter, Hanley (try). Substitutes: Byrne, Wane.
Halifax 12
Eadie (captain), Meredith, T Anderson (try), Wilkinson, Whitfield (2 goals), Grogan, Robinson, James (try), McCallion, Neller, Holliday, Dixon, Pendlebury. Substitutes: Fairbank, Scott.
Half-time: 16-0. Referee: GF Lindop (Wakefield). Attendance: 94,273.

Wigan in party mood after their Wembley victory in 1990. Lance Todd Trophy winner Andy Gregory, kneeling, extreme right, shares the moment with his young daughter.

PROFILE

Andy Gregory enjoyed a remarkable career, achieving success throughout most of it, particularly at his first three clubs Widnes, Warrington and Wigan. A highly competitive scrum-half, quick off the mark and a brilliant play-maker and passer of the ball, he joined Widnes from Wigan St Patrick's in 1979, after failing to agree terms with Salford (who his father Arthur had played for) following a trial match in late 1978. With Widnes, he appeared three times at Wembley, winning the Challenge Cup in 1981 and 1984 (being a runner-up in 1982 following a replay) and was successful in the Premiership Trophy Finals of 1982 and 1983. Following a dispute with Widnes, he was listed at £150,000, being out of action for almost five months before transferring to Warrington in a player-exchange deal at the start of 1985 where he won another Premiership Trophy medal in 1986.

He joined his hometown club Wigan in January 1987 for £130,000, Gregory having been at loggerheads with Warrington throughout the 1986/87 campaign. Whilst at Central Park he won the Championship (1986/87, 1989/90, 1990/91 and 1991/92), Challenge Cup (1988, 1989, 1990, 1991 and 1992), Premiership Trophy (1987), John Player Trophy (1988/89), Regal Trophy (1989/90) and Lancashire Cup (1987 and 1988). He also claimed victory in the World Club Challenge matches of 1987 and 1991 (being captain in the latter when Penrith Panthers were beaten at Anfield, Liverpool). He transferred to Leeds for £30,000 in 1992, finishing his career with Salford (1993-95) where he was also coach from 1995 to 1999. He also played for Australian side Illawarra Steelers during 1989. Gregory went on three Great Britain tours (1984, 1988 and 1992), appeared in 26 Tests (1981-92) and nine county games for Lancashire (1981-89).

Rugby League Challenge Cup Final 1990
Saturday 28 April at Wembley Stadium, London
Wigan 36
Hampson, Lydon (6 goals), K Iro (2 tries), Bell, Preston (2 tries), Edwards, A Gregory, Shelford, Dermott, Platt, Betts (try), Goodway, Hanley (captain, try). Substitutes: Goulding, Gildart.
Warrington 14
Lyon (try), Drummond, Mercer, Derbyshire (goal), Forster, Crompton, Bishop (2 goals), Burke, Mann, Harmon, Jackson, Sanderson, M Gregory (captain, try). Substitutes: McGinty, Thomas.
Half-time: 16-8. Referee: J Holdsworth (Kippax). Attendance: 77,729.

Andy Gregory plots his next move!

JACK GRUNDY (BARROW)
Lance Todd Trophy winner 1955

Jack Grundy became the only Barrow player, to date, to win the Lance Todd Trophy, following an inspiring second-half performance against Workington Town at Wembley in 1955. It was a match of contrasting halves. The first period was a nervous, dull affair, the two north-west clubs being tied at 2-2 when the interval arrived. Barrow's pack, led by a non-stop Grundy, then picked up the pace, opening up the game for the backs in an entertaining second-half that produced five tries; three for Barrow, two for Workington.

Barrow edged slowly ahead 6-2, thanks to a penalty and drop-goal from legendary skipper and stand-off Willie Horne. On the hour Workington spilled the ball on the halfway line close to the left touchline and, inevitably, it was Grundy that pounced on it, bursting through a

determined manner to provide the scoring pass for Frank Castle to go flying in down the left flank. The conversion by Horne put Barrow in control at 21-7, Workington registering a late consolation try from Eppie Gibson, insufficient to stop the Shipbuilders celebrating their only Challenge Cup win to date.

Rugby League Challenge Cup Final 1955
Saturday 30 April at Wembley Stadium, London
Barrow 21
Best, Lewthwaite, Jackson, Goodwin (try), Castle (try), Horne (captain, 6 goals), Toohey, Belshaw, McKeating (try), Barton, Grundy, Parker, Healey.
Workington Town 12
Vickers, Southward, Paskins (3 goals), Gibson (try), Faulder (try), Wookey, Roper, Hayton, Lymer, Key, Edgar, Mudge, Ivison (captain).
Half-time: 2-2. Referee: R Gelder (Wakefield).
Attendance: 66,513.

═══ PROFILE ═══

Second-row forward Jack Grundy began his professional career with hometown club St Helens in 1948. Moving to Barrow for a 'considerable transfer fee' in 1950, he played eleven seasons for the club, appearing in three Challenge Cup Finals (1951, 1955 and 1957), claiming victory in 1955. He also won the Lancashire Cup with Barrow in 1954. Although he had a reputation as the 'hard man' of the team, he was an intelligent, hard-working forward who was not short on pace. He represented Great Britain on 13 occasions (1955-57) including the 1957 World Cup held in Australia and Lancashire 11 times (1951-57). He later coached Barrow.

posse of defenders before turning the ball inside to send hooker Vince McKeating (who played in Workington's victorious 1952 Wembley outfit) charging over the line. There were protests that Grundy's pass was forward but referee Ron Gelder stood firm, Horne's goal stretching Barrow's lead to 11-2. Workington hung on gamely but with nine minutes left and the score standing at 16-7, Grundy was on hand for the killer blow. Loose forward Bill Healey, who also had an outstanding game for Barrow, made the initial break, Grundy continuing the move in

Jack Grundy, above left, holds the plinth, as Barrow celebrate at Wembley in 1955, led by skipper Willie Horne, seen lifting the trophy.

BOB HAIGH (BRADFORD NORTHERN)
Harry Sunderland Trophy winner 1978

Bob Haigh – Premiership Trophy in one hand and Harry Sunderland Trophy in the other – embraces his Bradford Northern coach Peter Fox after their 1978 triumph over Widnes.

Bob Haigh celebrated Bradford Northern's only Premiership Trophy success by becoming the oldest player, to date, to receive the coveted Harry Sunderland Trophy. Haigh's man of the match performance in Northern's 17-8 victory over Widnes at Swinton's Station Road ground completed a remarkable comeback for the 34-year-old veteran who had been forced out of the game following the 1975/76 season through a career threatening hamstring injury. Having regained fitness, Bradford tempted him back into action at the beginning of 1977, paying Leeds a modest £750 for his services and eventually making him club captain.

Widnes took an early 5-0 lead before Haigh restored Northern's aspirations in the 22nd minute by squeezing in near the posts after latching on to an Alan Redfearn pass, Keith Mumby's goal levelling the scores. The Yorkshire side then took control through a Peter Roe try on the half-hour followed by a John Wolford drop-goal to lead 9-5 at the turnaround.

Widnes – their ranks depleted by the loss of injured forwards Bill Ramsey and Glyn Shaw – fought back gamely, applying intense pressure before emergency second-rower Mal Aspey eventually went over after 54 minutes to reduce their arrears to just one point. Bradford's response was to turn the screw even tighter, scoring two more tries, David Redfearn placing the ball in the left corner to conclude a superb team effort that covered half the length of the field – Mumby adding a brilliant conversion – and David Barends diving in from acting half-back to close the scoring.

Haigh, who led his side superbly throughout the match, was typically modest about his Harry Sunderland award saying: 'I'm accepting it for the team as a whole. You only have to ask these lads to do something and they do it. I've had a good run, but you never get tired of success like this.'

Premiership Trophy Final 1978
Saturday 20 May at Station Road, Swinton
Bradford Northern 17
Mumby (2 goals), Barends (try), Roe (try), Austin, D Redfearn (try), Wolford (drop-goal), A Redfearn, van Bellen, Raistrick, Thompson, Joyce, Trotter, Haigh (captain, try). Substitutes: Fox, Forsyth.
Widnes 8
Eckersley, Wright, Hughes, Aspey (2 tries), Woods (goal), Gill, Bowden (captain), Mills, Elwell, Shaw, Adams, Hull, Laughton. Substitutes: George, Ramsey.
Half-time: 9-5. Referee: JE Jackson (Pudsey).
Attendance: 16,813.

PROFILE

Bob Haigh enjoyed a magnificent career with Wakefield Trinity, Leeds and Bradford Northern, the strong running second row or loose forward being noted for his try scoring exploits and his exceptional cover defence. A local lad, he signed for Wakefield in 1962 having emerged through the club's junior side, appearing in their Championship Final winning teams of 1967 and 1968 and playing at Wembley in the infamous 'Watersplash Final', won by Leeds. He also won the Yorkshire Cup with Trinity in 1964. He transferred to Leeds for £6,000 – a record sale for Wakefield – in 1970, creating a sensation in his first full season at Headingley (1970/71) by scoring an incredible 40 tries, a new record for a forward, making him Rugby League's joint leading try scorer for the season. With Leeds, he was to play in two more Challenge Cup Finals (1971 and 1972) losing both but sharing in the club's Championship success of 1971/72, although injury deprived him of his place in the final. There were plenty of other highlights, however, to celebrate with Leeds, including wins in finals for the BBC2 Floodlit Trophy (1970/71), Player's No.6 Trophy (1972/73) and Premiership Trophy (1975).

His last match for Leeds was in 1976, coming back a year later to join Bradford. It was a worthwhile return, earning the Harry Sunderland accolade in Northern's 1978 Premiership Trophy triumph and receiving the White Rose Trophy later that year as man of the match in the Yorkshire Cup Final win over York. He completed his playing career with Dewsbury (1979-80), returning to Wakefield as coach for a short period during 1984. Haigh played six times for Great Britain (1968-71) and was in the World Cup squads of 1968 (in Australia and New Zealand) and 1970 (in England – being in the line-up beaten by Australia in the final). He also played three times for England (1969-70) and twice for Yorkshire (1969 and 1971).

One of Bob Haigh's many career tries, this time against York in Bradford Northern's 1978 Yorkshire Cup Final win at Headingley.

ALBERT HALSALL (ST HELENS)
Harry Sunderland Trophy winner 1966

When a player scores three tries in a cup final it is something special. When that player happens to be a prop forward then it is extra-special! 22-year-old Albert Halsall achieved that feat on a hot, sunny afternoon in the 1966 Championship decider when his side St Helens hammered Halifax 35-12 at Station Road, Swinton. Halsall, pinched the ball from flying winger Johnny Freeman), and Halifax when last year's Harry Sunderland winner Terry Fogerty crashed over. It was then, after 29 minutes, that Halsall struck his first blow. Picking up from a play-the-ball, he crashed over the line just to the right of the posts. Surprisingly, Killeen missed the goal that

Albert Halsall, right, shows off his Harry Sunderland Trophy as he shares the spotlight with St Helens colleague Len Killeen, holder of the Lance Todd Trophy, following a momentous 1965/66 season for the Knowsley Road club.

virtually unknown before Saints signed him from Salford four months earlier, scored all three at key moments during the game to earn the Harry Sunderland Trophy, collecting 15 of the 16 votes cast.

As the half-hour approached Halifax were leading 7-3, both teams having scored a try; St Helens through the previous weekend's Lance Todd Trophy hero Len Killeen (after Halsall had would have put Saints in front, his kick hitting the upright. A few minutes later, St Helens did take the lead at 8-7 when skipper Alex Murphy dropped a goal from in front of the Halifax posts. With five minutes left before the break, Halsall put St Helens two scores in front when he raced in for a converted try from 20 yards out, the Yorkshire team's defence being fully stretched under Saints pressure.

With St Helens turning around 15-7 ahead, Halsall completed his hat-trick with a killer try just five minutes after the restart, charging through a Halifax line that was in disarray. St Helens then ran away with the match, adding three more tries (including two more from Killeen who also kicked six goals), Halifax gaining a consolation touchdown from Gordon Baker a minute from time. One incident of note, midway through the second half, occurred when tempers frayed with almost half the players becoming involved in a free-for-all, a St Helens woman racing onto the field wielding her handbag at a Halifax player!

The 1966 Championship Final was one of nine major finals held at Swinton's Station Road ground that concluded with the presentation of the Harry Sunderland Trophy.

Halifax, whose major strength lay with the pack, had finished tenth in the League table, outdoing last year's feat of reaching the final from seventh. St Helens – their opponents in 1965 – provided sterner opposition this time, winning their fourth major trophy of the season as they denied Halifax a second consecutive Championship. Harry Sunderland winner, Halsall, later recalled: 'It was like a dream come true. It was my season and I just couldn't put a foot wrong. Perhaps I shouldn't admit it, but that was the last time I scored three tries in a match!'

Northern Rugby League Championship Final 1966
Saturday 28 May at Station Road, Swinton
St Helens 35
F Barrow, A Barrow (try), Murphy (captain, goal), Benyon, Killeen (3 tries, 6 goals), Harvey, Bishop, Halsall (3 tries), Sayer, Watson, French, Warlow, Mantle. Substitute: Hitchen.
Halifax 12
Cooper (3 goals), Jones, Burnett (captain), Dixon, Freeman, Robinson, Baker (try), Roberts, Harrison, Scroby, Ramshaw, Fogerty (try), Renilson. Substitute: Duffy.
Half-time: 15-7. Referee: J Manley (Warrington). Attendance: 30,634.

ELLERY HANLEY (BRADFORD NORTHERN AND WIGAN)

Man of Steel Award winner 1985, 1987 and 1989
Lance Todd Trophy winner 1989

Ellery Hanley is the only person to achieve the incredible feat of winning the Man of Steel Award three times, once with Bradford Northern in 1985 and twice with Wigan in 1987 and 1989. In the latter year, he added the Lance Todd Trophy to his growing list of accolades. It was difficult to see beyond Hanley for the 1985 Man of Steel Award, his 55 tries – including 52 for Bradford where he played mostly at stand-off – during the campaign being the highest return since 1960/61. It also earned him a cheque for £5,000 from Man of Steel sponsor Greenall Whitley as the first to break the 50 barrier since Billy Boston got 51 in 1961/62. His try count incorporated a new First Division record of 40, all the more remarkable when it is realised that Bradford finished the Championship race mid-table in eighth place. He was honoured during March when given the captaincy of Great Britain for the first time, against France in Perpignan – his eleventh consecutive Test appearance. During the awards evening, held at the Willows Variety Centre, Salford, he was also voted First Division Player of the Year by a clear margin.

Ellery Hanley.

Two years later, following his transfer to Wigan, he became the first to win the Man of Steel Award a second time. If anything, he exceeded his performances of two year's earlier, his try scoring prowess again grabbing headlines with an incredible new personal high of 63 touchdowns in all matches. It was the most in British Rugby League since Lionel Cooper scored 66 for Huddersfield in the 1954/55 season. His 59 for Wigan even outdid Boston's best of 54 (1958/59) and was three short of Johnny Ring's club record 62 that had stood since 1925/26. Hanley certainly broke the mould as, hitherto, great try-scoring feats had been the preserve of flying wingers. None of Hanley's efforts came from the flank, 30 emanating from his new loose forward berth. He also broke his own record in scoring 44 First Division tries. Established as the regular Great Britain captain during the season, he took on the same role at Wigan in mid-term, leading the club to its first Championship since 1959/60 and first ever Premiership Trophy success, defeating Warrington 8-0 in the final at Old Trafford. Earlier in the season, he helped the Cherry and Whites lift the Lancashire Cup and John Player Special Trophy.

Hanley took the Man of Steel Award an unprecedented third time in 1989, having led

PROFILE

Many Rugby League observers consider Ellery Hanley the most outstanding British player to emerge in the sport over the past three decades. He commenced his professional career in 1978, signing for Bradford Northern as a 17-year-old from the Leeds-based Corpus Christi club, making his debut the same year. In 1981, he appeared in his only final with Northern, losing to Castleford in the Yorkshire Cup. Playing mostly at stand-off he began to grab headlines, culminating in an incredible 1984/85 season when he scored 55 tries. Following a dispute with Northern at the start of the following term, when he refused to play, Wigan captured his signature in September 1985 for a Rugby League record £85,000, the move valued at £150,000 with Steve Donlan and Phil Ford moving in the opposite direction.

He became Wigan captain during 1986/87, coach Graham Lowe switching him to loose forward midway through the campaign. The role suited Hanley perfectly, allowing him the freedom to dictate play and use his pace and power to even greater effect, finishing the season with an incredible 63 tries (59 for Wigan). With Wigan he won the Championship (1986/87, 1989/90, 1990/91), Challenge Cup (1988, 1989, 1990, 1991 – the latter three as the first captain of three consecutive Wembley winning sides), Premiership Trophy (1987), John Player Trophy (1985/86, 1986/87, 1988/89), Regal Trophy (1989/90), Lancashire Cup 1985, 1986, 1987, 1988) and World Club Challenge (1987). He transferred to Leeds in 1991 for a new Rugby League record of £250,000, leading his hometown club to the Challenge Cup Final at Wembley in 1994 and 1995 (his final match), losing both. He had several spells in Australia playing for Balmain (1988 – runner-up in that years Grand Final, 1996, 1997) and Western Suburbs (1989).

He toured with Great Britain in 1984, 1988 and 1992, the last two as captain, missing the opportunity to lead the 1990 tour through injury. He made 36 Test appearances (1984-93) including 19 as captain, played for England twice (1984 and 1992) and Yorkshire five times (1985-91). He was coach of Great Britain (1994-95), England (1994-95) and St Helens (1998-2000 – winning the 1999 Super League Grand Final), moving to Rugby Union where he was on the coaching staff of England, Bristol and Bath. In 2004, he temporarily returned to Rugby League as coaching consultant to Castleford. He received the MBE in 1990.

first success over the Aussies for ten years. Hanley was also skipper of the Yorkshire side that defeated Lancashire 24-14 in the annual War of the Roses clash, staged at Headingley. During the term, he raised his aggregate of First Division tries to 178, surpassing the previous best by Salford's Keith Fielding of 165 (1973-81).

Kneeling, centre stage behind the Challenge Cup, Ellery Hanley enjoys his duel 1989 Wembley success as winning Wigan captain and Lance Todd Trophy recipient.

Twelve days before completing his Man of Steel hat-trick, Hanley won the 1989 Lance Todd Trophy after scoring one of the most amazing tries seen at Wembley as Wigan won a one-sided Challenge Cup Final 27-0 against their keenest rivals St Helens. Receiving the ball just inside the St Helens half from Shaun Edwards in the 26th minute, Hanley outmanoeuvred five opponents in a bewildering run with typical speed and strength to score a try under the posts that had looked an impossibility just seconds earlier. He also had a key role in the opening try after three minutes, receiving the ball from Steve Hampson who had caught a goal-line drop out on the halfway line, Hanley shrugging off a Roy Haggerty tackle before drawing in Les Quirk to send Kevin Iro charging over. With Joe Lydon scoring a penalty and converting Hanley's try, Wigan led 12-0 at half-time.

Three more tries were added without reply following the break as Wigan continued to outclass their opposition, including a second effort from Kevin Iro – Hanley again being involved in the build-up – helping to place the Kiwi second in the press vote to decide the Lance Todd winner. Hanley also had the honour

Wigan to success in the Challenge Cup (winning the Lance Todd Trophy as Wigan retained the cup), John Player Special Trophy (voted man of the match) and Lancashire Cup (Wigan's fourth consecutive win). He also extended his run as Great Britain captain to nine successive Tests, a figure that incorporated leading the 1988 tour party to the Southern Hemisphere and winning the third Test against Australia in Sydney, the

Ellery Hanley goes down to a Neil Holding tackle in a Wigan-St Helens Challenge Cup meeting at Central Park in 1986.

of being presented with the Challenge Cup by the Right Honourable Viscount Whitelaw, the first of three successive occasions when he would lead the team up to the Royal Box as winning captain, thereby creating a Wembley record.

Greenalls Man of Steel Awards 1985
Wednesday 8 May at The Willows Variety Centre, Salford
Compered by Keith Macklin
Man of Steel: Ellery Hanley (Bradford Northern).
First Division Player of the Year: Ellery Hanley (Bradford Northern).
Second Division Player of the Year: Graham Steadman (York).
Young Player of the Year: Lee Crooks (Hull).
Coach of the Year: Roger Millward (Hull Kingston Rovers).
Referee of the Year: Ron Campbell (Widnes).

Greenalls Man of Steel Awards 1987
Wednesday 13 May at The Willows Variety Centre, Salford
Compered by Harry Gration
Man of Steel: Ellery Hanley (Wigan).
First Division Player of the Year: Andy Gregory (Wigan).
Second Division Player of the Year: John Cogger (Runcorn Highfield).

Young Player of the Year: Shaun Edwards (Wigan).
Coach of the Year: Graham Lowe (Wigan).
Referee of the Year: John Holdsworth (Kippax).

Greenalls Man of Steel Awards 1989
Thursday 11 May at The Willows Variety Centre, Salford
Compered by Harry Gration
Man of Steel: Ellery Hanley (Wigan).
First Division Player of the Year: David Hulme (Widnes).
Second Division Player of the Year: Daryl Powell (Sheffield Eagles).
Young Player of the Year: Paul Newlove (Featherstone Rovers).
Coach of the Year: Graham Lowe (Wigan).
Referee of the Year: John Holdsworth (Kippax).

Rugby League Challenge Cup Final 1989
Saturday 29 April at Wembley Stadium, London
Wigan 27
Hampson (try), T Iro, K Iro (2 tries), Bell, Lydon (3 goals), Edwards, Gregory (try, drop-goal), Lucas, Kiss, Shelford, Platt, Potter, Hanley (captain, try).
Substitutes: Betts, Goodway.
St Helens 0
Connolly, O'Connor, Veivers, Loughlin, Quirk, Cooper, Holding, Burke, Groves, Forber, Dwyer, Haggerty, Vautin (captain). Substitutes: Bloor, Evans.
Half-time: 12-0. Referee: R Tennant (Castleford).
Attendance: 78,000.

IESTYN HARRIS (LEEDS RHINOS)
Man of Steel Award winner 1998

=== PROFILE ===

Iestyn Harris laid down a marker for the future when declared player of the tournament for the 1995 World Cup when only 19, helping Wales reach the semi-finals. A dangerous attacker due to his adept passing game and sidestepping ability, proficient at full-back, centre, or stand-off, he is an intelligent player who reads the game well. He represented Wales 13 times (1994-2000) including the 2000 World Cup as captain when they again reached the last four. Born and bred in Oldham, he qualified through his grandfather, Norman Harris, who left Cross Keys Rugby Union to join Oldham in 1945. Due to his ancestry, the Welsh Rugby Union tempted him to the valleys in 2001, joining Cardiff and playing 25 times for Wales (2001-04).

He began his senior Rugby League career when Warrington signed him from Oldham St Annes in 1993, appearing for them in the 1994/95 Regal Trophy Final. In 1997, he looked all set to move to St Helens but eventually transferred to Leeds in a deal reportedly worth £375,000 (including a player-exchange).

Appointed captain at Leeds, he led them to two Challenge Cup Finals (1999 and 2000 – winning the former), and the Super League Grand Final loss of 1998. Following his Rugby Union sabbatical, he returned to Rugby League with Bradford Bulls in 2004, playing in his second Super League Grand Final later that year (against former club Leeds), although on the losing side once more. To date, he has played in 12 Tests for Great Britain (nine from 1996 to 1999 and three in the 2004 Tri-Nations series), and was a tourist in 1996.

Leeds Rhinos' captain Iestyn Harris took the Man of Steel Award for 1998 – the inaugural one held under the auspices of Super League Europe – being the first to receive a unanimous vote by the judging panel. The charismatic 22-year-old enjoyed a brilliant season, leading his club to the first ever Super League Grand Final (which they lost three days later to Wigan Warriors 10-4 at Old Trafford although giving an outstanding performance himself).

Operating mostly at full-back for Leeds he scored 283 points (13 tries, 114 goals, 3 drop-goals) for the Rhinos during the course of the season, incorporating 255 in Super League fixtures which made him the leading scorer in that competition. He subsequently made two appearances for Great Britain in the end-of-season Test series against the visiting New Zealanders and represented Wales against an Emerging England side at Widnes during July.

Iestyn Harris.

Harris made it a notable treble through being voted the Super League Players' Player of the Year during the ceremony, held at the prestigious Holiday Inn Crowne Plaza Midland Hotel in Manchester, and becoming the third recipient of the Rugby League Writers' Association Player of the Year award.

JJB Super League Man of Steel Awards 1998
Wednesday 21 October at the Holiday Inn Crowne Plaza Midland, Manchester
Compered by Eddie Hemmings and Mike Stephenson
Man of Steel: Iestyn Harris (Leeds Rhinos).
Super League Players' Player of the Year: Iestyn Harris (Leeds Rhinos).
Super League Young Player of the Year: Lee Gilmour (Wigan Warriors).
Super League Coach of the Year: John Pendlebury (Halifax Blue Sox).
Super League Referee of the Year: Russell Smith (Castleford).

TOMMY HARRIS (HULL)
Lance Todd Trophy winner 1960

=== PROFILE ===

Hull's Welsh hooker Tommy Harris was one of the most accomplished players in that position, a non-stop performer in the loose who won plentiful supplies of possession from the scrums. Testimony to his prowess is the fact he was virtually a regular as Great Britain's rake from 1954 to 1960 when making 25 Test appearances, encompassing the British Lions tours of 1954 and 1958 and the World Cup's of 1957 and 1960. He also played seven times for Wales (1952-53). Born in Crumlin, he signed for Hull in 1949 from Newbridge Rugby Union club, winning the Championship with them in 1955/56 and 1957/58 (suspension costing him a place in the final of the latter) and playing at Wembley in the defeated Challenge Cup Final teams of 1959 and 1960. He retired in 1962, taking up a coaching appointment at York where he later became a director.

For Tommy Harris, the 1960 Challenge Cup Final must have felt like the Battle of the Alamo as he and his Hull colleagues fought valiantly against the odds to repel the Wakefield Trinity hordes. Hull faced problems even before the match had started with injuries decimating their line-up, second-row forward Mike Smith making his debut! Harris reflected: 'Our strength was in the pack but, besides myself, Mick Scott and Johnny Whiteley were the only regulars to play at Wembley.' Despite the odds, Hull only trailed 7-5 at the interval, Harris receiving a knock five minutes before half-time, causing concussion and temporary loss of sight in one eye, bravely returning after several minutes off-field attention.

As anticipated, Trinity blitzed Hull after the interval but Harris never gave in. He controlled scrum possession and was everywhere in defence, tackling his heart out. Trinity added 15 of their 31 second-half points when Harris was eventually forced to quit with 13 minutes to go, being rushed to hospital with a head injury. 'They thought they would have to operate but in the end it didn't come to that' recalls Harris. 'My wife told me at the hospital on Saturday night that I had won the Lance Todd Trophy. I think they gave it to our coach Roy Francis to hand to me later.' The first hooker to win the Lance Todd, he regretted being unable to receive his medal from Her Majesty Queen Elizabeth II after the match. 'It was suggested that I would receive it from another member of The Royal Family, but nothing come of it' he said.

Rugby League Challenge Cup Final 1960
Saturday 14 May at Wembley Stadium, London
Wakefield Trinity 38
Round, Smith (try), Skene (2 tries), Fox (2 tries, 7 goals), Etty, Rollin (try), Holliday (2 tries), Wilkinson, Oakes, Vines, Firth, Chamberlain, Turner (captain).
Hull 5
Kershaw, Harrison, Cowan (try), Halifihi, Johnson, Broadhurst, Finn, Scott, Harris, Evans (goal), Sutton, Smith, Whiteley (captain).
Half-time: 7-5. Referee: E Clay (Leeds). Attendance: 79,773.

Tommy Harris.

Graham Morris

GERRY HELME (WARRINGTON)
Lance Todd Trophy winner 1950 and 1954

Warrington scrum-half Gerry Helme has the distinction of being the first player to win the Lance Todd Trophy a second time when he took the award in the historic 1954 Challenge Cup Final replay win over Halifax at Odsal Stadium, Bradford. It followed his success in 1950 when, as the first Lancashire born player to receive the honour, he was judged the outstanding performer in the Wembley triumph against local rivals Widnes.

played the ball back to his loose-forward Harold Palin who dropped a goal from in front of the posts after 15 minutes play to open the scoring. A penalty from Palin three minutes later began sewing the seeds of doubt in Widnes minds and their play become more jittery, Helme continuing to push Widnes back with his downfield kicks. Warrington capitalised with tries from their awesome Australian captain and second-row forward Harry Bath and centre Ron

Delighted Lance Todd Trophy winner Gerry Helme, holding plinth, looks on as skipper Harry Bath raises the Challenge Cup at Wembley in 1950.

The eagerly anticipated 1950 Challenge Cup Final between derby opponents Warrington and Widnes proved a disappointing one-sided affair. After Warrington withstood early pressure from the Widnes pack, Helme led the way with long, accurate kicks to touch, continually placing his side deep into opposition territory. It was from such a position that the quick-thinking Helme

Ryder, who dived over in the corner after receiving a neat Helme pass. Palin converted Bath's try and then added his second penalty two minutes before the break to put Warrington in a commanding 14-0 position at the turn around.

The second-half was contested more evenly but the damage was already done. Palin banged over a third penalty before Helme confirmed his

Warrington's 1950 Challenge Cup winning side. Gerry Helme is seated, extreme right.

man of the match status in the 67th minute with a perfect reverse pass, as he came away from a scrum, to stand-off partner Bryn Knowelden, who scored the final try of the afternoon for a decisive 19-0 victory.

THE RUGBY LEAGUE
CHALLENGE CUP COMPETITION
FINAL TIE
HALIFAX v. WARRINGTON

(Photo by courtesy of the Yorkshire Post)

ODSAL STADIUM, BRADFORD
WEDNESDAY, 5th MAY, 1954

Official Programme   -   Sixpence

The 1954 Challenge Cup Final replay at Odsal Stadium was seen by a, then, Rugby League world record attendance, officially recorded as 102,569

Four years later Warrington – and Helme – were back at Wembley, this time to face Halifax. The match, which finished 4-4, provided a poor advert for the game, the only scores being two first-half penalties from Halifax full-back Tyssul Griffiths, Bath responding in kind during the second period. The award for the Lance Todd

PROFILE

Gerry Helme joined Warrington from the Culcheth amateur club in 1945, making his debut the same year. The Leigh-born scrum-half, rated as one of the quickest number 7s in the game at the time, was an instant hit and included in the selection trials for the 1946 British tour squad. Although not picked on that occasion, he was included in the 1954 tour and the team that won the inaugural World Cup later that year in France, scoring a try in the final against the hosts. He played in 12 matches for Great Britain (1948-54), five for England (1948-53) and eleven for Lancashire (1948-54). His last match for Warrington was in 1957 after a career that had seen him share success in the Championship three times (1947/48, 1953/54 and 1954/55) and Challenge Cup twice (1950 and 1954). He later transferred to Keighley, playing twice in 1958. During the 1960s, he coached both Leigh and Oldham.

Trophy was put on hold until the replay – which was just as well! Even Helme and his normally brilliant Welsh outside-half Ray Price were well below par, the *Warrington Guardian* noting: 'Helme was completely out of touch and Price never found his true form and, of course, when the main cog of a machine is not functioning properly, there is little hope for the rest of it.'

The old adage of 'living to fight again another day' never rang so true, particularly in the case of Helme. The Odsal replay has gone down in the annals of Rugby League history, an official crowd of 102,569 creating unprecedented scenes of chaos outside and inside the stadium. The attendance was widely believed to have been closer to 120,000 but, either way, it was a world record for the sport. The following morning, Helme's name dominated the headlines. His astute kicks to touch had once more played a vital part in pushing back the opposition and, along with Price, he controlled play around the middle of the field. It was his scintillating touchdown, though, that grabbed the media attention. It was one of the most memorable seen in a Challenge Cup Final and came with 12 minutes left and the match finely balanced at 5-4 in Warrington's favour (their centre Jim Challinor having scored the only try, so far, in the 9th minute). Helme, who had already tested the Halifax defence with a 40-yard burst earlier in the second-half, broke from a similar position on halfway. Allan Cave of the *Daily Herald* wrote: 'He was on the ball like a swooping hawk as it came from a scrum. Two Halifax players bought a dummy and away went Gerry, finally to double somersault over the line for a try.' The journalists present voted in favour of Helme 'by a clear majority' his Lance Todd Trophy double not being emulated until Andy Gregory won it a second time 36 years later.

Rugby League Challenge Cup Final 1950
Saturday 6 May at Wembley Stadium, London
Warrington 19
Jones, Bevan, Ryder (try), A Naughton, Johnson, Knowelden (try), Helme, Derbyshire, Fishwick, Fisher, Bath (captain, try), Lowe, Palin (5 goals).
Widnes 0
Bradley, Parkes, Hutton, Sale (captain), Malone, Fleming, Anderson, Rowbottom, Band, Wilcox, Leigh, J Naughton, Reynolds.
Half-time: 14-0. Referee: AS Dobson (Pontefract).
Attendance: 94,249.

Rugby League Challenge Cup Final Replay 1954
Wednesday 5 May at Odsal Stadium, Bradford
Warrington 8
Frodsham (captain), B Bevan, Challinor (try), Ryder, McCormick, Price, Helme (try), D Naughton, Wright, Lowe, Bath (goal), Heathwood, Ryan.
Halifax 4
Griffiths (2 goals), Daniels, Lynch, Mather, D Bevan, Dean, Kielty, Thorley, Ackerley (captain), Wilkinson, Fearnley, Schofield, Clarkson.
Half-time: 3-2. Referee: R Gelder (Wakefield).
Attendance: 102,569.

Gerry Helme, kneeling right, as the 1954 Warrington squad show off their silverware collection of Championship Trophy, Challenge Cup and Lancashire League Trophy.

DAVID HOBBS (FEATHERSTONE ROVERS)
Lance Todd Trophy winner 1983

Featherstone Rovers produced one of Wembley's biggest upsets when they overcame hot favourites Hull 14-12 in the 1983 Challenge Cup Final. None did more for the cause than two-try second-row hero David Hobbs whose performance earned him the Lance Todd Trophy vote ahead of colleagues Peter Smith and captain Terry Hudson. His first touchdown came after just seven minutes play when, in a pre-planned move, he latched on to a delayed pass from a tap penalty by Hudson to burst through James Leuluai's attempted tackle and place the ball in the corner. Steve Quinn failed to add the extra two points but then succeeded with a penalty, Featherstone holding on gamely to lead 5-0 at half-time.

Hull began to live up to their tag of being the 4 to 1 on favourites in the second half as they took control and led by 12-5 with only 13 minutes left. Quinn pulled two points back with a penalty, Hobbs then going on an inspired

David Hobbs.

PROFILE

Born in Hemsworth, West Yorkshire, David Hobbs played for Featherstone Rovers Juniors before signing for the senior outfit, making his debut in 1978. A strong-running second-row forward, his powerful bursts and intelligent running earned him a Rovers club record of 21 tries by a forward in 1981/82. Prior to the clubs sensational Challenge Cup win in 1983, he helped them gain promotion as Division Two champions in 1979/80. In 1985, he transferred to Oldham for £40,000, gaining a runner-up medal for the 1986 Lancashire Cup Final defeat by Wigan, before moving again, to Bradford Northern in 1987 in a player-exchange deal. He spent almost seven years at Northern, where he became team captain and regular goal kicker, winning the Yorkshire Cup twice (1987 and 1989) and being player-coach for eighteen months during 1990 and 1991. He joined Wakefield Trinity in 1994 where he was appointed coach (1994-95), concluding his playing career with several matches at the start of 1994. In July 2005, he took over as Featherstone Rovers coach. He was a Great Britain tourist in 1984 and made 12 Test appearances in his career (1984-89), represented England once (1984) and Yorkshire seven times (1982-89).

rampaging run to tear a hole through a tiring Hull defence, running wide to become the first forward to grab a brace at Wembley. Quinn added the goal and the scores were sensationally level at 12-12. With eight minutes remaining, a second successive replay was looming. For Hobbs, however, the adrenalin was flowing, and he attempted a drop-goal which sailed between the Hull posts, Featherstone celebrations being curtailed when referee Robin Whitfield ruled

Featherstone Rovers pictured in 1984 with David Hobbs, standing, third from left.

for each team – seen in the Challenge Cup Final. Hobbs, who also pulled off a crucial try-saving tackle on Hull second-rower Lee Crooks near the posts, became the third Featherstone player to receive the Lance Todd Trophy, the team from the tiny mining community winning the Challenge Cup for the third time in five Wembley visits.

Rugby League Challenge Cup Final 1983
Saturday 7 May at Wembley Stadium, London
Featherstone Rovers 14
Barker, Marsden, Quinn (4 goals), Gilbert, K Kellett, Banks, Hudson (captain), Gibbins, Handscombe, Hankins, Hobbs (2 tries), Slatter, Smith. Substitutes: Lyman, Siddall.
Hull 12
Kemble, O'Hara, Evans, Leuluai (try), Prendiville, Topliss (captain), Harkin, Skerrett, Bridges, Stone, Rose, Crooks (try, 3 goals), Norton. Substitutes: Day, Crane.
Half-time: 5-0. Referee: R Whitfield (Widnes).
Attendance: 84,969.

the ball had touched a Hull player in flight. Drama then struck just three minutes from the end when a touch judge spotted Hull prop Charlie Stone butting Smith, Quinn scoring the match-winning penalty from 20 yards.

It was a memorable, although untidy, match, which produced the first sin-bin dismissals – one

David Hobbs takes on the French defence for Great Britain in 1984.

DICK HUDDART (ST HELENS)
Lance Todd Trophy winner 1961

Dick Huddart, standing fifth from left, helps hoist St Helens captain Vince Karalius aloft after the 1961 Wembley victory over Wigan.

The clash of Lancashire's two star studded giants, St Helens and Wigan, in the 1961 Challenge Cup Final took place in front of a shirt sleeved crowd on Wembley's hottest day yet, watched by a massive 94,672 attendance. It was Cumbrian second-row forward Dick Huddart who turned the tide in St Helens favour after a promising opening from Wigan, who led 2-0 through a Fred Griffiths penalty after four minutes. He made several surging runs into Wigan territory, an enterprising kick to his winger Mick Sullivan almost leading to a try by Brian McGinn. And it was Huddart, avoiding a Frank Collier tackle, that was on hand to put Alex Murphy over for the opening try after 32 minutes. Austin Rhodes missed the difficult conversion but his subsequent penalty goal made it 5-2. As half-time approached Huddart again made a tremendous break but was held up on that occasion.

With another Griffiths penalty five minutes into the second half making it 5-4, St Helens sealed their win in the 63rd minute when flying South African wing Tom van Vollenhoven scored one of Wembley's greatest tries, following an inter-passing move down the right flank with centre partner Ken Large that covered almost the length of the field. Huddart – ably supported in the pack by skipper Vince Karalius and Cliff Watson – continued to make his long menacing breaks, earning himself the Lance Todd Trophy having been, according to famous journalist and broadcaster Eddie Waring, 'a constant source of trouble to Wigan.'

PROFILE

Dick Huddart, born in Flimby, near Maryport, was one the greatest ever Cumbrian forwards, a powerfully built six feet tall, 14 stone-plus second-rower with a punishing hand-off. He originally joined Whitehaven from amateurs Risehow and Gillhead in 1955, transferring to St Helens for £7,250 in 1958. Whilst at St Helens he won the Championship (1958/59), Challenge Cup (1961) and Lancashire Cup (1960, 1961 and 1962). In 1964, he moved to Australia, joining Sydney club St George for £10,000, where he played from 1964 to 1968, being a member of their 1966 Grand Final winning side. He became player-coach of New South Wales country club Dubbo, later joining Macquarie United from the Newcastle district. During the 1970/71 season, aged 33, he unexpectedly returned to Britain, playing seven matches for Whitehaven before deciding to head back to Australia. A tourist in 1958 and 1962, he played in 16 Tests for Great Britain (1958-63), represented England once (1962) and Cumberland eleven times (1956-63).

Rugby League Challenge Cup Final 1961
Saturday 13 May at Wembley Stadium, London
St Helens 12
Rhodes (3 goals), van Vollenhoven (try), Large, McGinn, Sullivan, Murphy (try), Smith, Terry, Dagnall, Watson, Vines, Huddart, Karalius (captain).
Wigan 6
Griffiths (3 goals), Boston, Ashton (captain), Bootle, Carlton, Bolton, Entwistle, Barton, Sayer, McTigue, Lyon, Collier, Evans.
Half-time: 5-2. Referee: TW Watkinson (Swinton).
Attendance: 94,672.

DAVID HULME (WIDNES)
Harry Sunderland Trophy winner 1988

=== PROFILE ===

David Hulme signed for hometown club Widnes from local amateurs Halton Hornets in 1980. It commenced a highly successful 16 years at Naughton Park for Hulme, a competitive player with good handling skills who served the club with distinction in both half-back roles (he also appeared in the pack during the latter stages of his career). At Widnes, he won the Championship (1987/88 and 1988/89), Challenge Cup (1984 – he was a runner-up in 1993), Premiership Trophy (1983, 1988, 1989 and 1990), Lancashire Cup (1990) and World Club Challenge (1989 – man of the match against Canberra Raiders). He was a tourist in 1988, played in eight Test Matches (1988-89) and made two appearances for Lancashire (1987 and 1988). He joined Leeds in 1996 and subsequently played for Salford (1997-98) before returning to Widnes as player-coach (2000-01). He shared most of his glory years at Widnes with younger brother Paul who joined the club in 1983.

David Hulme claimed the 1988 Harry Sunderland Trophy award after a brilliant all-round scrum-half display as Widnes outplayed St Helens at a sun-drenched Old Trafford, the Chemics producing a record equalling Premiership Trophy Final score in winning 38-14. Hulme mesmerised and tormented the St Helens defence throughout the 80 minutes, his two tries – both created by loose forward Richard Eyres and which sandwiched the half-time break – being a just reward for his endeavour.

St Helens drew first blood with a Paul Loughlin penalty in the 4th minute, but then it was one way traffic after Widnes captain Kurt Sorenson burst through to register the first of Widnes' seven tries, Hulme supporting an Eyres break for the third as they built up a commanding 16-2 lead before the interval. Loughlin again opened the second half scoring with a St Helens penalty two minutes in, but revival hopes were shelved when Andy Currier made a powerful break before delivering an inside pass to the supporting Hulme, who transferred to Eyres, accepting his return pass to race over the whitewash and complete his brace.

Currier's goal made it 22-4 and Widnes had one hand firmly on the trophy.

With Hulme at the heart of their attacking machine, including a perfectly weighted scoring pass for flying winger Stuart Wright late in the game, Saints – despite claiming two second half touchdowns themselves – finished a well beaten side. For Widnes it was a record fourth Premiership Trophy win and incorporated their first Championship-Premiership double.

Premiership Trophy Final 1988
Sunday 15 May at Old Trafford, Manchester
Widnes 38
Platt (goal), Thackray, Currier (4 goals), Wright (2 tries), Offiah, Dowd, D Hulme (2 tries), Sorenson (captain, try), McKenzie (try), Grima, M O'Neill, P Hulme, R Eyres. Substitutes: Tait (try), S O'Neill.
St Helens 14
Loughlin (3 goals), Ledger (try), Tanner, Elia, Quirk, Bailey, Holding, Burke, Groves (captain), Evans, Forber, Fieldhouse, Haggerty (try). Substitutes: Allen, Dwyer.
Half-time: 16-2. Referee: J Holdsworth (Kippax).
Attendance: 35,252.

David Hulme.

BILLY IVISON (WORKINGTON TOWN)
Lance Todd Trophy winner 1952

Workington Town's Billy Ivison became the clearest Lance Todd Trophy winner so far after his contribution to the 18-10 Challenge Cup Final triumph over Feathestone Rovers in 1952. *The Sporting Chronicle* said 'Never has one man dominated as Ivison did. When his colleagues were jittery Ivison covered them.' The first Cumbrian to receive the award, Ivison instigated the opening try after 16 minutes when, from a play-the-ball, he quickly transferred to winger Johnny Lawrenson who, although tackled short of the line by Featherstone's Don Metcalfe, regained his feet, played the ball to himself and scored. Gus Risman's conversion, added to his first minute penalty, put Town seven points

Billy Ivison, in skull-cap, provides cover as the Workington Town halfback gets the ball away from the scrum during a League fixture.

attack by changing the direction of play. In the 57th minute and from his own 25-yard line, he shook off several would-be tacklers to charge downfield, breaking the defensive line to send second-row man John Mudge on a clear try-scoring run from halfway. Featherstone were broken and Town added two further tries from Lawrenson and George Wilson, Rovers scoring a late consolation touchdown. Ivison returned to Wembley in 1955, when he was 35 years old, as Workington captain but had to settle for second best to Barrow on that occasion.

clear. Two Fred Miller penalties reduced the margin to three points and, with 15 minutes remaining to the break, Featherstone piled tremendous pressure on Town's line. It was Ivison who stood up to be counted at this point, steadying the Workington line by continually running the ball out of defence in the face of Rovers' tough tackling pack.

When Featherstone captain Eric Batten's try levelled the scores three minutes after the interval, Ivison rallied his troops, varying the

Rugby League Challenge Cup Final 1952
Saturday 19 April at Wembley Stadium, London
Workington Town 18
Risman (captain, 3 goals), Lawrenson (2 tries), Paskins, Gibson, G Wilson (try), Thomas, A Pepperell, Hayton, McKeating, Wareing, Mudge (try), B Wilson, Ivison.
Featherstone Rovers 10
Miller (2 goals), Batten (captain, try), Metcalfe, Tennant, Mitchell, Cording, Evans (try), Welburn, Bradshaw, Daly, Hulme, Gant, Lambert.
Half-time: 7-4. Referee: CF Appleton (Warrington).
Attendance: 72,093.

Graham Morris

CHRIS JOYNT (ST HELENS)
Harry Sunderland Trophy winner 1993 and 2000

The valuable service and high level of performance given to St Helens by Chris Joynt over many seasons is illustrated by the fact that his two Harry Sunderland Trophy wins occurred seven years apart, easily the longest gap amongst the three players who have won the award twice. He had the satisfaction of accomplishing his feat against his hometown club Wigan on both occasions; as an upcoming 21-year-old in the 1993 Premiership Trophy Final, and as the captain in its successor, the Super League Grand Final, in 2000.

The 1993 contest was almost too close to call, the sound of the klaxon after the 80 minutes was up finally confirming that Wigan had gone down for the first time in 19 consecutive finals across various competitions, St Helens winning 10-4. The low scoring contest saw Saints centre Gary

Connolly contribute the only points of the first half with a try after being on hand to recover the ball from a Shane Cooper kick. With an hour gone, Mike Forshaw scored a try for Wigan to level the score before two Gus O'Donnell drop-goals gave St Helens a slender 6-4 lead. Five minutes from time, Paul Loughlin raced over the line for St Helens to close the scoring with the afternoon's third unconverted try.

Joynt, whose superb performance gave him

Chris Joynt.

PROFILE

Chris Joynt signed for Oldham from his local Wigan St Patrick's club in 1989, although it was not until the 1991/92 season that he featured regularly in the senior side. He was snapped up by St Helens at the start of the 1992/93 campaign, the non-stop second-row forward quickly commanding a place in Saints starting line-up and making his Great Britain debut in 1993. He was destined to appear in 25 Tests (the last in 2002) and was in the 1996 touring party to New Zealand, Papua New Guinea and Fiji. He played six times for England (1992-96, including the 1995 World Cup when he played in the final against Australia at Wembley) and once for Lancashire (2002). He also made four appearances for Ireland in the 2000 World Cup under the parent/grandparent rule. His committed, inspirational performances made him an ideal club captain and he led St Helens to victory in three Super League Grand Finals (1999, 2000 and 2002), plus a Challenge Cup-World Club Challenge double in 2001. He was also skipper of the side beaten in the 2002 Challenge Cup Final. Other honours with Saints include wins in the Challenge Cup (1996, 1997 and 2004), Super League (1996) and Premiership Trophy (1993). During 1995, he played for Australian side Newcastle Knights. He retired following the 2004 season.

the man of match verdict ahead of strong claims by team-mates Bernard Dwyer, Cooper and O'Donnell, said: 'It was a tough game, but it was our day and I think we deserved to win in a major final after losing out in the Championship by the narrowest of margins. Obviously I am delighted to have won the Harry Sunderland Trophy but I am pleased that we won the Premiership Trophy, it was a team effort.'

95

Joynt led his team out seven years later, one of only two survivors from the 1993 line-up (the other being substitute Sonny Nickle who had returned to St Helens after several seasons with Bradford Bulls). In a thrilling match, watched by

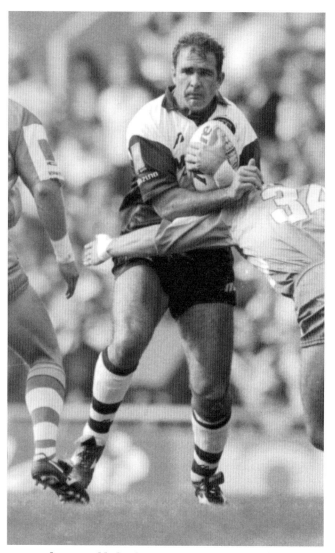

Despite being tackled, Chris Joynt still looks for support.

over 58,000 spectators – some 21,500 or so more than in 1993 – St Helens looked to have the match sewn up, leading 17-4 with 30 minutes left, Joynt having had a role in all three Saints tries up to that point. The first, in the 7th

minute, was scored by Sean Hoppe after Joynt resisted a tackle to somehow squeeze the ball out to him. Joynt got the next two himself; evading three defenders in the 28th minute before touching down and then, ten minutes after the interval, latching on to the end of a super break by Sean Long.

Wigan, to their credit, had everyone guessing the outcome when they dramatically fought back to close the gap to just one point at 17-16, St Helens sealing it with two late converted tries to win 29-16. Joynt fully deserved his second Harry Sunderland Trophy success having given a characteristically forceful performance, leading through example in attack and defence. The *St Helens Reporter* exclaimed: 'His tackling was straight out of the top drawer but he still found time – and energy – to drive forward.'

Premiership Trophy Final 1993
Sunday 16 May at Old Trafford, Manchester
St Helens 10
Lyon, Riley, Connolly (try), Loughlin (try), Hunte, Ropati, O'Donnell (2 drop-goals), Neill, Dwyer, Mann, Joynt, Nickle, Cooper (captain). Substitute: Griffiths.
Wigan 4
Atcheson, Robinson, Panapa, Farrar, Offiah, Botica, Edwards (captain), Cowie, Dermott, Skerrett, Cassidy, Farrell, Clarke. Substitutes: Forshaw (try), Gildart.
Half-time: 4-0. Referee: J Holdsworth (Kippax).
Attendance: 36,598.

Super League Grand Final 2000
Saturday 14 October at Old Trafford, Manchester
St Helens 29
Wellens, Hall, Iro, Hoppe (try), Sullivan, Martyn, Long (4 goals), Perelini, Cunningham, O'Neill, Joynt (captain, 2 tries), Jonkers (try), Sculthorpe (drop-goal). Substitutes: Tuilagi (try), Nickle, Stankevich.
Wigan Warriors 16
Robinson, Dallas, Radlinski, Renouf, Hodgson (try), Smith (try), Peters, O'Connor, Newton, Cowie, Cassidy, Betts, Farrell (captain, try, 2 goals). Substitutes: Malam, Mestrov, Chester, Gilmour.
Half-time: 11-4. Referee: R Smith (Castleford).
Attendance: 58,132.

Graham Morris

KEN KELLY (WARRINGTON)
Man of Steel Award winner 1981

=== PROFILE ===

Ken Kelly burst onto the scene with St Helens in 1969 as a clever, quick-witted 17-year-old scrum-half. The local schoolboy prodigy had signed the previous year after progressing through the St Helens 'B' and 'C' teams. It was at stand-off, however, that he established himself, a position he occupied most of his professional career, winning medals with Saints for the Championship (1971), Challenge Cup (1972) and BBC2 Floodlit Trophy (1971). He transferred to Bradford Northern in 1973 for £10,000, a Bradford record at that time, winning the Division Two Championship (1973/74). His form deserted him and, disillusioned, he drifted away from the club, his last first team game being in 1975. In 1977, his career revived through joining Warrington at the start of the year. It led to some of his finest performances, winning the Player's No.6 Trophy (1977/78), John Player Trophy (1980/81) and Lancashire Cup (1980 and 1982). He became club captain and resurrected his international and county status, his final tally being four Tests (1972-82), three England appearances (1979-81) and six for Lancashire (1972-81). The chance to travel with Great Britain was twice denied through a broken jaw; firstly, during a warm-up match ahead of the 1972 World Cup in France, and then before the 1979 tour to the Antipodes. He played his last match for Warrington in 1987.

for the Second Test against New Zealand at Odsal Stadium, in November. He earned further international recognition during the campaign with England in the European Championship, being man of the match in the 17-4 win over Wales at Craven Park, Hull during March.

Warrington skipper Ken Kelly accepts the John Player Trophy after victory in the 1980/81 final against Barrow at Central Park, a season that ended with him being named Man of Steel.

The award put the seal on an amazing revival in fortunes for Kelly whose playing career seemed to have ended prematurely after struggling at Bradford Northern, his Warrington comeback on New Years Day, 1977, under their, then, coach Alex Murphy being his first senior match for over a year.

Brilliant Warrington stand-off Ken Kelly scooped up two prizes at the 1981 Man of Steel Awards evening, being voted First Division Player of the Year by his fellow professionals and taking the major title of Man of Steel itself.

It followed a superb 1980/81 season in Warrington colours when, having been given the team captaincy, he led them to a double of Lancashire Cup (convincingly overcoming Wigan 26-10 in the final at St Helens) and John Player Trophy (Barrow 12-5 at Wigan). Warrington also came close to further honours during an impressive season, finishing runners-up by just two points to Bradford Northern in the First Division Championship race and losing to eventual winners Widnes in the Challenge Cup semi-final.

Kelly's excellent form earned him a Great Britain recall – his first appearance since 1972 –

Trumanns Man of Steel Awards 1981
Wednesday 13 May at the Golden Garter Theatre Club, Wythenshawe, Manchester
Compered by Keith Macklin
Man of Steel: Ken Kelly (Warrington).
First Division Player of the Year: Ken Kelly (Warrington).
Second Division Player of the Year: John Crossley (York).
Young Player of the Year: Des Drummond (Leigh).
Coach of the Year: Billy Benyon (Warrington).
Referee of the Year: John Holdsworth (Kippax).

BRETT KENNY (WIGAN)
Lance Todd Trophy winner 1985

PROFILE

The time that Australian Test star Brett Kenny spent in the British game covered only six months, but his impact with Wigan was unforgettable. The stand-off proved one of the most gifted players to emerge from the southern hemisphere, his anticipation, amazing acceleration and passing ability being of the highest order. Not surprisingly, given the time-scale, he was unable to add to his 1985 Challenge Cup success with Wigan, his career in Australia – where he played for Parramatta Eels from 1980 to 1993 – being more profitable, winning three Grand Finals (1981, 1982 and 1983). Born in Canterbury, Sydney, he played for Guildford at junior level before joining the Eels. Kenny toured Britain twice with the Kangaroos (1982 and 1986) and made 17 appearances each for Australia and New South Wales, both from 1982 to 1987. He retired as Parramatta's leading try scorer with 110 touchdowns.

It is difficult to think of a more dominant display than that of Wigan's Australian import Brett Kenny in the classic 1985 Challenge Cup Final against Hull. He put on a spell-binding show that won him the Lance Todd Trophy in a match that contained many outstanding performances. The 10-try extravaganza provided a spectacle of outstanding quality and the BBC repeated the highlights several times during the year and even transmitted a Christmas Special. Almost every try was out of the top drawer and it is doubtful a team played so well at Wembley as Hull did that day and still lost.

During a period when clubs annually flew Australian players – who had returned Down Under in February for their own competition – back to England for the Wembley occasion, stand-off Kenny, wingman John Ferguson (also Wigan) and Peter Sterling (Hull) - Kenny's half-back partner with Parramatta – repaid their clubs with interest for the cost of their air ticket.

It was Kenny who laid the foundations for the first Wigan try in the 17th minute, shrugging off three defenders near the Hull posts, before flipping the ball out to second-row forward Ian Potter, whose wide pass to the right sent Ferguson racing over in the right corner. Henderson Gill's tremendous touchline conversion brought the scores level at 6-6, Hull having taken an early lead. Kenny placed his mark firmly on the match ten minutes later with one of Wembley's greatest ever solo tries. Receiving the ball just inside his own half from Mike Ford, he burst through the line of defence, racing in an arc towards the left corner before evading Hull full-back Gary Kemble to touch down. It was a try of such electrifying brilliance that, had he done nothing of note for the rest of the match, he had placed one hand on the Lance Todd Trophy. David Stephenson's extra two points put Wigan 12-6 in front, a lead they would not surrender.

Brett Kenny.

The Aussie genius was again instrumental just before half-time when Gill scored another memorable try. From inside his own 25, Kenny whipped out a sharp pass, which cut out three defenders, to centre Stephenson on the left. Stephenson burst through the half-gap to send Gill on an exciting run down the left wing, evading the despairing tackle of Kemble to touch down. Gill's beaming smile as he looked

scorchers from their New Zealand centre James Leuluai. To Wigan's relief all three conversions failed, leaving the Humbersiders just short at 28-24 when the final hooter sounded.

After the match, Kenny said: 'The first half was really fast, I couldn't believe it. After the first ten minutes I was gone, I felt as if there was only ten minutes to go in the game! The last 40 (minutes) was the longest 40 I've ever played in

Brett Kenny eludes the Hull defence on the way to scoring his try during the 1985 Challenge Cup Final at Wembley.

up from the ground after placing the ball down produced an enduring image captured by most of the following days sports pages.

Ford and Kenny created the next try three minutes into the second half, with a well-worked move from a scrum 35 yards from the Hull posts. Ford fed Kenny who, having done a run-around, dummied his return pass to Ford, skipping out of a tackle by Sterling, before drawing Kemble and giving a well-timed pass to Shaun Edwards, who sprinted from the back of the scrum to race behind the posts. Gill's extra points made the score 22-8. Sterling gave Hull some hope when he put Steve Evans in at the corner but after Ferguson claimed a loose ball to charge over for his second try it looked all over. Gill added the difficult touchline kick and, with almost a half-hour left, Wigan held a comfortable 28-12 lead. Hull had other ideas, however, and came back with three excellent tries, including two

my life!' Having misled everyone by appearing to be completely disinterested in the whole affair during the pre-match presentation as he casually stood around with his hands in his pockets, Kenny became the first Australian to win the Lance Todd Trophy.

Rugby League Challenge Cup Final 1985
Saturday 4 May at Wembley Stadium, London
Wigan 28
Edwards (try), Ferguson (2 tries), Stephenson (goal), Donlan, Gill (try, 3 goals), Kenny (try), Ford, Courtney, Kiss, Case, West (captain), Dunn, Potter.
Substitute: Campbell.
Hull 24
Kemble, James (try), Evans (try), Leuluai (2 tries), O'Hara, Ah Kuoi, Sterling, Crooks (captain, 2 goals), Patrick, Puckering, Muggleton, Rose, Norton.
Substitutes: Schofield, Divorty (try).
Half-time: 16-8. Referee: R Campbell (Widnes).
Attendance: 97,801.

LEN KILLEEN (ST HELENS)
Lance Todd Trophy winner 1966

Len Killeen.

In 1966, St Helens flying left wingman Len Killeen became the first and, to date, only South African to win the Lance Todd Trophy, giving a stunning display against Wigan in a Challenge Cup Final which failed to live up to its classic billing. In truth, Wigan were badly handicapped through the suspension of their regular hooker Colin Clarke, Saints taking full advantage in rattling up a convincing 21-2 score-line. Killeen scored the second of St Helens' three tries in the 54th minute, cleanly gathering a grubber kick from his centre Billy Benyon to dive over at the corner. It was his amazing goal-kicking, however, that grabbed the headlines, the Wembley match programme writer being spot on in describing him as 'an exceptional kicker even at long and awkward distances.'

Watched by a Wembley record 98,536 for the 13-a-side code, the *Rugby Leaguer* newspaper pulled no punches in proclaiming 'Wonder-goal Killeen gets Lance Todd Trophy.' The goal in question – one of five in his 13-point contribution to the score – was his second penalty after just nine minutes. On a warm, sultry afternoon, he looked remarkably cool as he placed the ball a few yards in from the touchline and 65 yards from his target, before kicking a goal rated by many as the best ever seen at Wembley. He followed that up eight minutes later with another great touchline effort in converting John Mantle's try, taking the score to 9-0, a subsequent Laurie Gilfedder penalty for Wigan making it 9-2 at half-time.

Having increased Saints score with a straight-forward penalty, the left-footed Killeen, no doubt encourage by his first half effort, attempted one from 70 yards. The crowd gasped as the enormous kick, which achieved both height and distance, just sailed wide. Killeen

Len Killeen, about to secure his Wembley touchdown in 1966.

Len Killeen had two major assets; first, he was a brilliant attacking left wing-three-quarter possessing great flair, elusiveness and deadly speed and, second, he was a supreme goal-kicker who had tremendous power and accuracy in his boot. His prowess was perfectly illustrated in the 1965/66 season when he became the only player ever to top the Rugby League charts for tries (32), goals (120) and points (336). The South African flyer, born in Port Elizabeth, joined St Helens in 1962 from Uitenhage Rugby Union club, winning the Championship (1965/66), Challenge Cup (1966), Lancashire Cup (1963 and 1964) and short-lived Western Division Championship (1963/64). Following his last match for St Helens in 1967, he moved to Australia where he played for Balmain (1967-71, winning the 1969 Grand Final) and Penrith (1972), after which he returned to South Africa.

touchdown after 71 minutes. The scoring was completed by Alex Murphy, the Saints captain landing a drop-goal two minutes from the end. Killeen, who had scored all his team's points in the 12-5 semi-final victory over Dewsbury, was the first winger to win the Lance Todd Trophy and the second overseas player honoured following New Zealander Cec Mountford in 1951.

Rugby League Challenge Cup Final 1966
Saturday 21 May at Wembley Stadium, London
St Helens 21
Barrow, van Vollenhoven, Murphy (captain, goal), Benyon, Killeen (try, 5 goals), Harvey, Bishop (try), Halsall, Sayer, Watson, French, Warlow, Mantle (try).
Wigan 2
Ashby, Boston, D Stephens, Ashton (captain), Lake, C Hill, Parr, Gardiner, Woosey, McTigue, T Stephens, Gilfedder (goal), Major.
Half-time: 9-2. Referee: HG Hunt (Warrington).
Attendance: 98,536.

contributed his own try – rated as the best of the match – shortly after, failing with the difficult conversion attempt, being more successful in adding the extra two points to Tommy Bishop's

St Helens skipper Alex Murphy raises the Challenge Cup after the 1966 Wembley win. Lance Todd Trophy winner Len Killeen, left of the two players kneeling, is looking straight at the camera whilst future BBC Rugby League commentator Ray French, extreme right, admires his medal.

101

BILL KIRKBRIDE (CASTLEFORD)
Lance Todd Trophy winner 1970

PROFILE

Bill Kirkbride was born in Workington and played for the local United Steels team, joining Workington Town in 1964. Standing six feet, one inch and weighing 14 stone, he gained a reputation as a tough, agile second-row forward with a fair turn of speed. He transferred to Halifax in 1968 for £6,000, joined Castleford in 1969 for £5,750 (winning the 1970 Challenge Cup), followed by a £6,000 move to Salford in 1971. After a short loan spell with Leigh early in the 1973/74 season, he decided to move to Brisbane Souths in Australia's Queensland League in 1974. Returning to England, he joined Wakefield Trinity in 1976, being player-coach from 1979 to 1980, taking them to the 1979 Challenge Cup Final at Wembley, although not playing himself. He was player-coach at York (1980-82, his side winning the 1980/81 Division Two Championship) and Rochdale Hornets (1982-84) and coach at Mansfield Marksman (1985-86). He represented Cumberland seven times (1967-71).

Cumbrian second-row forward Bill Kirkbride celebrated the biggest game of his career by lifting the Lance Todd Trophy as he helped Castleford retain the Challenge Cup beating Wigan 7-2 in the 1970 final. Recovering from pre-match nerves after he 'suffered a severe attack of dressing room jitters which left his legs like jelly', Kirkbride played a major role in the only try after just 10 minutes. Hooker Clive Dickinson combined with Malcolm Reilly to send Kirkbride on a powerful 30-yard burst which took him inside Wigan's 25. Although tackled, he played the ball quickly before Wigan could reorganise their defensive line, allowing Brian Lockwood, Alan Hardisty and Ian Stenton to move the ball urgently, creating the overlap for Alan Lowndes to go round Keri Jones, placing the ball down in the right corner. Mick Redfearn missed the kick, his earlier penalty nosing Castleford 5-2 ahead at the break.

Kirkbride who, along with second-row partner Lockwood, dominated play after the interval, almost added another try (he also combined with Keith Hepworth to halt Bob Burdell near the Castleford posts in the closing

minutes) but the only second-half score was a 67th minute penalty by Redfearn. The match was not without controversy, Wigan full-back Colin Tyrer leaving the field after 16 minutes with concussion and a broken jaw following an incident with Hepworth, Cliff Hill subsequently becoming Wembley's first substitute.

The *Pontefract & Castleford Express* writer said of his Lance Todd success: 'Kirkbride received my vote for the trophy. Quickly over his attack of nerves, he ran onto the ball strongly, handled confidently and did his share of tackling.'

Rugby League Challenge Cup Final 1970
Saturday 9 May at Wembley Stadium, London
Castleford 7
Edwards, Briggs, Thomas, Stenton, Lowndes (try), Hardisty (captain), Hepworth (try), Hartley, Dickinson, Redfearn (2 goals), Kirkbride, Lockwood, Reilly. Substitute: Hargrave.
Wigan 2
Tyrer (goal), Jones, Francis, Rowe, Kevin O'Loughlin, D Hill, Parr, Ashcroft, Burdell, Hogan, Ashurst, Robinson, Laughton (captain). Substitute: C Hill.
Half-time: 5-2. Referee: GF Lindop (Wakefield).
Attendance: 95,255.

Bill Kirkbride celebrates a job well done in the Wembley dressing room in 1970.

DOUG LAUGHTON (WIDNES)
Man of Steel Award winner 1979

Doug Laughton.

Doug Laughton was the first person to receive the accolade of Man of Steel based on his achievements as a coach, rather than a player, the honour being conferred on him at the Wakefield Theatre Club in 1979 after another trophy-laden season for cup-Kings of the day, Widnes. In a dream start to his coaching career, having taken over – in the capacity of player-coach – from Frank Myler during May 1978, he led his charges to four wins from four cup final appearances across the 1978/79 campaign.

The first of those settled the destination of the Lancashire Cup during October, defeating Workington Town 15-13 at Wigan, followed by the BBC2 Floodlit Trophy, beating St Helens 13-7 at the Saints' Knowsley Road ground in December and the John Player Trophy, by overcoming Warrington 28-4 at St Helens in April, although not playing himself on that occasion. The biggest of the lot was at the climax of the season, during May, when Wakefield Trinity were vanquished 12-3 in the Challenge Cup Final at Wembley. Additionally, Widnes defeated the 1978 Australian touring side 11-10 in front of over 12,000 delirious fans at their Naughton Park enclosure on a magical Wednesday evening in October, one of only two

Widnes 1979. Doug Laughton is on the front row, third from right.

PROFILE

Widnes-born Doug Laughton was a skilful, ball-playing loose forward who possessed the ability to lead from the front, and packed a lot into his Rugby League career. As a player, he signed for St Helens from the Lowerhouse (Widnes) amateur club in 1962, winning the Championship (1965/66) and Lancashire Cup (1964) before transferring to Wigan in 1967 for £6,000. At Wigan, he was a winner in the final of the Lancashire Cup (1971) and BBC2 Floodlit Trophy (1968) but had to settle for runners-up medals in the Challenge Cup (1970) and Championship (1971). In 1973, he returned to his roots, joining Widnes for a £6,000 transfer fee, where he enjoyed his most successful period. He won the Challenge Cup (1976 and 1979, being a Wembley runner-up on two other occasions), Championship (1977/78), Lancashire Cup (1974, 1976 and 1978) and BBC2 Floodlit Trophy (1978). In 1974, he surrendered the chance to captain the Great Britain touring side to the Antipodes, spending the close-season with Australia club Canterbury-Bankstown instead, although he was a tourist in 1970 and 1979, being captain on the latter. He became Widnes player-coach in 1978, and continued to enjoy success as a coach (after playing his last match in 1979) until 1983, taking them to Wembley in 1981 (won) and 1982 (lost in a replay). He subsequently had two more spells as Widnes coach (1986-91 and 1995-97) and was in charge at Leeds (1991-95, taking them to Wembley twice). He represented Great Britain 15 times (1970-79, including the 1970 World Cup when he appeared in the final, losing to Australia at Headingley), England twice (1965 and 1977) and Lancashire on eleven occasions (1964-73).

retired at the start of the following season after one match, a knee injury sustained whilst captain of Great Britain's 1979 touring party Down Under convincing him that he should concentrate on consolidating his initial coaching successes.

Trumanns Man of Steel Awards 1979
Wednesday 16 May at the Wakefield Theatre Club
Compered by Keith Macklin
Man of Steel: Doug Laughton (Widnes).
First Division Player of the Year: Mick Adams (Widnes).
Second Division Player of the Year: Steve Norton (Hull).
Young Player of the Year: Steve Evans (Featherstone Rovers).
Coach of the Year: Doug Laughton (Widnes).
Referee of the Year: MJ (Mick) Naughton (Widnes).

A 1974 success for Doug Laughton, after leading Widnes to victory over Salford in the Lancashire Cup Final at Central Park.

clubs to do so during a tour that saw the Kangaroos colours lowered just three times.

His achievements brought him the Coach of the Year title – ahead of fellow nominees Billy Benyon (Warrington) and Arthur Bunting (Hull) – earlier in the evening before the main award took place. Effectively, it was Laughton's only full season of combining his role at loose-forward with coaching. The 35-year-old (the oldest winner of the Man of Steel to date)

Graham Morris

BRIAN LOCKWOOD (HULL KINGSTON ROVERS)
Lance Todd Trophy winner 1980

A moment of sheer class when delivering one of Wembley's most memorable try-scoring off-loads earned Brian Lockwood the Lance Todd Trophy in the all-Humberside Challenge Cup Final of 1980. Curiously, Lockwood – who appeared in five finals at the famous venue – plays down his contribution saying: 'I thought personally there were far better players playing on the day. I made a pass to Steve Hubbard, who scored an absolutely marvellous try, and I got the accolade for passing the ball. But people

Lance Todd Trophy hero Brian Lockwood is on the extreme right of this picture, clenching his fist in triumph as Hull Kingston Rovers skipper Roger Millward holds up the Challenge Cup.

don't understand that Steve ran 30 yards to take the ball to go another 30 yards to score the try and didn't get the accolade he should have. I got it because of the timing of the pass!' Whilst that may be true, Lockwood's perfect execution of

Brian Lockwood signed for his local team Castleford in 1963 having emerged through the Castleford junior ranks. He was a competitive, pacy, second-row forward who developed the skill to off-load the ball with devastating effect, particularly during the latter third of his playing career when he relocated to prop. He won the Challenge Cup with Castleford twice (1969 and 1970) but, having spent the 1974 close-season in Australia with Canterbury-Bankstown where he was a runner-up in that year's Grand Final, he left his hometown club in 1975, returning to Australia to join Balmain for three years (1975-77). Towards the end of 1976, he signed up with Wakefield Trinity as player-coach, having to leave them for nine months during 1977 to complete his Balmain contract. In 1978, he left Wakefield for Hull Kingston Rovers, where he won the Championship (1978/79) and Challenge Cup (1980). He joined Oldham in 1980, transferring to Widnes at the start of 1981, adding two further Challenge Cup Final appearances (1981 and 1982 – winning the former but losing the latter in a replay following a draw at Wembley) and enjoying success in the Premiership Trophy (1982). He played his last match for Widnes in 1983, afterwards coaching Huddersfield (1983-85) and Batley (1985-87). He appeared in nine Test matches for Great Britain (1972-79, including the 1972 World Cup and 1979 tour), played three times for England (1970-79) and five for Yorkshire (1969-73).

the move – pre-planned and imported from Lockwood's time in Australian club rugby – produced the key moment of a tense final. It opened the scoring in the eighth minute, Lockwood looking at first as though he was set to pass to the supporting Len Casey, tempting the Hull defence to move across and cover the Rovers loose forward. Hubbard, however, cut infield from the right wing to go on the inside of Casey, accepting Lockwood's delayed pass to burst through a huge gap and race diagonally across field to place the ball down in the left corner. He failed to convert his own try but referee Fred Lindop then awarded a penalty for a foul by Paul Woods as he touched down, Hubbard making no mistake with his second attempt and adding a second penalty five minutes later for a 7-0 lead. Although Rovers'

A unique day for Rugby League and the city of Hull.

Lockwood, despite his reservations and generosity in nominating Rovers scrum-half Allan Agar as his own choice, polled 19 of the 33 votes cast in winning the Lance Todd Trophy. *Daily Telegraph* writer Paul Rylance was typical of many in praising his 'superb display in attack and defence.' It was Lockwood's farewell appearance for Hull Kingston Rovers, against whom he played at Wembley the following year for Widnes, claiming his fourth Challenge Cup win, having won with Castleford in 1969 and 1970. It brought him a share of Alex Murphy's, then, record of four Wembley wins, the pair also having the distinction of winning the Challenge Cup with three different clubs at the famous venue.

Rugby League Challenge Cup Final 1980
Saturday 3 May at Wembley Stadium, London
Hull Kingston Rovers 10
Hall, Hubbard (try, 3 goals), Smith, Hartley, Sullivan, Millward (captain, drop-goal), Agar, Holdstock, Watkinson, Lockwood, Lowe, Rose, Casey. Substitutes: Hogan, Millington.
Hull 5
Woods, Bray, Walters, Wilby (try), Prendiville, Newlove, Pickerill, Tindall, Wileman, Stone, Birdsall, Lloyd (goal), Norton (captain). Substitutes: Hancock, Farrar.
Half-time: 8-3. Referee: GF Lindop (Wakefield).
Attendance: 95,000.

eventual winning margin was just five points, it was a pivotal phase of play in a low-scoring final full of handling errors.

SEAN LONG (ST HELENS)
Man of Steel Award winner 2000
Lance Todd Trophy winner 2001 and 2004

═══ PROFILE ═══

The precocious talent of Sean Long cost St Helens just £80,000 when they signed him from Widnes in 1997. It turned out to be a bargain price for one of the quickest half-backs around (in thought and on foot), his lightening breaks and exceptional kicking game making him one of Super League's most lethal attackers. His career started with his local club Wigan, who snapped him up from St Judes in 1993, but, dogged by injury problems, he was unable to gain a regular slot with the Cherry and Whites. He dropped down a division to join Widnes Vikings in April 1997, but quickly discovered his elusive form, St Helens recruiting him two months later. Since joining the Saints he has enjoyed wins in the World Club Challenge (2001), Super League Grand Final (1999, 2000, 2002) and Challenge Cup (2001, 2004). His only set-back, to date, is losing the 2002 Challenge Cup decider. At the time of writing, he has played in 11 Tests for Great Britain (1997-2004) and represented England five times (all in the 2000 World Cup).

Two-time Lance Todd Trophy winner Sean Long, when asked at the post-match press conference following his second success in 2004, if he had ambitions to become the first person to win the coveted trophy three times, replied: 'I've not thought about that, to be honest. It would be great to do it. If we do go there again it would be on my mind.' Who could argue against the dynamic scrum-half, a consistent match-winner since joining St Helens in 1997, and pre-match 4-1 favourite to take the 2004 award? Long himself said: 'I read before the match that Sean Long and Kris Radlinski are two players that could win it again and I thought "I may as well go out there and give it my best shot." To be part of it (winning the Lance Todd Trophy twice) with three other people is unbelievable especially when Andy Gregory (winner in 1988 and 1990) comes up to you and says "well done" – that means a lot to me.'

His first Lance Todd success was in 2001, during a miserable cold, rain soaked afternoon at Twickenham, making handling difficult. St Helens and Bradford Bulls still conjured up a

match worthy of the occasion, although with just two tries – both from the 13-6 winners St Helens – it was hardly a classic. Long was the architect each time, producing two perfectly judged kicks towards the Bulls line. Tommy Martyn (12th minute) was the first beneficiary, diving on the ball despite Henry Paul's tackle, after a neat chip to the right of the posts, Keiron Cunningham (26th minute) scooping the ball up 15 yards in front of goal for the second from Long's grubber kick. Long converted both.

The same tactic by Long came close to producing three other tries. The first – in the 10th minute – was thwarted when Shane Rigon obstructed Martyn's follow through resulting in

Sean Long.

the Bradford player being sin-binned, the move being successfully repeated two minutes later. The two other close calls occurred in the second half, Martyn being ruled offside and Tim Jonkers not grounding properly. Enterprisingly, coach Ian Millward utilised Long on the right

there was no disputing Long's massive influence on the outcome. On a hot day, his form sizzled as much as the sunshine and provided the crowd with a magical display in the arts of kicking, having a hand – or foot – in three of St Helens five tries.

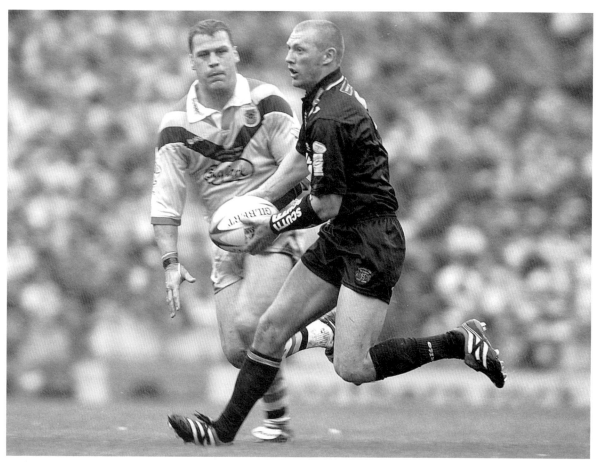

Sean Long attempts to outwit Bradford Bulls' James Lowes in the 2001 Challenge Cup Final at Twickenham. His performance brought him his first Lance Todd Trophy award.

flank in defence to negate the potential danger of Henry Paul's kicking. A clear winner of the man of the match award, Long showed he was just as sharp in defence beating two Bradford attackers to the touch-down after a Henry Paul kick in only the 4th minute and pulling off a vital tackle on Rigon in the 63rd minute who, having intercepted, looked a certain scorer.

Most felt his display in the 2004 Challenge Cup Final win, over Wigan Warriors in Cardiff, outshone that of 2001, his then familiar white headband (worn to keep his lengthy blonde locks off his face) seeming to appear everywhere. Despite the press coming up with one of the closest Lance Todd verdicts in years – four votes covering the top four candidates –

St Helens led 20-10 at half-time, the scores being tied 6-6 after 13 minutes – a 3rd minute Saints' try by Lee Gilmour in the left corner being augmented by an excellent goal by Long. Long's astute kicking became a major factor, the scrum-half landed a well struck 35 yard penalty in the 18th minute before – six minutes later – directing a short bobbling kick over the Wigan whitewash which stood up perfectly for Willie Talau to pounce on and score, Long again converting. Seconds from half-time, he got his fourth goal, tacking on two points to a Paul Wellens try near the posts.

After the interval, Long continued testing Wigan's defence, his inch-perfect grubber kicks to the in-goal area creating all sorts of problems, forcing several goal line drop-outs. Both St Helens' second half tries had Long's stamp on them. As acting half-back, he supported Sculthorpe's play-the-ball, the loose-forward being on hand to accept Long's scoring pass close to the try line (51st minute), Long then re-gathering his own chip kick, propelled from 10 yards inside the Saints half, Gilmour racing up in support to receive the short pass and send Talau in for his second (68th minute). Long converted Sculthorpe's try, adding a penalty four minutes later to complete a perfect afternoon's work with a personal tally of six goals from seven attempts.

Long preceded his Lance Todd exploits with the Man of Steel Award in 2000 following a scintillating, record breaking season, which was climaxed by St Helens winning the Super League Grand Final a second consecutive year. His total of 418 points for St Helens, comprising 24 tries and 161 goals, incorporated new Super League records of 390 points and 151 goals. It was a campaign that finished in marked contrast to the traumatic opening weeks when they were overwhelmed 44-6 by Melbourne Storm in the World Club Challenge, suffered an early Challenge Cup exit to Leeds Rhinos, and lost their opening Super League clash to Bradford Bulls 32-10 at Knowsley Road. More unsettling for Long at that stage was the apparent break up of his acclaimed half-back partnership with 1997 Lance Todd Trophy winner Martyn. Coach Ellery Hanley was no longer selecting Martyn, with Saints, reportedly, prepared to release him. In a dramatic turn of events, the St Helens board replaced Hanley one month into the season, former Leigh coach Ian Millward taking over who reinstated Martyn. With their irrepressible half-back pairing of Long and Martyn restored, St Helens fired back into life, their rejuvenated side dominating Super League V, the Saints losing just four more matches all season during their march to the title.

Tetley's Super League Man of Steel Awards 2000
Wednesday 11 October at the Crowne Plaza
Midland, Manchester
Compered by Eddie Hemmings and Mike Stephenson
Man of Steel: Sean Long (St Helens).
Super League Players' Player of the Year: Tommy Martyn (St Helens).
Super League Young Player of the Year: Stuart Fielden (Bradford Bulls).
Super League Coach of the Year: Frank Endacott
(Wigan).
Super League Referee of the Year: Russell Smith (Castleford).

Rugby League Challenge Cup Final 2001
Saturday 28 April at Twickenham, London
St Helens 13
Wellens, Hoppe, Iro, Newlove, Sullivan, Martyn (try, drop-goal), Long (2 goals), Nickle, Cunningham (try), Fairleigh, Joynt (captain), Shiels, Sculthorpe. Substitutes: Matautia, Jonkers, Hall.
Bradford Bulls 6
Withers, Vaikona, Naylor, Rigon, Pryce, H Paul (3 goals), R Paul (captain), Vagana, Lowes, McDermott, Peacock, Gartner, Forshaw. Substitutes: Anderson, Fielden, Gilmour, Deacon.
Half-time: 13-4. Referee: R Smith (Castleford). Attendance: 68,250.

Rugby League Challenge Cup Final 2004
Saturday 15 May at The Millennium Stadium, Cardiff
St Helens 32
Wellens (try), Gardner, Gleeson, Talau (2 tries), Albert, Hooper, Long (6 goals), Fozzard, Cunningham, Mason, Joynt, Gilmour (try), P Sculthorpe (captain, try). Substitutes: Edmondson, Feaunati, Wilkin, Bibey.
Wigan Warriors 16
Radlinski, Hodgson, O'Loughlin, Brown, Dallas (2 tries), Orr, Lam, Smith, Newton (try), Pongia, Tickle, Hock, Farrell (captain, 2 goals). Substitutes: O'Connor, D Sculthorpe, Cassidy, Wild.
Half-time: 20-10. Referee: K Kirkpatrick (Warrington). Attendance: 73,734.

In the thick of the action at Cardiff's Millennium Stadium, Sean Long on his way to a second Lance Todd Trophy accolade during St Helens 2004 Challenge Cup Final victory over Wigan Warriors.

JAMES LOWES (BRADFORD BULLS)
Man of Steel Award winner 1997

PROFILE

James Lowes began his professional career as a scrum-half with Hunslet, the Leeds-born player having signed in 1986 from Hunslet-Parkside. His transfer to Leeds in 1992 brought him under the influence of coach Doug Laughton, who moved him to hooker. It marked a new beginning for Lowes who appeared at Wembley as rake in the 1994 and 1995 Challenge Cup Finals, although losing both. In 1996, Bradford Bulls prised him away to become a key component in their awesome pack. His first Bradford success was winning the 1997 Super League, followed by appearances in four Super League Grand Finals (winning in 2001 and 2003) and four Challenge Cup Finals (winning in 2000 and 2003), being triumphant in the 2002 World Club Challenge. A Great Britain tourist in 1996 he appeared in five Test Matches (1997-2002), and, thanks to a Donegal-born grandmother, represented Ireland twice (1996 and 1997), and Yorkshire once (2001). Retiring after the 2003 Grand Final, he joined the Bulls coaching staff, moving to Salford City Reds as assistant-coach in 2005.

A classic action shot of James Lowes.

James Lowes.

The inspirational Bradford Bulls hooker James Lowes was a popular winner of the 1997 Man of Steel Award, contributing massively to his clubs Super League title that year. The first trophy won by the Bulls since the summer era began in 1996, they swept through their League programme, winning the first 20 matches to eventually finish seven points clear of runners-up London Broncos in the table.

A central cog in a well-drilled Bradford side, he also helped them reach the Challenge Cup Final at Wembley where they lost to St Helens for the second successive year, by 32-22. His late try was one of 17 he scored for the club during the campaign, making him their leading try-scorer, a testimony to his quick-thinking opportunism, particularly from acting half-back.

He was first choice for Great Britain in the subsequent three match Test series with Australia, played during November at Wembley (scoring a try), Old Trafford and Elland Road, respectively, the Aussies taking the series 2-1. The campaign also saw him wearing the green jersey of Ireland for the second time (following an initial appearance against Scotland in 1996) against France in Paris during May, again contributing a try that began a gritty Irish fight back from 30-16 down, to draw the match 30-30.

The first hooker to take the Man of Steel since Leeds' David Ward at the inaugural ceremony 20 years earlier, Lowes also received the Super League Player of the Year award.

Stones Gold Awards Dinner 1997
Thursday 25 September at the Holiday Inn Crowne Plaza Midland, Manchester
Compered by Eddie Hemmings and Mike Stephenson
Man of Steel: James Lowes (Bradford Bulls).
Super League Player of the Year: James Lowes (Bradford Bulls).
First Division Player of the Year: Tevita Vaikona (Hull Sharks).
Second Division Player of the Year: Richard Pachniuk (Rochdale Hornets).
Super League Young Player of the Year: Lee Briers (Warrington Wolves).
Super League Coach of the Year: Matthew Elliott (Bradford Bulls).
Referee of the Year: Russell Smith (Castleford).

JOE LYDON (WIDNES AND WIGAN)
Lance Todd Trophy winner 1984
Man of Steel Award winner 1984
Harry Sunderland Trophy winner 1987

Joe Lydon had a sensational season in 1983/84 culminating in his receiving the Lance Todd Trophy and Man of Steel Award after less than two years with Widnes. The 20-year-old set Wembley alight with two blistering length-of-field tries against Wigan in an otherwise pedestrian Challenge Cup Final. Lydon – who had appeared previously at Wembley in 1975 for Wigan under-11s against their Widnes counterparts in the schoolboy curtain raiser – scored his touchdowns 30 minutes into each half. The first occurred when Widnes second-row forward Les Gorley charged down an attempted Wigan chip-kick from inside his own 25. Recovering the ball, his short pass to Kevin Tamati was whipped out quickly to Lydon who sprinted down the left side off the field, his acceleration taking him clear of any opposition, to go under the posts having covered almost 80 yards. With Mick Burke adding the extra points it put Widnes 12-2 up at the turnaround, colleague Keiron O'Loughlin having already registered the opening try three minutes earlier.

Any uncertainty the assembled press had on where to cast their Lance Todd vote faded with Lydon's second effort, which even outshone his first. Wigan were again pressing inside the Widnes 25 when a dropped ball was quickly scooped up by Lydon who, darting through a gap in the defence, took on and beat full-back Shaun Edwards, and then rounded the

Joe Lydon – the emerging Widnes star of 1984.

despairing tackle of David Stephenson to touch down midway between the posts and left corner-flag, having covered some 85 yards. Although, Wigan got a late consolation try, the match was settled at that point. Lydon, who made five subsequent, victorious Wembley trips with Wigan, said of his Lance Todd success after the match: 'I didn't expect it at all. Mick Adams came over to me and said I'd won it. I'm over the moon! I had the breaks and a bit of luck on my side today. It was a beautiful ball off Kevin (Tamati) for the first one and I had acres of space. All I had to do was put it down! The second one I don't remember much about it! It all happened so quickly. I put my ears back and hoped for the best!' For Widnes, the 19-6 win was a record seventh at Wembley.

The following Wednesday, during the Man of Steel Awards evening held at the Willows Variety Centre, Salford, Lydon received three more accolades; First Division Player of the Year, Young Player of the Year and – the crème de la crème – the Man of Steel title itself. Bedsides his eye-catching Wembley debut, the rising star had registered 27 tries and 54 goals during the season in helping Widnes also reach the finals of the John Player Trophy against Leeds (scoring a try) and Lancashire Cup versus Barrow (try, two goals), although losing both. On a more personal level he represented Great Britain against France in Avignon during January, having appeared twice at under-24 level, also against the French, scoring a vital four goals in a 28-23 win in Villeneuve during November, and contributing a try and eight goals in the return at Oldham the following month, which resulted in a resounding 48-1 victory. To top it all off, the

moment of real excitement with a spectacular try five minutes before half-time. Wigan scrum-half and former Widnes team-mate Andy Gregory was the instigator, kicking the ball forward from inside his own 25 area. Lydon took up the chase, getting his boot to it three times as

Joe Lydon about to score the only try of the first Premiership Trophy Final to be staged at Old Trafford, on the way to earning himself the Harry Sunderland Trophy as Wigan defeat Warrington.

versatile back was selected to travel to the Antipodes with the 1984 Great Britain touring team at the end of the season.

Three years later, he became the first winger to receive the Harry Sunderland Trophy for his performance during the 1987 Premiership Trophy Final, staged at Manchester United's Old Trafford enclosure for the initial time. Following a record £100,000 transfer in 1986, he was appearing in the cherry and white of Wigan, the opposition being Warrington on a rain-soaked afternoon. In a dull affair, with both defences dominating, Lydon provided the only

he raced down the field towards the Warrington line. Despite being shadowed by the speedy Des Drummond, Lydon managed to gather the ball and dive over, thwarting late tackle attempts from two more defenders. In addition to his match-clinching try, Lydon contributed throughout with some excellent kicking, including a 70-yard effort to touch, gaining valuable territory on a day when a passing game was less effective. His Harry Sunderland award meant he became the second player to complete the prized trio of major individual honours

PROFILE

Wigan-born Joe Lydon commenced his professional career with Widnes, the speedy three-quarter – who later proved equally proficient at full-back – joining the club in 1982 from Wigan St Patrick's. His time at Naughton Park saw him gain winners' medals for the Premiership Trophy (1983) and Challenge Cup (1984) before transferring to Wigan for £100,000 in 1986. At Wigan, the honours flowed, Lydon being successful in the World Club Challenge (1987, 1991), Championship (1986/87, 1989/90, 1990/91, 1991/92, 1992/93, 1993/94), Challenge Cup (1988, 1989, 1990, 1992, 1993), Premiership Trophy (1987, 1992, 1994), John Player Trophy (1986/87, 1988/89), Regal Trophy (1989/90, 1992/93) and Lancashire Cup (1986, 1987, 1988, 1992).

A tourist with the Great Britain side in 1984, 1990 and 1992 (he was also selected in 1988 but had to withdraw), he made 30 Test appearances for Britain (1983-92) including the 1992 World Cup Final at Wembley against Australia. He also played four times for Lancashire (1985-88) and spent two periods in Australia with Eastern Suburbs (1987 and 1990). After retiring in 1994, he joined Wigan's coaching staff before taking on the role of Technical Director with the Rugby Football League, later joining the England Rugby Union coaching set-up.

Rugby League Challenge Cup Final 1984
Saturday 5 May at Wembley Stadium, London
Widnes 19
Burke (3 goals), Wright, Hughes (captain), Lydon (2 tries), Basnett, O'Loughlin (try), Gregory, S O'Neill (drop-goal), Elwell, Tamati, Gorley, M O'Neill, Adams. Substitutes: D Hulme, Whitfield.
Wigan 6
Edwards, Ramsdale, Stephenson, Whitfield (goal), Gill, Cannon, Stephens, Hemsley (try), Tamati, Case, West (captain), Scott, Pendlebury. Substitutes: Elvin, Juliff.
Half-time: 12-2. Referee: WH Thompson (Huddersfield). Attendance: 80,116.

Greenalls Man of Steel Awards 1984
Wednesday 9 May at The Willows Variety Centre, Salford
Compered by Keith Macklin
Man of Steel: Joe Lydon (Widnes).
First Division Player of the Year: Joe Lydon (Widnes).
Second Division Player of the Year: David Cairns (Barrow).

Young Player of the Year: Joe Lydon (Widnes).
Coach of the Year: Tommy Dawes (Barrow).
Referee of the Year: WH (Billy) Thompson (Huddersfield).

Premiership Trophy Final 1987
Sunday 17 May at Old Trafford, Manchester
Wigan 8
Hampson, Gill (goal), Stephenson (goal), Bell, Lydon (try), Edwards, A Gregory, Case, Kiss, Wane, Goodway, Potter, Hanley (captain). Substitutes: Russell, West.
Warrington 0
Johnson, Drummond, Ropati, Peters, Forster, Cullen, Bishop, Tamati, Roberts, Jackson (captain), Humphries, Sanderson, R Duane. Substitutes: M Gregory, Eccles.
Half-time: 6-0. Referee: K Allatt (Southport).
Attendance: 38,756.

Wembley 1993 – a delighted Joe Lydon holds the Challenge Cup after another Wigan success.

113

GREG MACKEY (HULL)
Harry Sunderland Trophy winner 1991

Greg Mackey.

The largest crowd to witness a Premiership Trophy Final (42,043) saw Hull captain and stand-off Greg Mackey dictate play as his side pulled off an unexpected 14-4 victory over Widnes in the 1991 decider. His performance guaranteed him the Harry Sunderland Trophy as, along with French scrum-half Patrick Entat, the Australian orchestrated Hull's attack to perfection as they tore into Widnes. Mackey set the Widnes alarm bells ringing in the 13th minute when, having feigned an 'up and under', he delivered a perfect pass to the supporting Richard Gay who evaded Kurt Sorenson's attempted tackle to dive over, Hull going on to build a worthwhile 8-0 interval lead.

When Martin Offiah touched down after the break making the score 8-4, the anticipated Widnes revival was quelled by a vigorous Hull pack allowing Mackey to seal victory ten minutes from time. With the Widnes line yards away, he squeezed the ball out for substitute Gary Nolan to score in the corner, Phil Eastwood being on target with a brilliant touchline kick to close the scoring.

An elated Mackey, in a *Rugby League Express* interview, said afterwards: 'It makes our season worthwhile. And the Harry Sunderland Trophy as well! What a rap, and I'm an Aussie too – I love it!' For Hull, it was to be their only success in the competition, having been runners-up four times during the 1980s.

Premiership Trophy Final 1991
Sunday 12 May at Old Trafford, Manchester
Hull 14
Gay (try), Eastwood (goal), McGarry, Webb, Turner, Mackey (captain), Entat, Harrison, Jackson, Dannatt, Marlow, Walker (try), Sharp. Substitutes: Nolan (try), Busby.
Widnes 4
Tait, Devereux, Currier, Davies (captain), Offiah (try), Dowd, D Hulme, Sorenson, McKenzie, Grima, P Hulme, Koloto, McCurrie. Substitutes: Wright, Howard.
Half-time: 8-0. Referee: J Holdsworth (Kippax). Attendance: 42,043.

PROFILE

The playing career of Sydney-born half-back Greg Mackey reached its peak when he arrived in England in August 1989 to play for Warrington. The former Mascot Juniors player had experienced a chequered career in his homeland having played in the senior grade for South Sydney (1981-83), Illawarra Steelers (1984-88) and Canterbury-Bankstown (1989). Mackey – who also had a spell in France playing for Paris club Chatillon during their 1983/84 season – elected to try his luck in England following his release by Canterbury. Having helped Warrington win the 1989 Lancashire Cup Final he joined Hull – much to Warrington's consternation – after just two months and nine matches with the Wilderspool side. At Hull, his organisational qualities shone through, his passing and kicking game coming to the fore as he led the side – as captain – to victory in the 1991 Premiership Trophy Final. Having spent three seasons on Humberside, he surprisingly rejoined Warrington in 1992, again taking on the mantle of skipper, being at the helm for the 1994/95 Regal Trophy Final defeat by Wigan. His stay with Warrington was somewhat longer the second time around, the truncated 1995/96 season (shortened due to the impending switch to summer rugby) being his last with Warrington. He returned to Australia and became involved in coaching at country club level.

BRIAN McTIGUE (WIGAN)
Lance Todd Trophy winner 1959

Brian McTigue.

lead on the back of four superb tries. The third of those, a 60-yard effort by David Bolton, following a typical rampaging run and perfectly timed pass from McTigue.

Wigan continued their dominance after the interval with only the boot of Hull's young full-back Arthur Keegan - who landed four penalties and converted Tom Finn's late try – keeping the score respectable. Showing great spirit, Hull twice came close to scoring tries at the start of the second-half but it was McTigue who rattled the Airlie Birds cage again as Wigan twice went close to scoring a try. The first chance came when McTigue broke through three defenders down the middle of the field setting up a certain looking try for winger Mick Sullivan who lost the opportunity when he fumbled the ball, the second was when McTigue created an opening for Keith Holden to dive over, referee Charlie Appleton being unhappy with the grounding. It was enough to shake Hull's new-found resolve and fittingly it was McTigue, who had proved a

Wigan's forwards were expected to be put under the cosh by Hull's mighty pack in the 1959 Challenge Cup Final but on the day it was the Wigan six, superbly led by Brian McTigue that took the upper hand. It was eventual Lance Todd Trophy winner McTigue – playing in the second row rather than his more accustomed prop position – that destroyed Hull as he provided a master class in ball handling skills, his long inch-perfect passing and amazing speed on the burst for a 15 stone-plus forward causing mayhem. Wigan raced to a 20-4 half-time

Lance Todd Trophy winner Brian McTigue registers Wigan's fifth try during their 1959 Wembley demolition of Hull.

constant menace to Hull all through the afternoon, that dived over for Wigan's fifth try after an hour's play, Holden and Bill Bretherton having prised an opening. McTigue polled twice the votes of any other nominee in winning the Lance Todd Trophy, Wigan prop John Barton praising his display, saying: 'He was absolutely magnificent in defence and attack and faultless with his passing from start to finish.' Wigan's 30-13 score was a Wembley record at the time.

Rugby League Challenge Cup Final 1959
Saturday 9 May at Wembley Stadium, London
Wigan 30
Griffiths (6 goals), Boston (2 tries), Ashton (captain),
Holden (try), Sullivan (try), Bolton (try), Thomas,
Bretherton, Sayer, Barton, McTigue (try),
Cherrington, Evans.
Hull 13
Keegan (5 goals), Cowan, Cooper, Saville, Watts,
Matthews, Finn (try), Scott, Harris, J Drake, Sykes,
B Drake, Whiteley (captain).
Half-time: 20-4. Referee: CF Appleton (Warrington).
Attendance: 79,811.

PROFILE

Brian McTigue started his Rugby League career when invited to play for the Giants Hall Colliery team where he worked, Wigan snapping up the locally born player just a few months later during 1950. Having signed as a centre, he was to have a phenomenal career as a tough, creative, ball-playing prop or second-row forward. With Wigan he appeared in a then record six Challenge Cup Finals at Wembley, a distinction shared with colleagues Eric Ashton and Billy Boston. He won on three of those occasions (1958, 1959 and 1965), adding the Championship title in 1959/60. He was a tourist in 1958 and 1962, and played in 25 Test Matches for Great Britain (1958-63), including the 1960 World Cup, and appeared 13 times for Lancashire (1957-62). After retiring in 1966, he returned for one match with Blackpool Borough in 1967 before travelling to Australia to coach New South Wales country club, Bathurst. He later returned to England.

This impressive looking 1966 Wigan line-up included Brian McTigue, standing, second from right.

TOMMY MARTYN (ST HELENS)
Lance Todd Trophy winner 1997

St Helens stand-off Tommy Martyn polled 21 of the 31 votes cast to walk away with the Lance Todd Trophy after a triumphant Wembley return against Bradford Bulls, having limped off the pitch with a knee injury 12 months earlier, lasting just 20 minutes after coming on as a substitute against the same opponents.

Relishing the occasion, Martyn scored St Helens opening tries in the 8th and 27th minutes. Both came when he pounced on neat grubber kicks from half-back partner and team captain, Bobbie Goulding. The first – which put Saints 4-0 up – was aimed from close to the line, the second angled across the face of goal covering 20 yards, augmented by Goulding himself to level the scores at 10-10, Bradford having earlier gone 10-4 ahead through tries from their centres Danny Peacock and former Saint Paul Loughlin. A Karle Hammond try in the 39th minute, Goulding adding the goal, put St Helens 16-10 in front at the interval.

Tommy Martyn.

PROFILE

Tommy Martyn was an intelligent, quick-thinking stand-off half, who provided both creativity and good support play. He signed professionally with Oldham from the Leigh Miners amateur club in 1989, and was in their side that won the 1990 Second Division Premiership Trophy at Old Trafford, when, aged 18, he scored a sensational late winning try against Hull Kingston Rovers. Having been selected four times for the Great Britain under-21s team (1991-92), he caught the attention of St Helens who signed him in 1993, starting an honour-laden career with the Knowsley Road side. With the Saints, he won the Super League title (1996, 1999, 2000 and 2002 – missing the Grand Final of the latter through injury), Challenge Cup (1996, 1997 and 2001 – he was a runner up in 2002) and World Club Challenge (2001). He transferred to his home club Leigh during the 2003 season, helping them win the 2004 National League One Grand Final in his final match (and thereby promotion to Super League), having secured victory in the National Cup earlier that season. Martyn – whose father (also Tommy) was a back-row forward who toured in 1979 – played eight times for Ireland (1997-2000) including the 2000 World Cup, qualifying through the parent/grandparent rule. Following his retirement as a player, he remained at Leigh on the coaching staff, quitting towards the end of the 2005 campaign.

Martyn was a try-saver five minutes into the second half through his acrobatic ankle tap on Peacock, who had looked certain to level the scores again. Minutes later Martyn turned provider when he put Chris Joynt and Anthony Sullivan in for tries. It occurred during an inspired four minute spell when Joynt scored near the posts after Martyn had put him through a gap 30 yards out, Sullivan then winning the sprint in pursuit of Martyn's perfectly judged kick 10 yards inside the Bulls half to claim the Saints fifth try. The latter was given amidst some controversy, as the wingman did not appear to ground the ball properly. Goulding converted both, his subsequent penalty placing St Helens in a commanding position at 30-10. Bradford brought respectability to the score, which finished at 32-22, scoring two tries in the last 17 minutes.

Recalling the occasion, Martyn said: 'When you hear your name being called as a Lance Todd winner it's something you can't begin to explain. It is only on the Tuesday at the Lance Todd dinner that it hits you.'

Rugby League Challenge Cup Final 1997
Saturday 3 May at Wembley Stadium, London
St Helens 32
Prescott, Arnold, Haigh, Newlove, Sullivan (try), Martyn (2 tries), Goulding (captain, 6 goals), Perelini, Cunningham, O'Neill, Joynt (try), McVey, Hammond (try). Substitutes: Pickavance, Morley, Matautia, Northey.
Bradford Bulls 22
Spruce, Ekoku, Peacock (try), Loughlin (try), Cook, Bradley, R Paul (captain), McDermott, Lowes (try), Reihana, Nickle, Dwyer, McNamara (3 goals). Substitutes: Medley, Calland, Tomlinson (try), Knox.
Half-time: 16-10. Referee: S Cummings (Widnes).
Attendance: 78,022.

Tommy Martyn was one of Rugby League's most innovative players.

MEL MASON (LEEDS)
Harry Sunderland Trophy winner 1975

=== PROFILE ===

Skilful, evasive stand-off Mel Mason rose to fame quickly at Featherstone Rovers, appearing in their Challenge Cup Final winning side of 1973, aged 19, as half-back partner to Great Britain Test star Steve Nash. Originating from Castleford he had developed through the Rovers junior side, being signed in 1970 and making his debut the same year. He missed Featherstone's Wembley return the following year, his form being affected by injuries. Leeds moved in with a £6,000 offer in January 1975 and four months later, the talented youngster was helping his new club win the Premiership Trophy. He continued to be dogged by injury, however, knee problems wiping out most of his 1975/76 term, and he transferred to Barrow at the start of the following campaign for £4,000. His time at Barrow was the longest of his professional career and he scored the Shipbuilders only try in their 1980/81 John Player Trophy defeat (12-5) by Warrington. He moved to Whitehaven in 1983, playing for the Cumbrians until 1985.

The first staging of the Premiership Trophy Final in 1975 saw Leeds stand-off Mel Mason walk away with the Harry Sunderland Trophy on a beautiful sunny afternoon at Wigan's former Central Park home. Leeds dominated the first half against opponents St Helens, scoring sixteen points without reply, the first of three tries during this period the result of a brilliant piece of magic from 22-year-old Mason who, having taken a short pass from second-row Ray Batten, completely bamboozled the Saints defence to score behind the posts after 14 minutes. Mason was also involved in the second, three minutes before the break, combining with scrum-half Keith Hepworth to put skipper Syd Hynes in.

St Helens (who had to drastically reorganise their pack after losing props John Warlow and John Mantle during the first half through injury) showed better form in the second half, scoring three tries to two. The first by Les Jones five minutes after the restart signalled a period of pressure by Saints, Mason showing his defensive mettle when racing back to deny Eddie Cunningham a try. Leeds had enough fuel left in the tank, however, holding out for a deserved 26-11 win.

The livewire Mason – a clear winner of the Harry Sunderland award – benefited from the go-forward of a Leeds pack, spearheaded by a young front-row combination of Roy Dickinson, David Ward and Steve Pitchford, taming a St Helens team who had been runaway Champions, leading the First Division 11 points clear of Wigan.

Premiership Trophy Final 1975
Saturday 17 May at Central Park, Wigan
Leeds 26
Holmes (2 goals), A Smith (try), Hynes (captain, try, drop-goal), Dyl, Atkinson (2 tries), Mason (try), Hepworth, Dickinson, Ward, Pitchford, Cookson, Batten, Haigh. Substitutes: Marshall (3 goals), Eccles.
St Helens 11
Pimblett, Jones (try), Wilson, Hull, Mathias (try), Walsh, Heaton (try), Warlow, Karalius, Mantle, E Chisnall, Nicholls, Coslett (captain, goal). Substitutes: Gwilliam, Cunningham.
Half-time: 16-0. Referee: WH Thompson (Huddersfield). Attendance: 14,531.

Harry Sunderland Trophy winner Mel Mason, lower right with scarf round neck, joins his Leeds colleague in celebrating their 1975 Premiership Trophy success over St Helens.

GAVIN MILLER (HULL KINGSTON ROVERS)
Man of Steel Award winner 1986

Hull Kingston Rovers' Australian loose forward Gavin Miller enjoyed a double celebration at the 1986 Man of Steel Awards evening becoming the first overseas winner of both the main award and First Division Player of the Year title. The skilful Aussie play-maker enjoyed a wonderfully consistent season, littered with man of the match prizes and was voted the Rovers' Player of the Year.

During October, he played a major roll in the Rovers' 22-18 Yorkshire Cup Final win over Castleford at Headingley, scoring their opening two tries and laying on the third for Garry Clark. Not surprisingly, he was awarded the White Rose Trophy as the games outstanding performer. He also starred in the end-of-season march to the Challenge Cup Final, winning two Silk Cut Awards as man of the match in both semi-final meetings with Leeds, Rovers winning a replay 17-0 after a 24-24 draw. On the eve of the final at Wembley in May, Miller injured a

Gavin Miller.

PROFILE

Australian loose-forward Gavin Miller was a talented ball-player who began his career in the top grade with Western Suburbs in 1977, having signed as a centre from the Goulburn club as an 18-year-old. He subsequently played for Eastern Suburbs (1978-79) and Cronulla-Sutherland (1980-83), returning to Eastern Suburbs for the 1984 season, where, having represented New South Wales twice in 1983, his form deteriorated. He moved to England, joining Hull Kingston Rovers in October 1984, producing the best performances of his career to date, winning the Championship (1984/85), John Player Trophy (1984/85) and Yorkshire Cup (1985), but suffering defeat in the 1986 Challenge Cup Final at Wembley. He rejoined Cronulla-Sutherland for the 1986 Australian season, continuing with them until 1992, during which time he showed incredible stamina by combining two further terms in England with Rovers (1986/87 and 1988/89). His performances for Cronulla resulted in him twice being picked for Australia in 1988 – including the 25-12 World Cup Final win over New Zealand in Auckland when he scored a try – followed by three more appearances for New South Wales in 1989 when he was also captain. In 1988 and 1989, he received the coveted Dally M award as the Australian player of the year. Born in Inverell, New South Wales, he returned to his former club, Goulburn, as captain-coach.

hamstring but, such was his value to the side, he still played, although heavily strapped up, a factor contributing to the narrow 15-14 defeat as Castleford gained ample revenge for the Yorkshire Cup loss. Miller and his colleagues also reached the John Player Trophy Final in January, suffering an 11-8 reverse to Wigan at Elland Road, Leeds.

Greenalls Man of Steel Awards 1986
Wednesday 14 May at The Willows Variety Centre, Salford
Compered by Elton Welsby
Man of Steel: Gavin Miller (Hull Kingston Rovers).
First Division Player of the Year: Gavin Miller (Hull Kingston Rovers).
Second Division Player of the Year: Derek Pyke (Leigh).
Young Player of the Year: Shaun Edwards (Wigan).
Coach of the Year: Chris Anderson (Halifax).
Referee of the Year: GF (Fred) Lindop (Wakefield).

Graham Morris

MICK MORGAN (CARLISLE)
Man of Steel Award winner 1982

Mick Morgan makes a break for Carlisle.

became the first Trinity player in eight years to receive a benefit. Interestingly and uniquely, it was announced his Man of Steel tribute had been bestowed, in part, for his unstinting participation in the *Sunday Mirror* Rugby League Roadshows, which, at the time, raised thousands of pounds each year towards players' benefits.

Trumanns Man of Steel Awards 1982
Wednesday 12 May at the Garter Theatre Club,
Wythenshawe, Manchester
Compered by Keith Macklin
Man of Steel: Mick Morgan (Carlisle).
First Division Player of the Year: Steve Norton (Hull).
Second Division Player of the Year: Mick Morgan (Carlisle).
Young Player of the Year: Des Drummond (Leigh).
Coach of the Year: Arthur Bunting (Hull).
Referee of the Year: GF (Fred) Lindop (Wakefield).

For the only time in its history, the Man of Steel Award winner came from outside of Rugby League's elite division, second division Carlisle's robust Yorkshire prop forward Mick Morgan taking the title after a record-breaking campaign. Assistant player-coach to Allan Agar in Carlisle's debut season, his incredible 25 tries easily created a new Rugby League record, the previous high from a prop being 17.

His inspirational play helped the Cumbrian club gain promotion to the senior division at the first attempt, finishing runners-up by four points to Oldham. He also captured the Second Division Player of The Year title – an award for which he had previously been nominated in 1978 whilst with York – his Carlisle team-mate and loose forward Dennis Boyd being one of the other two nominees.

His success was a real testimony for perseverance against the odds, having struggled at the beginning of his career to establish himself at his first club Wakefield Trinity. He succeeded to such an extent that, in 1976, he

PROFILE

Powerful, skirmishing forward Mick Morgan began his professional career with Wakefield Trinity in 1966 having previously played for the Featherstone Rovers Juniors side. Initially a centre, he was not a success in that role but developed into a powerful presence when moved to the pack, noted for his ability to outwit defenders in play-the-ball situations near the try-line. His stay with Trinity was a long one, lasting until 1977, although he was out of luck when it came to winning trophies, losing in three finals; Player's No.6 Trophy (1971/72) and Yorkshire Cup (1973 and 1974). He joined York in 1977, moving to his home club Featherstone Rovers in 1978, where, having played most of his rugby thus far in the back-row – with the occasionally match at hooker – he graduated to prop, helping them win the 1979/80 Division Two Championship. He joined newcomers Carlisle for the 1981/82 season as assistant player-coach to Allan Agar, taking over as head coach for the following campaign. However, he left in February 1983 to play for Oldham, his last match with them being in 1986. He played six times for England, all in 1975 – including four in the World Cup when he was in the squad that travelled to Australia and New Zealand – and made nine appearances for Yorkshire (1973-85).

CEC MOUNTFORD (WIGAN)
Lance Todd Trophy winner 1951

Cec Mountford became the first overseas winner of the Lance Todd Trophy in 1951, the Wigan captain standing out with his 'weaving runs through the Barrow defence' in a dour rain soaked Challenge Cup Final at Wembley. Whilst many players found conditions difficult underfoot, the gifted New Zealand stand-off still found the extra gear to make his trademark incisive runs across a slippery surface and test Barrow's resolute defence. A 6th minute Ken Gee penalty for Wigan separated the protagonists until the 59th minute when scrum half Tommy Bradshaw switched the direction of play. It wrong-footed Barrow loose-forward Hugh McGregor, who slipped on the wet turf, providing the opening for Mountford to exploit before transferring the ball to Jack Broome who put Jack Hilton in at the corner. This put Wigan into the ascendancy and, ten minutes from time, Gee seized a loose ball near the Barrow line to score a second and clinch the match, Mountford adding the goal.

Mountford, who was not fully fit, only just managed to stake his place in the final. In his compelling biography *Kiwis, Wigan & The Wire* (2003) Mountford, who had been injured in the previous weekend's Championship semi-final against Workington Town, revealed: 'I was a doubtful starter for the match right up to the Saturday. I travelled with the team to Brighton on the Thursday before the final with a possibility of playing, which I did, although only 85 per cent fit.'

Rugby League Challenge Cup Final 1951
Saturday 5 May at Wembley Stadium, London
Wigan 10
Cunliffe, Hilton (try), Broome, Roughley, Nordgren, Mountford (captain, goal), Bradshaw, Gee (try, goal), Curran, Barton, Silcock, Slevin, Blan.
Barrow 0
Stretch, Lewthwaite, Jackson, Goodwin, Castle, Horne (captain), Toohey, Longman, McKinnell, Hartley, Grundy, Atkinson, McGregor.
Half-time: 2-0. Referee: M Coates (Pudsey).
Attendance: 94,262.

Cec Mountford.

PROFILE

Stand-off Cec Mountford joined Wigan in 1946, forming a formidable half-back partnership with Tommy Bradshaw. Quick and evasive, he was known as the 'Blackball Bullet' after the name of the town he was born in, and club he played for, in New Zealand. He became captain of Wigan and, apart from his Challenge Cup triumphs (1948 and 1951), he helped the club win the Rugby League Championship (1946/47 and 1949/50) and Lancashire Cup (1946, 1948, 1949 and 1950). His 1951 Wembley appearance turned out to be his last for Wigan, joining Warrington as coach a few months later (he also played for Warrington during 1952 and 1953) where he enjoyed considerable success including the memorable 1954 Challenge Cup Final replay win at Odsal. He left Warrington in 1961, later coaching Blackpool Borough (in 1972/73) and New Zealand (1979 to 1982). His exile cost him the chance to play for New Zealand although he did represent Other Nationalities four times (1949-51). He received the MBE in 1987 for services to New Zealand Rugby League and was made an inaugural member of the New Zealand Sports Hall of Fame in 1990.

Graham Morris

ALEX MURPHY (LEIGH)
Lance Todd Trophy winner 1971

The Wembley success of Alex Murphy and Leigh in 1971 produced one of the most memorable and controversial Challenge Cup Finals ever. There was no doubting Leigh's superiority as they upset the odds to beat Leeds 24-7, or Murphy's right to be named recipient of the Lance Todd Trophy after stamping his dominant personality on the match from the opening minutes. It was also the only time in four visits that Murphy appeared in his usual position of scrum-half, being stand-off (1961) and centre (1966) with St Helens, and stand-off

again with Warrington (1974). In the build up to the 1971 final, Murphy said: 'So many people have tipped Leeds they will think they only have to step on the field to win. We want to stop them getting into their stride in the first quarter of the game whilst we will be looking for a few quick points.' He was certainly true to his word, attempting an ambitious 40-yard drop-goal from a difficult angle after only three minutes, which fell well short. Murphy was in the wars after 15 minutes, play being stopped while he received treatment near the touchline following an incident on the blind side as a scrum broke up.

The stadium erupted after 26 minutes when a scrum near the Leeds posts was won by Leigh against the head, Murphy racing around the back of the scrum with the ball to emerge on the right. After accelerating towards the try line through a melee of defenders, he put centre Stan Dorrington over for a simple try ten yards to the right of the posts. Stuart Ferguson's goal, added to his earlier penalty and a 5th minute drop-goal by prop Jim Fiddler – that had opened the scoring – put Leigh 9-0 up. Six minutes before half-time, Murphy struck again with a perfect 35-yard drop-goal from in front of the posts, the ball being passed back to him in a pre-planned move by Kevin Ashcroft from a play-the-ball. A glorious 60-yard penalty by Ferguson, from near the right touchline

Alex Murphy leaps in the air to celebrate a Leigh try at Wembley in 1971.

123

some 60 yards out, made Leigh unlikely leaders by 13-0 at the break.

Leeds gained some encouragement through a John Holmes penalty eight minutes into the second-half but Murphy responded with a drop-goal that was again set up in front of the posts in collusion with Ashcroft from acting half-back, this time covering some 40 yards. A third Ferguson penalty put Leigh into a commanding 17-2 lead, followed – with 15 minutes to go – by one of Wembley's most controversial and, even today, most talked of moments. Put in simple terms, Murphy lay prostrate on the ground, apparently head-butted by the Leeds captain Syd Hynes. Subsequent claims by Hynes were that he never made contact and that Murphy fell back feigning concussion. Murphy's recollection is somewhat different, saying 'People say I was carried off, winking, laughing, while I was going down the tunnel, but that was all part of playing that game – winning the Challenge Cup and then being told you had won the Lance Todd Trophy. Two cups in one day and I can't remember both of them!' Televised by the BBC, in an era that preceded multi-angle shots, the incident was just off camera and therefore unable to provide answers. Either way, Hynes became the first player to be dismissed at Wembley in a Challenge Cup Final, Murphy being taken off on a stretcher to the Leigh dressing room where he was attended to by both Leigh and Wembley doctors. With five minutes to go Murphy, who had been replaced on the pitch by Les Chisnall, was greeted by a tremendous cheer when he returned up the tunnel and sat on the bench. He did not return to the fray, a David Eckersley drop-goal and try – converted by Ferguson – adding to the Leigh score in his absence, Tony Wainwright getting a last minute obstruction try for Leeds.

When the final whistle went, the Leigh players rushed over to where Murphy was sat, arms raised to greet the man who had master-minded their moment of triumph. Murphy recently said of his Lance Todd Trophy achievement: 'It wasn't the fact I won it, it was the manner in which I won it. It was the first time I'd played in my own position when I'd been at Wembley. The feeling going off the field – even though I didn't feel in the best of ways because I'd had a knock – is a feeling you want

A key moment at Wembley in 1971 after Alex Murphy (7) had opened up the Leeds defence for Leigh centre Stan Dorrington to score the opening try.

to enjoy and be a part of it. It is the proudest moment of your life. The Lance Todd Trophy is probably the trophy that 99 per-cent of players want to win.'

Rugby League Challenge Cup Final 1971
Saturday 15 May at Wembley Stadium, London
Leigh 24
Eckersley (try, goal), Ferguson (5 goals), Dorrington (try), Collins, Walsh, Barrow, Murphy (captain, 2 goals), Watts, Ashcroft, Fiddler (goal), Grimes, Clarkson, Smethurst. Substitute: Chisnall.
Leeds 7
Holmes (2 goals), Langley, Hynes (captain), Cowan, Atkinson, Wainwright (try), Seabourne, Burke, Fisher, Barnard, Hick, Haigh, Ramsey. Substitute: Dyl.
Half-time: 13-0. Referee: WH Thompson (Huddersfield). Attendance: 85,514.

A great day for Leigh as Alex Murphy shows off the Challenge Cup at Wembley in 1971.

Alex Murphy – inducted into the Rugby League Hall of Fame in 1988 – is one of the true greats of the sport; a fiery, cocky scrum-half who was extremely quick off the mark, a supreme timer of a pass, a good tactical kicker, and exceptional motivator. He was born at Thatto Heath, St Helens, learning his rugby skills at St Austin's School, St Helens signing him as a 16-year-old in 1955 for £80. With the Saints, he won the Challenge Cup (1961, 1966), Championship (1958/59, 1965/66), Western Division Championship (1963/64), and Lancashire Cup (1960, 1961, 1963, 1964, missing the 1962 success through injury). A tourist in 1958 and 1962 and member of Great Britain's victorious 1960 World Cup side, he represented Great Britain in 27 Tests (1958-71), England twice (both 1969) and Lancashire 14 times (1958-71). He quit St Helens to take over as Leigh coach in 1966, although it was not until the following year that his former club agreed to his transfer as a player, the fee being £5,500. Following unprecedented success in which he led Leigh to victory in the BBC2 Floodlit Trophy (1969), Lancashire Cup (1970) and Challenge Cup (1971), he moved to Warrington in 1971 as player-coach. He again revived the fortunes of an ailing club, Warrington winning four trophies in 1973/74; the short-lived Club Championship, Challenge Cup, Player's No.6 Trophy, and Captain Morgan Trophy (another fleeting event), Murphy not appearing in the finals of the latter two. Retiring as a player in 1975, he continued as Warrington coach until 1978, followed by similar appointments at Salford (1978-80), Leigh (1980-82), Wigan (1982-84), Leigh (1985), St Helens (1985-90), Leigh (1990-91) and Huddersfield (1991-94). His love affair with Wembley continued as Warrington (1975), Wigan (1984), and St Helens (1987 and 1989) all reached the Challenge Cup Final under his influence, although failing to win each time. He also acted as coach to England (1975 – including that years World Cup) and Lancashire (1973-78 and 1985-88). Awarded the OBE in 1999, he returned to Leigh for a fifth time in 2003, taking on the role of Director of Rugby.

FRANK MYLER (ST HELENS)
Harry Sunderland Trophy winner 1970

St Helens upset the pre-match forecast with a powerful performance against Leeds in a memorable 1970 Championship Final held at Odsal Stadium. Trailing 8-7 at half-time, the Saints produced an awesome second-half display

St Helens captain Cliff Watson lifts the Championship Trophy in 1970 following the victory over Leeds at Odsal. Harry Sunderland winner Frank Myler is to the left of Watson, his arm placed on his skipper.

– described by one newspaper as 'Saints best performance in years' – to finish comfortable 24-12 victors. The match was a personal triumph for their 31-year-old stand-off Frank Myler, who took the Harry Sunderland Trophy after a wonderful demonstration in the art of good support play.

Alan Smith gave Leeds the perfect start with a try after only six minutes, but five minutes later St Helens took a 5-3 lead when Bill Sayer received a scoring pass from Myler, who had raced up in support of an Eric Chisnall break,

Kel Coslett adding the goal. In a see-saw opening Leeds regained their advantage in the 17th minute, Ron Cowan scored a spectacular solo try, John Holmes converting. The score encouraged the Headingley side to exert tremendous pressure in a bid to retain their title, but Saints held out, registering the only points of the half's remaining 23 minutes when Coslett hit a 24th minute penalty to trail 7-8 at the break.

When St Helens' centre John Walsh banged over a 25-yard drop-goal six minutes after the restart, it was a pivotal moment, giving Saints a lead, at 9-8, which they would not surrender. Six minutes later, St Helens emphasised their Championship credentials and sank Leeds hearts, scoring the try of the match as the ball travelled through six pairs of hands in dazzling fashion before Myler backed up yet again to send Eric Prescott over with a reverse pass, Coslett's conversion attempt hitting the post. Whilst Leeds played their part in an entertaining match, it was the signal for a virtuoso finish from St Helens, further tries coming from Walsh and Prescott.

For man of the match, Myler, it was the perfect send-off on the eve of his departure Down Under as captain of the Great Britain touring team, during which Britain was destined to win an Ashes series against Australia for the last time to date.

126

St Helens in 1969 with the Lancashire Cup and Lancashire League Trophy. Frank Myler is seated, extreme right.

PROFILE

Frank Myler was one of the most talented players ever produced by Widnes, a brilliant stand-off or centre, and proven match winner who broke the clubs try-scoring record with 34 touchdowns in 1958/59. He played in 24 Tests for Great Britain (1960-70) and was captain of the 1970 touring party to the Antipodes and the World Cup side that reached the final of the competition played in England later that year. He also toured in 1966 and was a member of the victorious 1960 World Cup side in the first tournament to be held in England. Myler – who also appeared 20 times for Lancashire (1959-70) – was a local product, having played for Widnes St Patrick's before joining the town's senior club in 1955. Although silverware at Widnes was sparse, his time at the club provided one of the biggest moments of his career, scoring a try under the posts as Hull Kingston Rovers were beaten 13-5 in the 1964 Challenge Cup Final at Wembley. He moved to St Helens in 1967 where he spent four years, being a winner in the finals of the Championship (1970) and Lancashire Cup (1968). In 1971, he joined Rochdale Hornets as player-coach, leading them to the final of the 1971/72 BBC2 Floodlit Trophy where they lost 8-2 to his former club St Helens. He played his last match for Hornets in 1973, continuing as coach until 1974. He returned to Widnes as coach in 1975, taking them to Wembley in 1976 and 1977. He stepped down in 1978, having been voted Coach of the Year at that years Man of Steel Awards evening. He subsequently took charge at Swinton (1980-81), Oldham (1981-83 and 1984-87) and, finally, Widnes (1991-92). He also looked after Great Britain (1982-84 including the 1984 tour) and England (1977-78).

Northern Rugby League Championship Final 1970
Saturday 16 May at Odsal Stadium, Bradford
St Helens 24
F Barrow, Jones, Benyon, Walsh (try, 2 goals), Prescott (2 tries), Myler, Heaton, Halsall, Sayer (try), Watson (captain), Mantle, E Chisnall, Coslett (4 goals).
Leeds 12
Holmes (3 goals), A Smith (try), Hynes, Cowan (try), Atkinson, Shoebottom, Seabourne (captain), Burke, Crosby, A Eyre, Ramsey, Eccles, Batten. Substitute: Hick.
Half-time: 7-8. Referee: WH Thompson (Huddersfield). Attendance: 26,358.

TONY MYLER (WIDNES)
Harry Sunderland Trophy winner 1983

Tony Myler.

Widnes' brilliant 21-year-old stand-off Tony Myler emulated his famous uncle, Frank Myler, by winning the Harry Sunderland Trophy in the 1983 Premiership Trophy Final against Hull, scoring a try and being influential in two others. He gave an early warning of his flair, kicking a loose ball from his own half that winged its way into the Hull 25, Dane O'Hara just beating him to the touch down. After that hiccup, Hull got into their stride to lead 7-2 after 20 minutes, Myler bringing Widnes into contention on the half-hour, accepting a long pass from Mick Adams to race round Gary Kemble to score under the posts. Joe Lydon converted to level matters at 7-7, a further try apiece squaring the half-time score to 10-10.

After the break, the match belonged to Widnes, scoring 12 points without reply to win 22-10, Myler creating both of his side's second half tries. He made a tremendous break in the

57th minute to set up winger John Basnett, who flew over in the corner, and was to the fore again in the 62nd minute when, having been held short, he somehow slipped the ball inside to the supporting Andy Gregory who dived over the line for Widnes' fourth touchdown.

Myler – who had scored a hat-trick of tries in the semi-final success over Hull Kingston Rovers – was a runaway winner of the man of the match award, receiving all the votes after standing out with his strong, powerful running and masterly distribution. Understating his feelings after the match, he said 'I've really enjoyed myself today!'

Premiership Trophy Final 1983
Saturday 14 May at Headingley, Leeds
Widnes 22
Burke, Linton, Hughes (captain), Lydon (5 goals), Basnett (2 tries), Myler (try), Gregory (try), M O'Neill, Elwell, Gorley, Whitfield, Prescott, Adams. Substitutes: D Hulme, S O'Neill.
Hull 10
Kemble, O'Hara (try), Day, Leuluai, Evans, Topliss (captain, try), Dean, Skerrett, Bridges, Stone, Rose, Crooks (2 goals), Norton. Substitutes: Solal, Crane.
Half-time: 10-10. Referee: GF Lindop (Wakefield). Attendance: 17,813.

PROFILE

Stand-off half Tony Myler signed for Widnes in 1978, playing for his local club until 1992. An excellent ball-player and leader, capable of powerful match-winning breaks, he had previously been attached to Widnes Rugby Union club. At Widnes, he won the World Club Challenge (1990), Championship (1987/88 and 1988/89), Premiership Trophy (1982, 1983, 1989 and 1990) and Lancashire Cup (1990, as captain). He was unlucky in the Challenge Cup, experiencing frustration at Wembley in 1982 (when the match was drawn), and missing the 1984 win over Wigan after tearing a knee cartilage in the semi-final. In the latter case, he recovered in time to take his place in that year's Great Britain tour to Australasia. Altogether, he appeared in fourteen Test Matches (1983-86) and played twice for Lancashire (1982 and 1985). He played for Australian club Balmain Tigers (1986) and later coached Widnes (1994-95). His brother John played for Widnes in the 1981 Challenge Cup Final.

STEVE NASH (FEATHERSTONE ROVERS)
Lance Todd Trophy winner 1973

Steve Nash was born within a stone's throw of the Featherstone Rovers ground, signing in 1967 after graduating through the Featherstone junior system. He was a tough competitor and, although only five feet, five inches tall, was a determined tackler who enjoyed running at the opposition, often being referred to as the seventh forward. With Featherstone he appeared in two Challenge Cup Finals (1973 and 1974), joining Salford in 1975 for a Rugby League record £15,000, winning the Championship (1975/76) and becoming team captain. He retired in 1984 but came back with Rochdale Hornets (1985-88), later coaching the now defunct Mansfield Marksman (1988-89), appearing for them once in 1989. He played in 24 Tests for Great Britain (1971-82) being captain on the last occasion, and was a tourist in 1974 and 1979, representing Britain in the World Cup's of 1972 and 1977. He also played seven times for England (1975-81) including the 1975 World Cup, and ten times for Yorkshire (1971-81).

With half-backs Steve Nash and Mel Mason teeing up a continuous barrage of forward power from a pack led by Vince Farrar, Alan Rhodes and Jim Thompson, Featherstone Rovers virtually sealed their 1973 Challenge Cup win over Bradford Northern in the opening 20 minutes. Lance Todd Trophy winner Nash recalls 'We were 17 points up and I was so confident of victory that I went over to the captain, John Newlove, and said "The cups ours, they can't beat us now." Our coach Peter Fox overheard me from the touchline and at half-time he gave me a right telling off!'

It was the promptings of Nash – who landed a drop-goal ten minutes from time when, at 24-14 Bradford were threatening to rally – that sealed his man of the match verdict. He claimed one-third of the votes on a day of many heroes in the Rovers ranks, none more so than 34-year-old full-back Cyril Kellett who landed a Wembley record eight goals. Nash, Great Britain's first choice scrum-half at that time, said of his Lance Todd success: 'I hadn't given any thought to winning that award and it was a surprise when David Coleman, or was it Frank Bough? – I can't

recall which – told me I had got it during the BBC television interview straight after the game.' A year later Featherstone were back, but lost to Warrington. 'Losing at Wembley is the worst thing I have experienced in Rugby League. Within 12 months I had my happiest and saddest moments in the game – and both at Wembley!' said Nash.

Rugby League Challenge Cup Final 1973
Saturday 12 May at Wembley Stadium, London
Featherstone Rovers 33
C Kellett (8 goals), Coventry, Smith (try), Newlove (captain, 2 tries), K Kellett, Mason, Nash (goal), Tonks, Bridges, Farrar (try), Rhodes, Thompson, Stone. Substitutes: Hartley (try), Hollis.
Bradford Northern 14
Tees (captain, 4 goals), Lamb, Stockwell, Watson, Redfearn (try), Blacker, Seabourne, Hogan, Dunn, Earl, Joyce, Pattinson, Fearnley (try). Substitutes: Treasure, Long.
Half-time: 17-6. Referee: MJ Naughton (Widnes).
Attendance: 72,395.

Steve Nash.

GEORGE NICHOLLS (ST HELENS)

Harry Sunderland Trophy winner 1976
Lance Todd Trophy winner 1978
Man of Steel Award winner 1978

George Nicholls.

St Helens second-row forward George Nicholls is one of only two players (the other being Joe Lydon) to have won all three of Rugby League's major individual awards; Lance Todd Trophy, Harry Sunderland Trophy and Man of Steel.

The first to have his name engraved on it was the Harry Sunderland award, earned during the 1976 Premiership Trophy Final. It was a match billed as a 'Clash of the Champions', opponents Salford having just secured the Rugby League Championship by virtue of topping the First Division and St Helens cock-a-hoop after their Challenge Cup success over Widnes two weeks earlier. In fact, the 15-2 victory over Salford bore similarities to their Wembley win, a three-try blitz sinking their opposition in the final 12 minutes of both matches. With the scores tied at 2-2, Nicholls – who had been instrumental in the Saints pack increasing their pressure on Salford

after the interval – sent Peter Glynn in for the opening try in the 68th minute. Geoff Pimblett's goal attempt hit the post, but they now had the bit between their teeth with Glynn, minutes later, just failing to hold on to another potential try-scoring pass from Nicholls. It was only a respite for Salford, who looked a beaten team, and Eric Chisnall, accepting another precision pass by Nicholls, and Tony Karalius – who also had an outstanding game – added further tries, as St Helens completed their late 13-point salvo. One writer observed: 'Nicholls was a leading figure in a pack which never stopped working.' Commenting on his team's belated surge, Nicholls said: 'It is experience that counts. We know how to contain sides and then, when the moment is right, we can play a bit.'

Nicholls was 31 years old when he took that award and, two years later, he won the Lance Todd Trophy, despite being in a St Helens side beaten at Wembley by Leeds in a scintillating 1978 Challenge Cup Final. He gave scant concession to his veteran status by being involved in making the opening four tackles of the game. As usual, Nicholls was to the fore in driving St Helens forward and they quickly built up a 10-0 lead after only 13 minutes play, leading

---

PROFILE

George Nicholls signed for his local club Widnes in 1966, having previously played for the Derby Arms (Widnes) side. A tough, dynamic second-row forward, he was an industrious tackler who possessed good ball distribution skills and ran with awesome power. In 1973, he transferred to St Helens where he was to secure all his accolades at club level, winning the Championship (1974/75), Challenge Cup (1976 – he was a Wembley runner-up in 1978), Premiership Trophy (1976, 1977) and BBC2 Floodlit Trophy (1975). He made 29 Test appearances for Great Britain (1971-79, incorporating the 1974 and 1979 tours and the 1972 and 1977 World Cup competitions), played four times for England (1975-78, including the 1975 World Cup), and 16 times for Lancashire (1969-79). After leaving St Helens in 1981, he concluded his career with Cardiff City (1981-82) and Salford (1982-84).

12-5 at half-time. Leeds, however, repeated their Wembley feat of a year earlier (against Widnes) by staging a second half comeback, retaining the Challenge Cup 14-12, despite the efforts of Nicholls, who gave a superb all-round performance, being well supported throughout by Welsh prop Mel James.

George Nicholls hands off Kevin Dick of Leeds in the 1978 Challenge Cup Final at Wembley, a match St Helens were destined to lose despite Nicholls taking the Lance Todd Trophy.

Ten days later, at the Wakefield Theatre Club he became the second Man of Steel recipient, having been confirmed as First Division Player of the Year earlier that evening. It was a wonderful achievement for a man who, by rights, should have been past his best, but instead had performed consistently well throughout the season inspiring his St Helens colleagues to reach the finals of the Challenge Cup and BBC2 Floodlit Trophy, although both were lost. His fine form earned him a place in the England side, answering his countries call by taking on the demanding and unfamiliar position of blind-side prop. Unfazed by the change, he won the man of the match award against France in Toulouse, England becoming that season's European Champions. He also starred in the Lancashire county team – playing in his more accustomed back-row slot – that trounced Yorkshire 33-8 at Widnes during October. In accepting his prize, Nicholls said: 'I am really made up with these awards. I was very happy just to be nominated for the First Division award, but to win the overall award is really fantastic.'

Premiership Trophy Final 1976
Saturday 22 May at Station Road, Swinton
St Helens 15
Pimblett (3 goals), Jones, Glynn (try), Noonan, Mathias, Benyon, Heaton, Mantle, Karalius (try), James, Nicholls, E Chisnall (try), Coslett (captain). Substitute: Gwilliam.
Salford 2
Watkins (2 drop-goals), Fielding, Richards, Hesketh (captain), Graham, Butler, Nash, Coulman, Raistrick, Sheffield, Knighton, Dixon, Prescott. Substitute: Turnbull.
Half-time: 0-1. Referee: MJ Naughton (Widnes). Attendance: 18,082.

Rugby League Challenge Cup Final 1978
Saturday 13 May at Wembley Stadium, London
Leeds 14
Oulton (goal), D Smith (try), Hague, Dyl, Atkinson (try), Holmes (drop-goal), Sanderson, Harrison, Ward (captain, 2 drop-goals), Pitchford, Eccles, Cookson (try), Crane. Substitutes: Dick, Dickinson.
St Helens 12
Pimblett (captain, 3 goals), Jones, Noonan, Glynn, Mathias, Francis (try), Gwilliam, D Chisnall, Liptrot (try), James, Nicholls, Cunningham, Pinner.
Half-time: 5-12. Referee: WH Thompson (Huddersfield). Attendance: 95,872.

Trumanns Man of Steel Awards 1978
Wednesday 17 May at the Wakefield Theatre Club
Compered by Keith Macklin
Man of Steel: George Nicholls (St Helens).
First Division Player of the Year: George Nicholls (St Helens).
Second Division Player of the Year: John Woods (Leigh).
Young Player of the Year: John Woods (Leigh).
Coach of the Year: Frank Myler (Widnes).
Referee of the Year: WH (Billy) Thompson (Huddersfield).

MARTIN OFFIAH (WIDNES AND WIGAN)
Man of Steel Award winner 1988
Lance Todd Trophy winner 1992 and 1994

Martin Offiah.

At a time when high scoring wingers were thought to be past their sell by date, Martin Offiah burst onto the Rugby League scene during the 1987/88 season in spectacular fashion, climaxing his debut season by winning the 1988 Man of Steel Award. The talk of the sport throughout 1987/88, his 42 tries for Widnes shattered the previous club record, helping his side win its first Championship for ten years and claim the Premiership Trophy, beating St Helens 38-16 in the final at Old Trafford. Offiah waited until his third Widnes match before grabbing his first try, commencing a run that saw him cross the whitewash in 15 consecutive matches.

Such was his impact that he appeared in his first representative match only six and a half weeks after his Widnes debut, playing for Lancashire against the touring Papua New

Guinea team, a 22-22 draw at St Helens in October. He increased his tally during the term to an impressive 44 with a try each for Great Britain (on his Test debut at Avignon during January, Britain winning 28-14) and a Chairman's XIII (defeating an Auckland touring side 12-6 at Headingley in November), crowning a fantastic first season with inclusion in the 1988 Great Britain touring team bound for Australasia.

Following his high profile move to Wigan in 1992, he fulfilled his ambition to appear at Wembley in a Challenge Cup Final, being in the winning side with the Cherry and Whites for four consecutive years from 1992, the icing on his cake being his two Lance Todd awards, in 1992 and 1994. Predictably, he won them through producing tries out of the top drawer, setting Wembley alight each time on a stage that was perfect for him to show off his unique talent. He scored two tries in both finals, adding a further dimension to his match-winning performance of 1992 when his quickness off the mark saved a certain try from opponents Castleford.

It took Offiah just five minutes to strike the first blow in 1992, sending an innocuous looking kick over the Castleford line, the normally cool Graham Steadman fumbling the ball as Offiah, having raced through two defenders, speeded towards him, to tap the ball out of the full backs reach and score. Offiah notched Wigan's third try a minute before the break, again after pursuing a kick that initially looked a lost cause. It was the boot of Shaun Edwards that propelled the missile from just inside Castleford's half into their in-goal area, Offiah beating two defenders to dive on the ball to the left of the posts, as Wigan built up a substantial 19-0 half-time lead.

Despite his success, Offiah felt aggrieved at not becoming the first player to register a Wembley Challenge Cup hat-trick, having a try disallowed in the 52nd minute after picking up a loose ball on the halfway line and racing over

PROFILE

virtually unopposed. With referee Robin Whitfield about to award the score, a touch judge claimed Offiah had knocked on when collecting the ball, although video replays indicate that Offiah picked the ball up cleanly. Undeterred, he performed his try saving feat minutes later when outpacing St John Ellis, who had kicked towards the Wigan line, beating the Castleford winger to the touchdown. It was a vital stop with Castleford threatening a revival with the score at 19-6, Wigan eventually winning 28-12.

Offiah, who received 20 of the 33 votes to take the Lance Todd Trophy, told the BBC's Ray Stubbs after the match: 'I would like to have got the three tries. I was a little disappointed. I suppose you can't be too upset if you've won the Lance Todd.'

Two years later Offiah again scored twice, his tries coming at vital moments during the 1994 triumph over Leeds by 26-16. Both were stunning efforts, but the first, which opened the scoring in the 13th minute, has to be rated the best individual try seen at Wembley. Accepting a pass just five yards in front of his own posts, he accelerated through a gap to go racing down the right touchline, eventually swerving past the stranded Leeds full-back Alan Tait on the outside for a an unforgettable try in the corner.

Wigan led 12-0 at half-time, but Leeds showed their mettle at the start of the second period, being back in contention at 14-10 before Offiah delivered the killer blow in the 62nd

Martin Offiah, about to complete his sensational 13th minute touchdown run for Wigan against Leeds at Wembley in 1994, rated as one of Wembley's greatest ever tries.

A moment to savour for Martin Offiah after his incredible length-of-field try that opened the Wembley scoring in 1994. It staked his claim for a second Lance Todd Trophy honour.

minute. It started when Mick Cassidy made a brilliant break from just inside the Wigan 25 arcing to the left side of the field, before off-loading to the supporting wing ace who left the Leeds defence in his wake as he sprinted for the line from half-way. Offiah, who became the third player to win the Lance Todd Trophy a second time, praised his colleagues after the game, playing down his own contribution, saying of his spectacular first try: 'I was just made up to score

it on such a big occasion.'

Greenalls Man of Steel Awards 1988
Thursday 12 May at The Willows Variety Centre, Salford
Compered by Harry Gration
Man of Steel: Martin Offiah (Widnes).
First Division Player of the Year: Steve Hampson (Wigan).
Second Division Player of the Year: Peter Smith (Featherstone Rovers).
Young Player of the Year: Shaun Edwards (Wigan).
Coach of the Year: Doug Laughton (Widnes).
Referee of the Year: GF (Fred) Lindop (Wakefield).

Rugby League Challenge Cup Final 1992
Saturday 2 May at Wembley Stadium, London
Wigan 28
Lydon (2 drop-goals), Botica (5 goals), Bell (captain), Miles, Offiah (2 tries), Edwards (try), Gregory, Skerrett, Dermott, Platt, Betts, McGinty, Clarke. Substitutes: Hampson (try), Cowie.
Castleford 12
Steadman, Wray, Ellis, Blackmore (try), Nelson, Anderson, Ford, Crooks (captain), Southernwood, England (try), Bradley, Ketteridge (2 goals), Nikau. Substitutes: Smith, Sampson.
Half-time: 19-0. Referee: R Whitfield (Widnes).
Attendance: 77,286.

Rugby League Challenge Cup Final 1994
Saturday 30 April at Wembley Stadium, London
Wigan 26
Connolly, Tuigamala, Bell (captain), Mather, Offiah (2 tries), Botica (5 goals), Edwards, Skerrett, Dermott, Platt, Betts, Farrell (try), Clarke. Substitutes: Panapa (try), Cassidy.
Leeds 16
Tait, Fallon (try), Iro, Innes, Cummins (try), Holroyd (2 goals), Schofield (try), Harmon, Lowes, Howard, Mercer, Eyres, Hanley (captain). Substitutes: Vassilakopoulos, O'Neill.
Half-time: 12-0. Referee: D Campbell (Widnes).
Attendance: 78,348.

RAY OWEN (WAKEFIELD TRINITY)
Harry Sunderland Trophy winner 1967

=== **PROFILE** ===

Ray Owen joined hometown Widnes from the local amateur scene in 1960, following the footsteps of his father Harry who played for the club at Wembley in 1930 and 1934. The same destiny awaited the quick-witted scrum-half who featured in the side that won the 1964 Challenge Cup. Known as 'Ginger' Owen, he transferred to Wakefield Trinity shortly after, winning the Championship (1966/67 and 1967/68) and Yorkshire Cup (1964). He made a Wembley return in 1968, settling for a runners-up medal. His transfer to Rochdale Hornets was reported in 1969, although he does not appear to have figured in any first team matches. In the late 1980s he became chairman of Widnes, a position he held for four seasons, a period that included the club's World Club Challenge success of 1989.

The 1967 Harry Sunderland recipient, Wakefield Trinity scrum-half Ray Owen, became the only player to receive the award in a replayed final, the first meeting with St Helens, played in heavy rain, finishing 7-7 at Headingley, Leeds. Ironically, it was Owen's controversial penalty try, seven minutes from time, that forced the replay, played four days later, on a Wednesday evening at Station Road, Swinton, the two protagonists facing each other in dryer, firmer conditions.

Owen began his man of the match performance by jinking and dummying his way over from acting half-back for the first try after just nine minutes but, in a pulsating first half, St Helens fought back to lead 7-6 when, three minutes from the interval, Owen had a hand in Trinity's third try of the half. Again, it was his alertness from acting half-back at a play-the-ball, passing inside for stand-off Harold Poynton to cross the whitewash. Neil Fox added the extra points, Wakefield returning to the changing rooms 11-7 to the good.

In the second half, Len Killeen's penalty reduced Saints deficit to two points before Owen – who had earlier made a crucial try-saving tackle on Tommy Bishop – was involved in Wakefield's fourth try in the 57th minute. A typical Owen dummy produced the opening, sending centre Ian Brooke in for his second try of the match, Wakefield going on to claim the title 21-9.

Bob Pemberton noted in the *Daily Telegraph* that 'Owen's lively play around the scrum earned him the Harry Sunderland Trophy as man of the match, and Poynton was a close second in the vote by the pressmen present.'

Northern Rugby League Championship Final Replay 1967
Wednesday 10 May at Station Road, Swinton
Wakefield Trinity 21
Cooper, Hirst (try), Brooke (2 tries), N Fox (3 goals), Coetzer, Poynton (captain, try), Owen (try), Bath, Prior, Campbell, Clarkson, Haigh, D Fox.
St Helens 9
F Barrow, van Vollenhoven (captain, try), A Barrow, Smith, Killeen (2 goals), Douglas, Bishop (goal), Warlow, Sayer, Watson, French, Hogan, Mantle.
Half-time: 11-7. Referee: J Manley (Warrington).
Attendance: 33,537.

Ray Owen.

135

SAM PANAPA (WIGAN)
Harry Sunderland Trophy winner 1994

Sam Panapa.

Versatile Wigan player Sam Panapa became the first New Zealand recipient of the Harry Sunderland Trophy after a sterling performance in the 1994 Premiership Trophy Final win over Castleford at Old Trafford. Playing in the centre, Panapa capped a wonderful all-round display in scoring a vital second try for Wigan, after racing clear off a Shaun Edwards pass and outpacing the chasing defence, putting the Cherry and Whites ahead for the first time. It came after the Yorkshire side had taken a surprise opening quarter 8-0 lead, Wigan coming back with three tries before half-time in a 12-minute blitz through Andrew Farrell, then Panapa's effort, and Frano Botica, whose two conversions sent Wigan back to their changing quarters with a 16-8 advantage.

In an uninspired second period, Wigan extended their lead to 24-8, Castleford bringing respectability to the scoreboard with two late converted tries. Despite the win, it was an unhappy afternoon for Wigan prop Kelvin

Skerrett, who suffered a badly broken jaw after 55 minutes in an incident with Dean Sampson. Panapa, who proved his worth with a great defensive effort as Castleford threatened to come back at the end, told the *Wigan Observer*: 'It's an honour to be named man of the match, but I just went out and gave my all as I always do.' Despite the back-slapping, it was his last Wigan match on English soil, transferring to Salford following the 1994 World Club Challenge match in Brisbane, to create space on the overseas quota for the incoming Henry Paul.

Premiership Trophy Final 1994
Sunday 22 May at Old Trafford, Manchester
Wigan 24
Atcheson, Robinson, Panapa (try), Connolly, Offiah, Botica (try, 4 goals), Edwards (captain), Skerrett, Hall, Cowie, Betts (try), Farrell (try), Clarke. Substitutes: Lydon, Cassidy.
Castleford 20
Ellis, C Smith, Blackmore, T Smith, Middleton, Steadman (try, 2 goals), Ford, Crooks (captain, 2 goals), Russell, Sampson (try), Ketteridge, Hay, Nikau. Substitutes: Smales, Sykes (try).
Half-time: 16-8. Referee: S Cummings (Widnes). Attendance: 35,644.

PROFILE

Centre-cum-loose forward Sam Panapa originally came to England for the 1984/85 season, when he played for Sheffield Eagles. Born in Auckland, New Zealand, he was attached to Auckland-based Glenora at that time. In 1990, having made his international debut and represented Auckland in provincial matches, he re-signed for Sheffield, this time from Te Atatu, another Auckland side. He spent 12 months with the Eagles before transferring to Wigan in 1991. His three-year stint with Wigan saw him win the World Club Challenge (1991 and 1994), Championship (1992/93 and 1993/94), Challenge Cup (1993 and 1994), Premiership Trophy (1992 and 1994) and Regal Trophy (1992/93). He transferred to Salford in 1994, helping them capture the Division One (formerly Division Two) title twice (1995/96 and 1996), and win the Divisional Premiership Final (1996), earning the club a Super League place in his final match. He played in eight Test Matches for New Zealand (1990-91) and in their touring side that visited Australia and Papua New Guinea in 1987.

HENRY PAUL (BRADFORD BULLS)

Harry Sunderland Trophy winner 1999
Lance Todd Trophy winner 2000

When New Zealand stand-off Henry Paul won the Lance Todd Trophy with Bradford Bulls in 2000, be became the first and, to date, only, overseas player to complete the man of the match double, having been awarded the Harry Sunderland Trophy in the previous year. His Lance Todd success also meant he and his brother Robbie – who won the award in 1996 and was his half-back partner in 2000 – emulated Don and Neil Fox, who both received the coveted trophy during the 1960s.

With the 2000 Challenge Cup Final being staged at Murrayfield, Edinburgh, due to Wembley being rebuilt, Paul became the second player to win the Lance Todd Trophy away from the twin towers, Gerry Helme having received it following the 1954 Odsal replay. Bradford's

Henry Paul.

PROFILE

British fans became aware of the talent of Henry Paul in 1993 when, as a 19-year-old, he toured with the Junior Kiwis. He did so well he was drafted into the injury hit senior New Zealand party touring Britain and France at the same time. Wakefield Trinity realised the potential of the speedy, clever stand-off, signing him in December 1993 until the end of the 1993/94 season. Wigan captured his signature during August 1994, winning a dispute with Auckland Warriors who also claimed him. At Wigan, Paul won the Championship (1994/95, 1995/96), Challenge Cup (1995 – he was a runner-up in 1998), Premiership Trophy (1995, 1996, 1997), Regal Trophy (1994/95, 1995/96) and Super League Grand Final (1998). In 1999, he joined brother Robbie at Bradford Bulls, setting new club records there in 2001 for goals (208) and points (457) in a season, adding to his honours list with wins in the Challenge Cup (2000 – losing in the 2001 final) and Super League Grand Final (2001 – being a runner-up in 1999). Following the 2001 season, he moved to Rugby Union with Gloucester (he had played for Bath RU during the 1996/97 close season), and, to date, has made six appearances for England (2002-04). Born in Tokoroa, he played Rugby League for Auckland side Te Atatu prior to his career in England. He was picked 23 times for New Zealand (1995-2001) including the 1995 and 2000 World Cup competitions, losing in the final of the latter to Australia.

opponents were fierce rivals Leeds Rhinos and, although the Bulls entered the arena as clear favourites with the bookies, the result – 24-18 to Bradford – was closer than predicted. Paul won the vote primarily for his kicking tactics, his sky-high kicks into the left corner – policed by previous Lance Todd winner Leroy Rivett – being his favoured target. He hoisted seven in that direction during the final to produce three of his side's four tries, the first in the 10th minute catching Rivett out as Tevita Vaikona recovered the missile to put Michael Withers over in the left corner. Encouraged by that outcome, Paul repeated the bombardment seven minutes later, the ball hitting Ritchie Blackmore's leg, Withers recovering it for his second try. Paul missed both conversions, but an 8th minute penalty – which opened the scoring after he was judged to have been fouled by Barrie McDermott – plus a brilliant Nathan McAvoy effort eleven minutes before the interval, when he recovered his own chip kick, put Bradford comfortably ahead 14-2 at half-time.

A proud day for the Paul brothers as Lance Todd Trophy winner Henry (right) and Bradford Bulls skipper Robbie celebrate winning the 2000 Challenge Cup Final at Murrayfield.

Eight minutes into the second half Paul again kicked to the left from close in, Jamie Fielden claiming the ball to score Bradford's final try, Paul adding the goal. The score was 20-4 at that point, the Rhinos then staging a fight back that almost swung the result. Paul helped keep Bradford one step ahead with two more penalties to complete their scoring, the last – with two minutes remaining – after Leeds had rallied to a disconcerting 22-18. Paul said the win was 'a fantastic feeling' but admitted to being very tired at the end, having travelled back from Australia with brother Robbie after playing in a Test Match in Australia the previous weekend. For Bradford it was the club's first Challenge Cup success in 51 years.

In contrast, the 1999 Super League Grand Final was a much tighter affair, Bradford losing by the narrowest of margins, 8-6 to St Helens on a rain-soaked evening. The Bulls were again favourites and led 6-2 at the interval, all the points coming from Paul who stood out as a clear man of the match, even in defeat. His contribution came in the 18th minute, evading Sonny Nickle and Paul Atcheson as he sped 65 yards direct from a scrum to slide beneath the posts, the try – which he converted – being all the more remarkable as he lost a boot on the way. That was the last time they troubled the scoreboard, having two subsequent efforts disallowed by the video referee as St Helens inched their way towards victory, Sean Long's touchline goal, following Kevin Iro's 65th minute try in the corner, providing the difference.

Super League Grand Final 1999
Saturday 9 October at Old Trafford, Manchester
St Helens 8
Atcheson, Smith, Iro (try), Newlove, Sullivan, Sculthorpe, Martyn, Perelini, Cunningham, O'Neill, Tuilagi, Nickle, Joynt (captain). Substitutes: Matautia, Long (2 goals), Hoppe, Wellens.
Bradford Bulls 6
Spruce, Vaikona, Naylor, Withers, Pryce, H Paul (try, goal), R Paul (captain), Anderson, Lowes, Fielden, Boyle, Dwyer, McNamara. Substitutes: Forshaw, McDermott, Deacon.
Half-time: 2-6. Referee: S Cummings (Widnes).
Attendance: 50,717.

Rugby League Challenge Cup Final 2000
Saturday 29 April at Murrayfield, Edinburgh
Bradford Bulls 24
Spruce, McAvoy (try), Naylor, Withers (2 tries), Vaikona, H Paul (4 goals), R Paul (captain), Brian McDermott, Lowes, Anderson, Peacock, Forshaw, Mackay. Substitutes: Fielden (try), Boyle, Pryce, Dwyer.
Leeds Rhinos 18
Harris (captain, 5 goals), Rivett, Blackmore, Senior, Cummins, Powell, Sheridan, Fleary, Lawford, Barrie McDermott, Morley, Farrell, Hay (try). Substitutes: Mathiou, Jackson, Barnhill, St Hilaire (try).
Half-time: 14-2. Referee: S Presley (Castleford).
Attendance: 67,247.

Graham Morris

ROBBIE PAUL (BRADFORD BULLS)
Lance Todd Trophy winner 1996

Robbie Paul.

Robbie Paul had a sensational Challenge Cup Final debut with Bradford Bulls in 1996, perfect in every way, excepting the result, which went in St Helens' favour. It is doubtful that a player from the losing side ever made such an impact as Paul, who scored the first Wembley hat-trick of tries – the last qualifying as one of the stadiums greatest ever solo efforts – to rubber stamp his status as Lance Todd Trophy winner. The youngest captain of a Wembley side at 20 years and three months old, Paul's performance throughout a thrilling cup final was exceptional, proving an inspiration to his colleagues and a constant threat to St Helens with his ability to exploit every half-chance.

The final ebbed and flowed like no Wembley occasion before it, St Helens leading 8-0 after 17 minutes, Bradford gamely fighting back with four tries, including Paul's first two, to go ahead 26-12 after 53 minutes. It was then St Helens turn to stage a comeback, eventually winning 40-

32, the verdict confirmed when Apollo Perelini scored St Helens last try five minutes from time.

Paul's first try came three minutes before the interval, charging under the posts after being first receiver at a play-the ball close to the try line. Thirteen minutes after the break he got his second, spinning and twisting his way through three defenders from acting half-back near the right hand corner. He completed his trio ten minutes from time, taking a pass five yards inside his own half to go on a mesmerising run to the try-line past four defenders, guaranteeing a nerve tingling finish.

Rugby League Challenge Cup Final 1996
Saturday 27 April at Wembley Stadium, London
St Helens 40
Prescott (2 tries), Arnold (2 tries), Gibbs, Newlove, Sullivan, Hammond, Goulding (captain, 4 goals), Perelini (try), Cunningham (try), Leathem, Joynt, Booth (try), Northey. Substitutes: Martyn, Pickavance (try), Matautia, Hunte.
Bradford Bulls 32
Graham, Cook (6 goals), Calland, Loughlin, Scales (try), Bradley, R Paul (captain, 3 tries), McDermott, Dwyer (try), Hamer, Donougher, Nickle, Knox. Substitutes: Fairbank, Medley, Donohue, Hassan. Half-time: 12-14. Referee: S Cummings (Widnes). Attendance: 75,994.

PROFILE

Robbie Paul was in at the start of the Bradford Bulls rise to power, joining the club in 1994, aged 18, his 1994/95 debut season being their last as Bradford Northern. A powerful scrum-half and an explosive runner, he can motivate and lift colleagues, being appointed captain in the 1995/96 season. He has won the Challenge Cup twice (2000 and 2003, being runner-up 1996, 1997 and 2001) and Super League Grand Final twice (2001 and 2003, runner-up in 1999, 2002 and 2004). He also shared Super League success in 1997, prior to the play-off system being instigated, and won the World Club Challenge in 2002, missing the 2004 win through injury. Born in Tokoroa, he previously played for Waitakere. A former Junior Kiwi, he has, to date, represented New Zealand 26 times at senior level (1997-2004), including the 2000 World Cup when he appeared in the final. During the 1996/97 winter break he played for Harlequins Rugby Union club.

JAMIE PEACOCK (BRADFORD BULLS)
Man of Steel Award winner 2003

It is difficult to visualise how Jamie Peacock's 2003 campaign could have been any better than it was. Apart from winning that year's Man of Steel Award, the Bradford Bulls' accomplished second-row forward monopolised the individual accolades and enjoyed a clean sweep of team honours in the Bulls colours as well.

On the same evening that he received the Man of Steel trophy, he was announced as the Super League Players' Player of the Year, further plaudits coming his way when voted the Rugby League Writers' Association Player of the Year and through being included in the mythical Tetley's Super League Dream Team for 2003.

Jamie Peacock.

He also came within one vote of taking the Lance Todd Trophy in April's Challenge Cup Final, having made a massive contribution to Bradford's 22-20 defeat of Leeds at Cardiff's Millennium Stadium.

Bradford also took the season's remaining team honours, heading the Super League table

PROFILE

Born in the Bramley district of Leeds, Jamie Peacock joined Bradford Bulls in 1997 from the Leeds-based Stanningley amateur club. The accomplished, power-packed second-row forward eased his way into senior Rugby League, playing in Australia for Wollongong University, near Sydney (where he was studying) and for a New South Wales country club. On returning, he was loaned to Featherstone Rovers at the end of 1998, making his Bulls debut as a 21-year-old in 1999. His honours tally with the Bulls cover two wins each in the Challenge Cup (2000 and 2003), Super League Grand Final (2001 and 2003) and World Club Challenge (2002 and 2004 – being captain in the latter against Penrith). He was also a runner-up in the Challenge Cup in 2001 and Super League Grand Finals of 2002 and 2004. His representative honours, so far, embrace 14 Test appearances for Great Britain (2001-04), five for England (2000-01 including the 2000 World Cup) and four for Yorkshire (2001-03). He has agreed to join Leeds Rhinos from 2006.

three points clear of Leeds to win the Minor Premiership – and with it the League Leaders' Shield – and securing the Super League Grand Final trophy through disposing of Wigan 25-12 at Old Trafford, Peacock claiming a winners' ring five days after his Man of Steel success. Having appeared for Yorkshire in July's County of Origin match, when Lancashire were slammed 56-6 at Odsal Stadium, Peacock took part in Great Britain's three match Test series against Australia which closed the season. It provided the only real negative of Peacock's year, the visiting Kangaroos winning all three clashes.

Tetley's Super League Man of Steel Awards 2003
Monday 13 October at the Le Meridian Palace Hotel, Manchester
Compered by John Champion
Man of Steel: Jamie Peacock (Bradford Bulls).
Super League Players' Player of the Year: Jamie Peacock (Bradford Bulls).
Super League Young Player of the Year: Gareth Hock (Wigan Warriors).
Super League Coach of the Year: Brian Noble (Bradford Bulls).
Super League Referee of the Year: Karl Kirkpatrick (Warrington).

BARRY PHILBIN (WARRINGTON)
Harry Sunderland Trophy winner 1974

PROFILE

Loose forward Barry Philbin followed elder brother Mike to Warrington in 1974, the St Helens-born pair having begun their professional careers with Swinton. He made his Swinton debut in 1970, appearing in their side that lost the 1972 Lancashire Cup Final to Salford. With Warrington the honours came fast, winning the Challenge Cup (1974, runner-up in 1975), Club Championship (1974), Player's No.6 Trophy (1973/74 and 1977/78) and Captain Morgan Trophy (1973/74). Earning a reputation for his powerful attacking bursts and the tenacity of his defence, he was picked three times by Lancashire in 1974 and included by England for the 1975 World Cup match against France at Headingley. Dogged by injury, his form declined, and he attempted to resurrect his career by following former Warrington coach, Alex Murphy, to Salford, but managed only 11 matches during 1978/79 before suffering a broken leg.

Barry Philbin.

Warrington loose-forward Barry Philbin took the 1974 Harry Sunderland award after starring in the only final of the Club Merit Championship, against St Helens. Played at Central Park, Wigan, it produced a stirring contest, Warrington hanging on in a tight finish to win 13-12. Philbin earned his reward with a gutsy, storming show, Warrington's commanding front three of David Chisnall, Kevin Ashcroft and Brian Brady providing the launching pad for Philbin's powerful, thrusting runs.

Warrington held a slim 8-7 advantage after the opening half, increasing their lead to 13-7 eleven minutes into the second period when Derek Noonan finished off some good work by John Bevan, Derek Whitehead augmenting. With 15 minutes left St Helens centre Frank

Wilson set pulses racing when he scored his second try of the match, Kel Coslett's conversion closing the gap to just one point. A flurry of missed drop-goal attempts followed, including six by Murphy and three from Ashcroft for Warrington, whilst a heart-stopping last second effort by Coslett just sailed wide, but there was no further scoring.

Barry Philbin in action for Warrington at Wembley in 1974.

Philbin collected seven of the 18 votes, three ahead of team mates Alan Whittle and Brady, the *St Helens Newspaper & Advertiser* admitting: 'Barry Philbin, a bargain-buy from Swinton earlier this year, ripped the St Helens midfield to shreds with breath-taking runs and full-blooded tackling.' Played in heavy rain the victory completed one of the most successful seasons in Warrington's history, having won the Challenge Cup, Player's No. 6 Trophy and Captain Morgan Trophy.

Club Championship Final 1974
Saturday 18 May at Central Park, Wigan
Warrington 13
Whitehead (2 goals), M Philbin (try), Noonan (try), Pickup, Bevan, Whittle, A Murphy (captain), D Chisnall, Ashcroft, Brady (try), Wanbon, Mather, B Philbin. Substitutes: Lowe, Gaskell.
St Helens 12
Pimblett, Brown, Wills, Wilson (2 tries), Mathias, Eckersley, Heaton, Mantle, Liptrot, M Murphy, E Chisnall, Nicholls, Coslett (captain, 3 goals).
Substitute: Warlow.
Half-time: 8-7. Referee: P Geraghty (York).
Attendance: 18,040.

GEOFF PIMBLETT (ST HELENS)
Lance Todd Trophy winner 1976
Harry Sunderland Trophy winner 1977

When St Helens full-back Geoff Pimblett won the Harry Sunderland Trophy in 1977, he became the first player to achieve the notable double of being voted man of the match in both of British Rugby League's major finals, having won the Lance Todd Trophy the previous year. He completed his twosome at Swinton in a sun-baked Premiership Trophy Final clash with Warrington, his 17 points from a try – he had a leading role in three others – and seven goals securing his award. Saints won 32-20, nine of the games ten tries coming during a free-flowing second half, partly due to the dismissal of Harry Pinner (St Helens) and Alan Gwilliam (Warrington) shortly after the break, reducing the occasion to a 12-a-side encounter.

Geoff Pimblett.

Warrington led 5-4 after a low-key first half, Pimblett's two penalties – in the 12th and 36th minutes – being the only response to a Warrington try from Alan Gwilliam, converted by Steve Hesford. St Helens took the lead five minutes into the second half when Pimblett put Billy Benyon over and added the extra two points. A Hesford penalty, two minutes later, proved insufficient as Pimblett raced into the corner in the 53rd minute to end a stunning move initiated by an Eric Chisnall break, Pimblett being involved in another exciting Saints attack five minutes later, Roy Mathias touching down. With Pimblett converting his own effort with a magnificent touch-line kick, Saints were in command at 17-7. As the tackles dropped off in the hot conditions, the two depleted defences conceded three tries each in the final 15 minutes, including a Ken Gwilliam effort after Pimblett shrugged off a tackle to put him through, Saints retaining the trophy, having appeared in all three Premiership deciders since its 1975 inception.

The sun was also sizzling in the Wembley skies in 1976 for a 'shirt sleeved' Challenge Cup Final as Pimblett completed the opening leg of his double, becoming the third consecutive full-back to be awarded the Lance Todd Trophy as St Helens eventually crushed pre-match favourites and holders Widnes 20-5. With both half-backs and four of their forwards – including the entire front-row – aged over 30, St Helens were not expected to go the distance against the younger Widnes side in the extreme heat beating down inside the stadium. In the event, the first half belonged to St Helens, with Pimblett continually making inroads with penetrating runs from the back and Saints halves Jeff Heaton and Billy Benyon also giving outstanding performances. Pimblett converted centre Eddie

Cunningham's 12th minute try and also produced a timely drop-goal six minutes before the interval, St Helens turning round with their noses just in front at 6-4.

Keith Elwell reduced the margin to a nerve-wracking one point ten minutes into the second half with a drop-goal, St Helens then suffering a setback when Benyon was forced to quit with just over 15 minutes remaining due to a cut on his head, to be replaced by Peter Glynn. Rather than wilt in the heat, Saints 'Dad's Army' pack suddenly took control, skipper Kel Coslett having a try disallowed for not grounding properly and winger Roy Mathias being held up in the corner, Pimblett signalling the opening of the floodgates with his second drop-goal with 12 minutes remaining. From the restart, Pimblett took the ball to go racing down the field with a dazzling run. Although tackled by Ray Dutton, his quick play-the-ball enabled Derek Noonan and Tony Karalius to send Heaton over near the posts. Pimblett was involved again as he combined with Karalius to put Glynn in for a further try, his conversion of both efforts putting Saints 17-5 ahead, 'super-sub' Glynn completing the scoring with a touchdown two minutes from time.

Geoff Pimblett (left) holds the Harry Sunderland Trophy, whilst St Helens skipper Billy Benyon takes care of the Premiership Trophy following the 1977 win over Warrington at Station Road, Swinton.

PROFILE

Locally born Geoff Pimblett swapped codes in 1971, leaving St Helens Rugby Union club in favour of the 13-a-side game at Knowsley Road. He was an exciting full-back with an exhilarating side-step that often took him through gaps as he set up counter-attacks for his three-quarter line. Reliable on defence and a competent goal-kicker, he was no slouch at contributing vital drop-goals when needed. He was unlucky in that there were several outstanding full-backs around in the 1970s, limiting him to one appearance each for England (1978) and Lancashire (1977). At club level, he enjoyed a productive career with St Helens, winning the Championship (1970/71 and 1974/75), Challenge Cup (1972 and 1976, visiting Wembley a third time in 1978 as captain but losing on that occasion), Premiership Trophy (1976 and 1977) and BBC2 Floodlit Trophy (1971 and 1975). He made his farewell Saints appearance in 1979.

Pimblett recalls the day fondly, saying: 'I vividly remember walking up the steps to the Royal Box afterwards and looking over to the scoreboard and seeing "Lance Todd winner Geoff Pimblett." At the top of the steps where you turn towards the Royal Box, who was there but my dad waiting to shake my hand! Wembley is an emotional place anyway and I thought "I've won the Lance Todd Trophy, I've won the cup winners medal and my dads here!" I can't beat that!'

Rugby League Challenge Cup Final 1976
Saturday 8 May at Wembley Stadium, London
St Helens 20
Pimblett (3 goals, 2 drop-goals), Jones, Cunningham (try), Noonan, Mathias, Benyon, Heaton (try), Mantle, Karalius, Coslett (captain), Nicholls, E Chisnall, Hull. Substitutes: Glynn (2 tries), James.
Widnes 5
Dutton (2 goals), Prescott, Hughes, George, Jenkins, Eckersley, Bowden (captain), Nelson, Elwell (drop-goal), Wood, Foran, Adams, Laughton. Substitutes: D O'Neill, Sheridan.
Half-time: 6-4. Referee: R Moore (Wakefield).
Attendance: 89,982.

Premiership Trophy Final 1977
Saturday 28 May at Station Road, Swinton
St Helens 32
Pimblett (try, 7 goals), Jones, Benyon (captain, try), Cunningham (try), Mathias (try), Glynn, K Gwilliam (try), D Chisnall, Liptrot, James (try), Nicholls, E Chisnall, Pinner. Substitutes: Ashton, Karalius.

Warrington 20
Finningan, Curling, Bevan, Hesford (4 goals), Kelly, A Gwilliam (try), Gordon (captain, try), Weavill (try), Price, Case, Lester, Martyn, B Philbin (try). Substitutes: Cunliffe, Peers.
Half-time: 4-5. Referee: GF Lindop (Wakefield). Attendance: 11,178.

St Helens 1977, with Geoff Pimblett on the back row, extreme left.

Graham Morris

HARRY PINNER (ST HELENS)
Harry Sunderland Trophy winner 1985

PROFILE

Harry Pinner was not the biggest of loose forwards in stature but his on-field presence was immense, the inventive, ball playing packman being as effective in the tackle as on offence. Born in St Helens, he was an outstanding schoolboy prospect who signed for his local club from their Colts side in 1974. He made his first team bow in 1976, progressing quickly to earn a Lancashire call in 1977, making seven county appearances in all, the last in 1981. With St Helens he won the Premiership Trophy (1977 and 1985) and Lancashire Cup (1984), being a runner-up in his only Challenge Cup Final (1978). A Great Britain tourist in 1984, he made seven Test appearances (1980-86, four as captain) and represented England three times (1980-81). He subsequently played for Widnes (1986-88 – leaving midway through their 1987/88 Championship season having taken part in 12 League fixtures), Leigh (1988), Bradford Northern (1988-89) and Carlisle (1989).

St Helens loose forward and captain Harry Pinner shone in a thrilling, spectacular 1985 Premiership Trophy Final against holders Hull Kingston Rovers, which produced a ten-try 52-points feast. Pinner won the vote for the Harry Sunderland Trophy after an outstanding authoritative performance in which he scored one and engineered four of the Saints tries, their remaining two being the result of interceptions by giant Australian centre Mal Meninga.

St Helens hooker Gary Ainsworth got the first after two minutes play, set up by an astute Pinner pass, Sean Day adding the goal. George Fairbairn retaliated, converting his own try to level the scores before Pinner again opened up the Rovers defence, his pass to the alert Phil Veivers, who raced up in support, producing Saints' second touchdown, Day augmenting for a 12-6 lead after 12 minutes. The two adversaries shared four more tries during the second quarter, the half-time score standing at 22-14 in St Helens favour.

The scoring spree eased after the break with only a Fairbairn penalty – bringing Rovers within six points – troubling the scorekeeper until the final 15 minutes. St Helens then let rip with a closing flurry, Meninga's runaway try being followed six minutes later by Pinner swerving his way over the whitewash, and then being influential in Barry Ledger's last minute score, Saints finishing the match 36-16 victors.

Pinner said afterwards: 'I never had any doubts that we wouldn't win. We played smashing football and beat them well. I was delighted to pick up the man of the match award, but it could have gone to any of the lads.'

Premiership Trophy Final 1985
Saturday 11 May at Elland Road, Leeds
St Helens 36
Veivers (try), Ledger (2 tries), Peters, Meninga (2 tries), Day (4 goals), Arkwright, Holding, Burke, Ainsworth (try), Gorley, Platt, Haggerty, Pinner (captain, try). Substitutes: Allen, Forber.
Hull Kingston Rovers 16
Fairbairn (try, 2 goals), Clark, Robinson (try), Prohm, Laws (try), M Smith, G Smith, Broadhurst, Watkinson (captain), Ema, Kelly, Hogan, Hall. Substitutes: Harkin, Lydiat.
Half-time: 22-14. Referee: S Wall (Leigh).
Attendance: 15,518.

Harry Pinner breaks through for St Helens during the emphatic Premiership Trophy Final victory over Hull Kingston Rovers in 1985.

STEVE PITCHFORD (LEEDS)
Lance Todd Trophy winner 1977

Steve Pitchford gets stuck in for Leeds during the 1977 Challenge Cup Final against Widnes.

Leeds powerhouse prop Steve Pichford was an unlikely pre-match candidate to win the 1977 Lance Todd Trophy, his barn-storming runs throughout the second-half of an intriguing Challenge Cup Final conjuring up an everlasting image for those who witnessed them. Opponents Widnes were creating their own piece of history, emulating Bradford Northern's feat – some 30 years earlier – of reaching three consecutive Wembley finals. Unfortunately for the Chemics' frustrated fans, their team repeated the previous year's failing by unexpectedly losing.

Pitchford served notice of what was in store when he bulldozed Ray Dutton out of the way in the opening minutes, although his resultant 'try-scoring' pass to John Atkinson was judged as being forward. Having turned around 7-5 behind, Leeds took control in the second half, aided by an unfortunate and accidental intervention from referee Vince Moss in the 53rd minute. After taking a tap restart on his own 25-yard line, Widnes scrum-half and captain Reg Bowden hit the official, who was stood at his side, with his pass. According to the rules, the referee had to form a scrum, Leeds winning the resultant possession, Les Dyl going over like a bullet to put his side 8-7 up. From that moment, the Headingley outfit, aided by the irresistible surges of Pitchford, became masters of their own destiny. One of Pitchford's steam-roller runs, in the 61st minute, was halted by a desperate Widnes defence just short of the try

Steve Pitchford (right), winner of the Lance Todd Trophy in 1977, congratulates successor George Nicholls of St Helens on his 1978 award.

146

PROFILE

Standing five feet nine inches tall and weighing close to 16 stone, Leeds prop forward Steve Pitchford – known as the 'Bionic Barrel' due to his square-set frame – was a tough, no-nonsense type of player who tackled hard and ran with power, taking the direct route towards the opposition line. He was born in the Hunslet district of Leeds, graduating through the Leeds Intermediates side before signing professionally for the Headingley outfit in 1968. Having paid his dues in the reserve side, he came to the fore during the mid-1970s, earning winners medals in the Challenge Cup (1977, 1978), Premiership Trophy (1975, 1979) and Yorkshire Cup (1975, 1976, 1979, 1980). He also contributed towards the clubs Championship win of 1971/72, although not taking part in the final itself. He played four times for Great Britain (all in the 1977 World Cup) and twice for Yorkshire (both 1978). In 1984, he was transferred to Bramley, playing for them until 1986.

A typical rampaging run from Steve Pitchford during a League encounter.

line. He played the ball to Dick, who cheekily dummied his way over the line for Leeds' third and final touchdown, which he converted himself, adding a drop goal and penalty in the last four minutes.

Pitchford was a popular winner of the Lance Todd Trophy whilst colleague Dick – making his first Challenge Cup appearance after being brought into the side following the tragic death of Chris Sanderson in a match two weeks earlier – was a close second having contributed ten points towards Leeds' 16-7 victory.

Rugby League Challenge Cup Final 1977
Saturday 7 May at Wembley Stadium, London
Leeds 16
Murrell, A Smith, Hague, Dyl (try), Atkinson (try), Holmes, Dick (try, 3 goals, drop-goal), Harrison, Ward (captain), Pitchford, Eccles, Cookson, Fearnley. Substitutes: D Smith, Dickinson.
Widnes 7
Dutton (2 goals), Wright, Aspey (try), Eckersley, D O'Neill, Hughes, Bowden (captain), Ramsey, Elwell, Mills, Dearden, Adams, Laughton. Substitutes: George, Foran.
Half-time: 5-7. Referee: V Moss (Manchester).
Attendance: 80,871.

ANDY PLATT (WIGAN)

Harry Sunderland Trophy winner 1992
Man of Steel Award winner 1993

Andy Platt.

major trophies; First Division Championship, Rugby League Challenge Cup (beating Widnes 20-14 in the final), Regal Trophy (Bradford Northern 15-8) and Lancashire Cup (St Helens 5-4). He was also in the side that lost 22-8 to Brisbane Broncos in the World Club Challenge at Wigan's Central Park ground in October 1992. In a repeat of 1990, Platt was also one of the three nominees for the First Division Player of the Year on the same awards evening.

In contrast to the formal, calmer atmosphere of the Man of Steel Awards Ceremony, Platt received the Harry Sunderland Trophy after sweating it out in the baking heat of a hot, sunny Old Trafford, as Wigan overcame St Helens 48-

Andy Platt confirmed his status as one of Britain's greatest ever prop forwards when he concluded a perfect 12 months as a popular winner of the 1993 Man of Steel Award. Over the past year he had enhanced his reputation on the international stage, having been voted the outstanding performer on Great Britain's 1992 tour of Australia, New Zealand and Papua New Guinea when playing in all six Test matches, being rewarded with the captaincy for the 72-6 hammering of France at Headingley during April 1993. Voted the world's leading prop that year, he also appeared for Britain in a dramatic World Cup Final against Australia at Wembley during October 1992, narrowly losing 10-6.

At club level, Platt proved as solid as a rock in Wigan's pack as the club continued its domination of the British game, capturing four

---

PROFILE

Andy Platt began his career as a second-row forward with St Helens, eventually developing into one of British Rugby League's best ever props. Born in Billinge, midway between St Helens and Wigan, he joined the Saints from Wigan St Patrick's in 1982. His Knowsley Road career saw him gain winners' medals for the Premiership Trophy (1985), John Player Trophy (1987/88) and Lancashire Cup (1984), experiencing the heartbreak of a Wembley defeat to Halifax in the 1987 Challenge Cup Final. In 1988, he switched his allegiance to Wigan, the Central Park outfit paying £140,000 to secure his services. Whilst at Wigan he was a winner in the World Club Challenge (1991), Championship (five times from 1989/90 to 1993/94), Challenge Cup (six wins from 1989 to 1994), Premiership Trophy (1992), Regal Trophy (1989/90 and 1992/93) and Lancashire Cup (1988 and 1992). After the 1993/94 season concluded, he followed former Wigan coach John Monie to Auckland Warriors, playing for them during 1995 and 1996. He interrupted his stay with Auckland to return to England, playing for Widnes during part of the 1995/96 British season, reportedly to gain a place in England's 1995 World Cup squad, which he achieved, playing in four matches including the final. After leaving Auckland, he joined Salford (1997-98), transferring to Workington Town in October 1998 as player-coach where he played in just four matches before resigning in July 1999 and returning to Australia. He toured with Great Britain twice (1988 and 1992 – withdrawing from the 1990 tour) and appeared in 25 Tests (1985-93) plus three matches for Lancashire (1986-1991).

12 to win the 1992 Premiership Trophy Final. Wigan's score set a record for a final in any competition, although it hardly looked likely when St Helens led 12-10 with 28 minutes left to play, at which point the Cherry and White's defied the stifling conditions to score the first of seven second half tries.

Platt received his man of the match award for a typically industrious performance, the inspirational prop having worked overtime during the first 40 minutes when St Helens had threatened to take control. He also showed his early determination when dummying his way over the try-line from close range in the 23rd minute for Wigan's only first half try, and his second touchdown of the season. Augmented by Frano Botica's goal, who also got two earlier penalties, it propelled them 10-2 in front, St Helens staging a mini-revival with two tries of their own before the break. For Platt and his colleagues, the result marked the 25th consecutive win of the campaign.

Premiership Trophy Final 1992
Sunday 17 May at Old Trafford, Manchester
Wigan 48
Hampson, Lydon, Bell (captain), Miles (try), Offiah (2 tries), Botica (10 goals), Edwards, Cowie, Dermott, Platt (try), Betts (2 tries), McGinty, Clarke. Substitutes: Myers (try), Panapa.
St Helens 16
Veivers, Hunte, Connolly, Loughlin (try, 2 goals), Sullivan (2 tries), Ropati, Bishop, Neill, Dwyer, Ward, Nickle, Mann, Cooper (captain). Substitutes: Griffiths, Groves.
Half-time: 10-12. Referee: J Holdsworth (Kippax). Attendance: 33,157.

Stones Bitter Man of Steel Awards 1993
Friday 14 May at the Holiday Inn Crowne Plaza Midland, Manchester
Compered by Eddie Hemmings.
Man of Steel: Andy Platt (Wigan).
First Division Player of the Year: Tea Ropati (St Helens).
Second Division Player of the Year: Paul Newlove (Featherstone Rovers).
Third Division Player of the Year: Martin Wood (Keighley Cougars).
Young Player of the Year: Jason Robinson (Wigan).
Coach of the Year: John Monie (Wigan).
Referee of the Year: John Connolly (Wigan).

Wigan's Andy Platt takes centre stage, holding the Harry Sunderland Trophy at the 1992 Rugby League Writers' Association annual dinner. He is flanked by Gary Hetherington (left), accepting the Tom Bergin Trophy on behalf of absent Sheffield Eagles colleague Daryl Powell, and St Helens' Alan Hunte, seen with the Jack Bentley Trophy.

149

HAROLD POYNTON (WAKEFIELD TRINITY)
Lance Todd Trophy winner 1963

The 1963 Challenge Cup Final was a stunning triumph for Wakefield Trinity and their gifted stand-off and Lance Todd Trophy winner Harold Poynton. The 25-10 victory over Wigan defied all pre-match forecasts with Wakefield, despite Wembley wins in 1960 and 1962, the underdogs, putting out a much changed and less experienced line-up than before. For Poynton, who did so much for his side's cause, tormenting the Cherry and Whites with an all action display that almost defied defenders to lay a hand on him, it made up for missing the 1960 final, when an injury robbed him of his great Wembley day out.

Despite the aggregate tally of 35 points, it was not until two minutes before half-time that Malcolm Sampson opened the scoring with a try, settling Wakefield down after a nervous half that had generally seen Wigan on top. It was Poynton that scored another crucial try in the 67th minute when Trinity, leading 12-7, were facing a rejuvenated Wigan attack. David Bolton broke away with Billy Boston and Eric Ashton in support with only Poynton barring the way to the try line. As Bolton attempted to pass inside to Ashton, Poynton pounced in a flash to

Harold Poynton, at Wembley in 1963 when he won the Lance Todd Trophy.

intercept and race away unopposed for a try. Neil Fox's kick made it 17-7 and Wigan looked beaten.

Commenting on the Lance Todd verdict, Phil King of *The People* wrote: 'Poynton emerged with the most decisive margin since the award was introduced. He was the White Pimpernel. Wigan sought him here, there, everywhere – and found him nowhere. He was saucy with his sorcery.'

Rugby League Challenge Cup Final 1963
Saturday 11 May at Wembley Stadium, London
Wakefield Trinity 25
Round, Greenwood, Brooke (try), Fox (5 goals), Coetzer (2 tries), Poynton (try), Holliday, Wilkinson, Kosanovic, Sampson (try), Vines, Turner (captain), Pearman.
Wigan 10
Bolton, Boston, Ashton (captain, 2 goals), Davies, Carlton (try), McLeod, Pitchford (try), Barton, Sayer, McTigue, Collier, Lyon, Evans.
Half-time: 5-0. Referee: DTH Davies (Manchester). Attendance: 84,492.

PROFILE

Excelling as a scrum-half with Snapethorpe School in Wakefield, Harold Poynton showed a preference for his other love, soccer, after leaving school. On completing his National Service he was invited to Wakefield Trinity for trials in 1958, aged 21, club scouts remembering his prowess as a youngster. He signed, making his senior debut at stand-off – the position in which he would establish himself – that year following three reserve outings. Missing the 1960 Challenge Cup Final through injury, he was in the winning teams of 1962 and 1963, and captain when losing to Leeds in 1968. Other successes included the Championship (1966/67 and 1967/68 – captain on both occasions) and Yorkshire Cup (1960, 1961 and 1964). A creative player and deadly accurate passer, he was a non-stop performer always in the midst of the action. He was a Great Britain tourist in 1962, during which he made his three Test appearances, and represented Yorkshire once (1960). He retired in 1969.

Graham Morris

ALAN PRESCOTT (ST HELENS)
Lance Todd Trophy winner 1956

Alan Prescott.

Although not leading to a try, it demonstrated that the Halifax defence was wavering. Five minutes later, the breakthrough came, St Helens winger Frank Carlton scoring the first points of the afternoon with a brilliant try following good work by his centre Brian Howard who had sucked in the opposing winger to create the overlap. Four minutes further on Welsh winger Stewart Llewellyn scored on the other flank and, with Austin Rhodes converting both their efforts, Saints suddenly led 10-0.

PROFILE

Alan Prescott began his career as a wing three-quarter, joining Halifax in 1943 from his local St Marie's club in Widnes. After four years, and putting on weight, Halifax moved him to loose forward where his reputation grew, St Helens signing him in 1948 for £2,275. Within a season, he relocated to prop where his skill, guile and handling ability was to become an asset for club and country. His qualities as an inspiring leader were recognised by St Helens who made him captain in 1955, Great Britain following suit as he led the 1957 World Cup squad in Australia and the 1958 tourists. Prescott, who also toured in 1954, played in 31 international matches for Great Britain (1951-58), his most famous being the 1958 Test against Australia in Brisbane when he played most of the game with a broken right arm, inspiring his side to victory. He also represented England 10 times (1950-55) and Lancashire 15 (1949-57). With St Helens, he won the Championship (1952/53 and 1958/59), appeared twice at Wembley (losing in 1953, winning in 1956) and won the Lancashire Cup (1953). He later coached St Helens (leading them to Wembley success in 1961) and Leigh.

For over 65 minutes, the 1956 Challenge Cup Final between St Helens and Halifax was deadlocked, neither side having scored in a bruising contest, dominated by the two packs. Throughout the conflict, St Helens captain Alan Prescott continually urged his team on when they showed signs of weakness against his former club. It was Prescott – who had a good turn of pace for a prop forward – that made a tremendous charge through the Yorkshire side's cover midway through the second-half.

Tyssul Griffiths – later discovered to have played with a fractured cheekbone picked up in an earlier match although not realised at the time – pulled back two points for the pre-match favourites with a penalty. It set the stage for Prescott to seal his Lance Todd Trophy winning performance with one of the most memorable tries of his career as he crashed over the line in the final minute. Having headed back to St Helens the following Monday feeling tired and hungry, Prescott delayed a planned official

Alan Prescott receives the Challenge Cup from the Earl Alexander of Tunis after St Helens' 1956 Wembley triumph.

reception and dinner to address the gathering throng of fans in the towns Victoria Square, saying: 'This hour of triumph belongs to the supporters. We ought not to delay it a moment longer than we can. After all I believe some of the supporters went without food to encourage us at Wembley. What's food at a time like this?'

Rugby League Challenge Cup Final 1956
Saturday 28 April at Wembley Stadium, London
St Helens 13
Moses, Llewellyn (try), Greenall, Howard, Carlton (try), Finnan, Rhodes (2 goals), Prescott (captain, try), McIntyre, Silcock, Parsons, Robinson, Karalius.
Halifax 2
Griffiths (goal), Daniels, Lynch, Palmer, Freeman, Dean, Kielty, Wilkinson, Ackerley (captain), Henderson, Fearnley, Pearce, Trail.
Half-time: 0-0. Referee: R Gelder (Wakefield).
Attendance: 79,341.

Halifax captain Alvin Ackerley sportingly congratulates St Helens skipper Alan Prescott following the 1956 Challenge Cup Final.

KRIS RADLINSKI (WIGAN/WIGAN WARRIORS)
Harry Sunderland Trophy winner 1995
Lance Todd Trophy winner 2002

Wigan's brilliant attacking full-back Kris Radlinski is, at the time of writing, the most recent player to complete the Harry Sunderland/Lance Todd man of the match double. His was also the longest wait of the seven players to achieve the feat, his Lance Todd award being seven years after he became the youngest-ever recipient, at 19 years old, of the Harry Sunderland Trophy. His two performances contrasted sharply; in the 1995 Premiership Trophy Final, it was his attacking flair that stood out, whereas, in the 2002 Challenge Cup Final, his award was based on a determined, gutsy defensive showing.

He took possession of the Harry Sunderland Trophy following the biggest score ever recorded in a senior Rugby League final for any competition, Wigan hammering luckless Leeds 69-12 in the 1995 Premiership decider at Old Trafford. Radlinski had been drafted in at centre as a late replacement for Va'aiga Tuigamala who withdrew to attend a family funeral in New Zealand. The teenager grabbed his chance and, along with co-centre Gary Connolly, became the first to achieve a Premiership Final try hat-trick, on the back of some great support play.

It was Radlinski that began the scoring riot in the 8th minute, finishing off a magnificent attacking move involving five players, Frano Botica adding the conversion on the way to equalling his Premiership Final record of 10 goals and 20 points, set three years earlier. Leeds drew level 6-6 through a Richard Eyres try six minutes later but that was as close

as they got, Kelvin Skerrett crossing in the 17th minute, the unlucky prop then having to quit his second successive Premiership Final, this time through broken ribs. Wigan added four more touchdowns before half-time including Radlinski's second effort on 24 minutes, set up by a brilliant piece of play from skipper Shaun Edwards.

Three minutes after the interval Radlinski completed his hat-trick by recovering a Henry Paul grubber kick into the corner, Wigan

Kris Radlinski – at Old Trafford in 1995 holding the Harry Sunderland Trophy on high.

Kris Radlinski signed for Wigan in 1993 from the club's Academy side, having previously played for local amateurs St Judes and St Patrick's. A dependable and brave full-back, who can also perform capably in the centre, he made his debut the same year. His Wigan career, to date, has produced wins in the Championship (1994/95 and 1995/96), Super League Grand Final (1998, being a runner-up in 2000, 2001 and 2003), Challenge Cup (2002, runner-up in 1998 and 2004), Premiership Trophy (1995, 1996 and 1997) and Regal Trophy (1995/96). At the time of writing, he has made 20 Test Match appearances for Great Britain (1996-2003), being a tourist in 1996. His ten matches with England (1995-2001) embrace the 1995 and 2000 World Cups, appearing in the final at the former event. He has also represented Lancashire three times in the County of Origin series with Yorkshire (2001-02).

last thing on Radlinski's mind in the days leading up to the 2002 Challenge Cup Final in Edinburgh, having been hospitalised with a badly swollen right foot, thought to be due to an insect bite. In fact, he later admitted his lack of training caught up with him towards the end of the final, saying: 'I was dead on my feet! I had been in hospital all week and so I think that took its toll. It was only in the morning the doctor made a small cut in my foot and then declared I was fit to play.'

However, any worries he or his Wigan colleagues may have harboured about his sharpness were soon dispelled and, although his support play was less evident than usual – probably due to his condition – his defensive

The vast Old Trafford crowd celebrate as Kris Radlinski dives over for one of his three Wigan tries against Leeds in the 1995 Premiership Trophy Final.

crossing the Leeds line six times during the second half. Radlinski, who also defended well and reverted to his customary full-back slot when Paul went off on the hour, said: 'I just went out there determined to do well and the chances came my way.'

The Lance Todd Trophy was probably the

commitment was an inspiration. He made an early try-saving tackle on Tim Jonkers before setting up the move that led to the first try on 11 minutes from Australian winger Brett Dallas, releasing the ball in a two-man tackle. Radlinski then turned defensive hero again in the 25th minute, saving what could have been a crucial try – the score then standing at 12-4 for Wigan – by getting his (good) left foot underneath the ball as Keiron Cunningham attempted to place it down on the line, although St Helens disputed the decision, made by the video referee. Saints continued to press, however, and pulled back to 12-8 by half-time.

In a thrilling second-half, Radlinski was again the hero, highlighted by another outstanding try-line tackle on Jonkers in the 62nd minute with the score finely balanced at 18-12 for Wigan and Saints fighting back with great vigour. It turned the match with Adrian Lam dropping a vital goal four minutes later.

Radlinski realised he had won the Lance Todd Trophy whilst the match was still in progress, saying: 'They announced who won the man of the match pretty early. I looked up and I saw it on the big screen after about 72 minutes. I saw my face on it and it said underneath (I'd won it). It was a big shock – disbelief really. It was a huge emotional day for me.'

Premiership Trophy Final 1995
Sunday 21 May at Old Trafford, Manchester
Wigan 69
Paul (try), Robinson, Radlinski (3 tries), Connolly (3 tries), Offiah, Botica (10 goals), Edwards (captain, try), Skerrett (try), Hall (try), Cowie, Betts (try), Farrell (drop-goal), Clarke. Substitutes: Haughton (try), Cassidy.
Leeds 12
Tait, Fallon, Iro (captain), Hassan, Cummins, Innes (try), Holroyd (2 goals), Howard, Lowes, Faimalo, Mann, Eyres (try), Mercer. Substitutes: Vassilakopoulos, Harmon.
Half-time: 36-6. Referee: S Cummings (Widnes).
Attendance: 30,160.

Rugby League Challenge Cup Final 2002
Saturday 27 April at Murrayfield, Edinburgh
Wigan Warriors 21
Radlinski, Dallas (try), Connolly (try), Ainscough, Johnson, O'Neill, Lam (try, drop-goal), O'Connor,

Perfect poise from Kris Radlinski.

Newton, C Smith, Cassidy, Furner, Farrell (captain, 4 goals). Substitutes: Bibey, Hodgson, M Smith, Carney.
St Helens 12
Wellens, Albert (try), Gleeson (try), Newlove, Stewart, Martyn, Long, Britt, Cunningham, Shiels, Joynt (captain), Jonkers, Sculthorpe (try). Substitutes: Ward, Stankevitch, Hoppe, Higham.
Half-time: 12-8. Referee: S Cummings (Widnes).
Attendance: 62,140.

PETER RAMSDEN (HUDDERSFIELD)
Lance Todd Trophy winner 1953

The story of Peter Ramsden's Wembley success with Huddersfield in 1953 would not have looked out of place as a story from *Boys' Own*. Having established a regular place in the latter half of the 1952/53 season, he remains the youngest winner of the Lance Todd Trophy, the Challenge Cup Final against St Helens taking place on his 19th birthday.

In a match where the Saints were accused of having an over-physical approach, the teenage stand-off left the field with blood pouring from a suspected broken nose after only six minutes but returned five minutes later, undaunted and in true hero fashion, to score two vital tries. And

> ### PROFILE
>
> *Peter Ramsden was a product of local junior Rugby League, being signed by Huddersfield from the Birkby Civic Youth Club as a 16-year-old in January 1951, and making his debut later that year. With the Fartowners, he won the Championship (1961/62), Challenge Cup (1953) and Yorkshire Cup (1952 and 1957). A gutsy player, quick to exploit any gaps in the opposition defence, he began his professional career as a stand-off half, but operated as a loose forward from 1960, the position in which he made his second Challenge Cup Final appearance when Huddersfield lost to Wakefield Trinity in 1962. He later played for York from 1964 to 1966.*

what crucial tries they were! The first one broke the stalemate after 29 minutes of play, Ramsden receiving the ball from prop Ted Slevin 25 yards out before bursting through the Saints defence. Although he had two men in support, Ramsden elected to go it alone, being tackled from behind by Alan Prescott as he placed the ball down and, despite protests that he had grounded short, the try stood. Pat Devery's conversion put Huddersfield 5-0 up, St Helens levelling at 5-5 before the half-time whistle.

Ramsden almost got over again after the restart but Glyn Moses somehow managed to pull off a try-saving tackle. Huddersfield received a set-back after 63 minutes when full-back John Hunter was taken off on a stretcher

suffering from concussion, but returned ten minutes later. Despite his absence, Huddersfield held out, the score-line seesawing its way to 10-10. With only five minutes remaining, the stage was set for Ramsden's

Peter Ramsden.

second strike, darting across the line after forwards Dave Valentine and Jim Bowden had combined to break down the wilting St Helens defence. Lionel Cooper added the goal and the day belonged to Huddersfield, winning 15-10.

The press vote for Ramsden was almost unanimous, the shy teenager, simply telling his

adoring fans before the official reception in Huddersfield: 'I don't deserve this!' As a postscript, he added a third Wembley try, playing loose forward as the only survivor in Huddersfield's team beaten by Wakefield Trinity in the 1962 Challenge Cup Final.

Rugby League Challenge Cup Final 1953
Saturday 25 April at Wembley Stadium, London
Huddersfield 15
Hunter, Henderson, R Pepperell (captain), Devery (goal), Cooper (2 goals), Ramsden (2 tries), Banks (try), Slevin, Curran, Bowden, Brown, Large, Valentine.
St Helens 10
Moses, Llewellyn (try), Greenall (captain), Gullick, McCormick, Honey, Langfield (try, 2 goals), Prescott, Blakemore, Parr, Parsons, Bretherton, Cale.
Half-time: 5-5. Referee: GS Phillips (Widnes).
Attendance: 89,588.

Peter Ramsden clinches victory for Huddersfield in the 1953 Challenge Cup Final at Wembley, sinking St Helens hearts with his second try five minutes from time.

Huddersfield in 1953. Peter Ramsden is kneeling, third from right.

STUART REARDON (BRADFORD BULLS)
Harry Sunderland Trophy winner 2003

= PROFILE =

Local lad Stuart Reardon waited patiently for his opportunity with Bradford Bulls, being catapulted into the limelight in 2003 after making his first appearance at the start of the year. Signed from the West Bowling club in 2000, his confidence grew quickly following successful loan spells with Featherstone Rovers and Salford City Reds during 2002. He was a winner in the 2003 Super League Grand Final, being a runner-up in 2004, and in the team that won the 2004 World Club Challenge against Penrith Panthers. A powerful runner and resolute defender, he has proved his worth as a full-back and in the three-quarter line. To date, he has represented Great Britain five times, all of them in the 2004 Tri-Nations series. He has signed with Warrington Wolves for 2006.

Bradford Bulls' Stuart Reardon concluded a 'rags to riches' season in 2003 by walking away with the Harry Sunderland Trophy after starring in the Grand Final win over Wigan Warriors. The 22-year-old had begun the season as a virtually unknown member of the Bradford squad, coming in to the side at full-back due to the long-term injuries sustained by prime choices Michael Withers and Robbie Paul. So well had Reardon performed that the illustrious pair were accommodated elsewhere when they returned.

It was Reardon's 51st minute try that put Bradford ahead for the first time, having fought back from a 6-0 deficit to go level on the back of three Paul Deacon penalties. The try came when Bradford prop Joe Vagana broke through from some 25 yards out, Reardon racing up in support to accept the pass to dive over the line despite the attention of several defenders and appearing to trip up at one point. Deacon's goal made it 12-6, giving Bradford a lead they would not relinquish as their rampant pack took control to win the match comfortably 25-12.

Aside from offering valuable support in attack, Reardon showed his mettle in defence, producing a try-saving tackle on David Hodgson in the 12th minute, as Wigan got on top in the early stages. His outstanding performance made

him the third consecutive Bulls player to win the Harry Sunderland award and the fourth in five seasons. The result meant Bradford became the first club to complete a Super League Grand Final and Challenge Cup double.

Super League Grand Final 2003
Saturday 18 October at Old Trafford, Manchester
Bradford Bulls 25
Reardon (try), Vaikona, Withers, Hape (try), Vainikolo, Pratt, Deacon (6 goals, drop-goal), Vagana, Lowes (try), Fielden, Gartner, Peacock, Forshaw. Substitutes: Anderson, Radford, Pryce, R Paul (captain).
Wigan Warriors 12
Radlinski (try), Carney, Aspinwall, Hodgson, Dallas, O'Loughlin, Robinson, Pongia, Newton, C Smith, Cassidy, Tickle (try), Farrell (captain, 2 goals). Substitutes: P Johnson, O'Connor, Hock, M Smith. Half-time: 4-6. Referee: K Kirkpatrick (Warrington). Attendance: 65,537.

Stuart Reardon.

Graham Morris

MALCOLM REILLY (CASTLEFORD)
Lance Todd Trophy winner 1969

Malcolm Reilly.

recalled: 'Just prior to the kick-off the hairs were standing up on the back of my neck. I felt ten feet tall – it was tremendous. I was pretty fortunate to be there at such a tender age.'

Rugby League Challenge Cup Final 1969
Saturday 17 May at Wembley Stadium, London
Castleford 11
Edwards, Briggs, Howe (try), Thomas, Lowndes, Hardisty (captain, try), Hepworth (try), Hartley, Dickinson, Ward, Redfearn (goal), Lockwood, Reilly.
Salford 6
Gwilliam, Burgess, Whitehead, Hesketh, Jackson, Watkins (captain), Brennan, Ogden, Dickens, Bott, Coulman, Dixon, Hill (3 goals).
Half-time: 3-4. Referee: DS Brown (Preston).
Attendance: 97,939.

Pure genius by Castleford's Malcolm Reilly in the 53rd minute altered the course of the 1969 Challenge Cup Final against a dogged Salford. Trailing 4-3, the 21-year-old made the vital breakthrough after receiving the ball 35 yards from the Salford try line. He avoided one defender before shrugging off a Jack Brennan tackle – almost throwing him over his shoulder in the process – to race through a gap, resisting three more would-be tacklers to give a perfect pass to the supporting Alan Hardisty who raced under the posts from ten yards out. Mick Redfearn's kick made it 8-4 to the Yorkshire side and, although Salford reduced the margin with a third Ron Hill penalty, the momentum was with Castleford, adding a final try from Keith Hepworth two minutes from the end.

Reilly's Lance Todd Trophy winning performance fulfilled the pre-match prophecy of skipper Hardisty, *The Sun's* Paul Harrison noting: 'He was all over the field in an attempt to find the vital breakthrough.' Reilly himself later

---

PROFILE

Malcolm Reilly, brought up in Allerton Bywater, joined Castleford in 1967 from Kippax Welfare. One of the most outstanding loose forwards of his era, he had a reputation as a fierce competitor, but was a skilled ball distributor with good pace, capable of producing deft kicks into enemy territory, gaining winners' medals for the Challenge Cup (1969, 1970) and BBC2 Floodlit Trophy (1967/68). He played in nine Tests (all 1970, including Great Britain's tour and the World Cup), appearing for England (1970) and Yorkshire (1968) twice each. In 1971 he transferred to Manly in Australia for, a then, world record A$30,000, (£15,000 approximately), becoming a Grand Final winner in 1972 and 1973.

He returned to Castleford in late 1974 as player-coach, interrupting his comeback during 1975 to conclude his Manly obligations. Back with Castleford, he enjoyed success in the Player's No.6 Trophy (1976/77), BBC2 Floodlit Trophy (1976/77) and Yorkshire Cup (1977). Under his tenure, they captured the Challenge Cup in 1986 although not playing himself (his last match being a month earlier) and won the Yorkshire Cup again (1981 and 1986) without his on-field presence. He left in 1987, becoming Great Britain coach until 1994 (covering the 1988 and 1992 tours), combining as England coach (1992-93). He coached Leeds (1988-89) and Halifax (1993-94), moving back to Australia to take charge at Newcastle (1995-98, winning the 1997 Grand Final). Returning to England, he took over at Huddersfield (1998-99) and was later on the coaching staff at Leeds (2001-03) and Hull Kingston Rovers (2004). He received the OBE in 1991.

BEV RISMAN (LEEDS)
Harry Sunderland Trophy winner 1969

Bev Risman, kneeling, extreme left, with his Leeds colleagues before the 1969 Championship Final against Castleford, played at Odsal.

Leeds full-back Bev Risman won the Harry Sunderland Trophy after setting up a dramatic late try – and adding the conversion – in the 1969 Championship Final against Castleford on a dismal, overcast afternoon at Odsal Stadium, Bradford. In a tense, closely fought and often physical encounter that saw Castleford prop Dennis Hartley dismissed for a foul on Mick Shoebottom towards the end, it looked as though the Championship trophy was heading towards Wheldon Road for the first time. With only five minutes remaining and Leeds trailing 14-11, Castleford second-row man Mick Redfearn launched a high kick into the Headingley side's 25 area. Risman recovered the ball on the bounce and raced forward to find himself in acres of space as he covered some 30 yards in reaching the Castleford half of the field before drawing the cover and sending a perfectly placed kick towards the left corner. The ball stood up perfectly for John Atkinson who placed it some 15 yards to the left of the posts to level the score. In Phil Hodgson's book *Headingley Heroes* (2004) Risman recalled the pressure he was under to land the conversion, saying: 'I had a tendency to hook the ball across the uprights with my left foot, so the kick wasn't all that easy for me. To add to the pressure, we were due to go on holiday to Cornwall the following day. If I missed, the match would be replayed and the holiday would be off! Luckily I sneaked it over.' With no time for a tiring Castleford to respond, it secured for Leeds the second Championship in the clubs history (the first being 1960/61).

Castleford had led 11-7 at half-time, Risman, despite failing with a tricky touchline effort following a Ron Cowan try, keeping Leeds in arms reach with two penalty efforts, both after Keith Hepworth was judged guilty of illegal scrum-feeding. After the break, Risman added a third penalty, reducing the deficit to two points.

PROFILE

Bev Risman was an established England Rugby Union fly-half star when Leigh offered him a reported £6,000 contract to switch codes from Loughborough Colleges in 1961. Born in Salford, he was the son of Welsh Rugby League legend Gus Risman, and had represented England six times (1959-61) and a member of the British Lions 1959 tour of Australia and New Zealand, appearing in four of the Tests. The closest he came to honours at Leigh was as a runner-up in the 1963 Lancashire Cup Final, earning greater glory after transferring to Leeds in 1966 for £4,000, where he established himself as one of Rugby League's leading full-backs, possessing good positional awareness, a neat side-step, and the capability of always looking calm under pressure. With Leeds he won the Challenge Cup (1968), Championship (1968/69) and Yorkshire Cup (1968) gaining international recognition in the 13-a-side code by playing five times for Great Britain in 1968, including that year's World Cup competition staged Down Under when he was captain of the British squad. He retired in 1970, but has continued his involvement with the sport at various levels, and was team manager of Fulham from 1988 to 1989.

Northern Rugby League Championship Final 1969
Saturday 24 May at Odsal Stadium, Bradford
Leeds 16
Risman (4 goals), Cowan (try), Hynes, Watson, Atkinson (try), Shoebottom, Seabourne (captain), Clark, Crosby, K Eyre, Joyce, Ramsey (goal), Batten.
Substitutes: Langley, Hick.
Castleford 14
Edwards, Briggs, Howe, Thomas, Lowndes, Hardisty (captain, try, goal), Hepworth, Hartley, Dickinson (try), Ward, Redfearn (3 goals), Lockwood, Reilly.
Substitute: Fox.
Half-time: 7-11. Referee: WH Thompson (Huddersfield). Attendance: 28,442.

Bev Risman in action against Salford during Leeds' 1969 Championship semi-final win over Salford at Headingley.

When Castleford skipper Alan Hardisty intercepted a Mick Joyce pass, it looked as though it was all over but a determined, persistent Risman had other ideas and forced him to touch down in the corner providing Redfearn with a difficult kick and one that he subsequently missed. Bill Ramsey then popped over a drop-goal to bring Leeds within three points, creating the platform for Risman's match-winning finale.

The result gave Leeds their fourth major trophy of the season, Risman's four goals bringing his total for the season to 165, just one short of Lewis Jones' club record set in 1956/57.

LEROY RIVETT (LEEDS RHINOS)
Lance Todd Trophy winner 1999

Just three years after Robbie Paul achieved what so many had failed to do – score a hat-trick of tries at Wembley – Leeds Rhinos winger Leroy Rivett went one better in the 1999 Challenge Cup Final against London Broncos, his quartet including the last try at the stadium prior to it being rebuilt.

Rivett got his first in the 26th minute, Daryl Powell making a superb break 40 yards out before delivering an overhead pass that was just out of Martin Offiah's reach, Rivett cutting inside to score with John Timu wrapped around

Leroy Rivett completes his quartet of tries at Wembley in 1999 as Leeds Rhinos crush a gallant London Broncos.

a Ritchie Blackmore pass, shrugging off two defenders on a 35-yard run before placing the ball near the corner flag.

For London Broncos it was not the happiest of Challenge Cup Final debuts, losing by a record Wembley score of 52-18, despite trailing only 12-10 at half-time after taking a surprise 10-0 lead in the opening 12 minutes. They were back in front 16-12 three minutes after the resumption but it was short-lived, Leeds hitting them with seven tries. Rivett, who had never scored more than two in a match during his senior career, said afterwards: 'Last night I was dreaming about scoring a hat-trick and winning the Lance Todd Trophy. I can't believe it all came true!'

his legs. His remaining touchdowns followed the break in the 60th, 69th and 79th minute. The first resulted from a breathtaking 70-yard Ryan Sheridan run from the base of a scrum, a quick play-the-ball creating the overlap for Rivett to race over in the corner. For the next, he intercepted Karle Hammond's long pass to sprint 90 yards with five defenders in vain pursuit, completing his foursome after receiving

Rugby League Challenge Cup Final 1999
Saturday 1 May at Wembley Stadium, London
Leeds Rhinos 52
Harris (captain, try, 8 goals), Rivett (4 tries), Blackmore, Godden (try), Cummins (try), Powell, Sheridan, McDermott (try), Newton, Fleary, Morley, Farrell, Glanville. Substitutes: Jackson, Mathiou, St Hilaire (try), Hay.
London Broncos 16
Tollett, Smyth (2 goals), Fleming (try), Timu, Offiah (try), Hammond, Edwards (captain), Retchless, Beazley, Salter, Millard, Simpson (try), Gill. Substitutes: Toshack, Ryan, Callaway, Air. Half-time: 12-10. Referee: R Smith (Castleford). Attendance: 73,242.

JASON ROBINSON (WIGAN/WIGAN WARRIORS)

Lance Todd Trophy winner 1995
Harry Sunderland Trophy winner 1998

Jason Robinson.

right side of the Wigan attacking machine to send Jason Robinson on a 35-yard dash to the right corner, shaking off Francis Cummins and evading three other defenders en route. Frano Botica's goal made it 6-2, Leeds destined not to regain the lead and going in at the interval 12-4 down. Five minutes into the second half, Robinson got his second try, scooping the ball up from the acting half-back position on the halfway line to capitalise on poor covering

PROFILE

Jason Robinson signed for Wigan from Hunslet Parkside – based in his native Leeds – as a 17-year-old scrum-half in 1991, but, with half-back opportunities limited at Central Park, he built his reputation as a right-winger whose elusive running, particularly in broken play, created mayhem in opposition defences. Standing at five feet five inches and known as 'Billy Whizz', he made his first team debut in 1992, being voted Rugby League's Young Player of the Year in 1993. At Wigan he won the Championship (1992/93, 1993/94, 1994/95 and 1995/96), Super League (1998), Challenge Cup (1993 and 1995), Premiership Trophy (1994, 1995, 1996 and 1997), Regal Trophy (1992/93, 1994/95 and 1995/96), Lancashire Cup (1992) and World Club Challenge (1994). He represented Great Britain 12 times (1993-99, including the 1999 Tri-Nations series in Australasia), and England seven (1995-96, including the 1995 World Cup in which he played in the final against Australia at Wembley).

He made national headlines by joining Sale Rugby Union club in October 2000 (he had played for Bath RU during 1996/97). It led to his inclusion in the British Lions tour to Australia in 2001, followed in 2003 by his scoring England's only try in the World Cup Final victory over Australia in Sydney, subsequently receiving the MBE in 2004. He made his second Lions tour in 2005 to New Zealand and, at the time of writing, has made 38 England appearances since his 2001 debut.

Jason Robinson ably demonstrated his explosive running style when voted Lance Todd and Harry Sunderland winner in 1995 and 1998, respectively. On both occasions he engineered a try from a set-piece position that took spectators, media and – most importantly – the opposition completely by surprise.

The 1995 Challenge Cup Final brought the curtain down on Wigan's incredible run of eight consecutive Wembley wins, defeating Leeds 30-10 in a re-match of the previous year's decider. Intent on extracting revenge for that loss, Leeds took an early 2-0 lead, courtesy of a Graham Holroyd penalty. It was Robinson – in the 18th minute – that scored the first of five Wigan tries on the day, Martin Offiah popping up on the

around the play-the-ball area and burst through half a dozen defenders, who seemed rooted to the spot, for a fabulous try. It effectively killed off any hope Leeds had nurtured of a second half revival, a recharged Wigan crossing their line twice more during the next 20 minutes to build up a 30-4 lead, a late consolation try for Leeds by hooker James Lowes completing the score. For Robinson – who recovered from a broken bone in his foot in time to play – the Lance Todd success made up for the disappointment of being omitted from the 1994 Wembley line-up by the, then, coach John Dorahy. He said after the match: 'I just can't believe it. Earlier in the week I didn't think I was

A determined burst from Jason Robinson.

going to be playing but I got together with Inga (Va'aiga Tuigamala) and we've been praying all week and it just paid off.'

Three years later, Robinson took the Harry Sunderland Trophy as the outstanding player in the first Super League Grand Final, Leeds again providing the opposition. It was a desperately tight and physical contest, played on a wet, windswept evening under the Old Trafford floodlights, with the result in doubt until the

end. Leeds looked the most likely winners for much of the first half, and with the interval only two minutes away led 4-0 through a 21st minute Ritchie Blackmore try. It was then that Robinson took everyone unaware and, effectively, determined the destination of the trophy, with a brilliant solo try. In was the key moment of the evening, repeating his aforementioned Wembley ploy – except this time the distance was around 20 yards – picking up the ball from acting half-back to race through a posse of unsuspecting defenders to cross the try line. Andrew Farrell's goal gave Wigan a 6-4 half-time lead that contradicted the general run of play.

If the first half had belonged to Leeds, Robinson's try swung the pendulum for the second half. With conditions making tries difficult to come by, the only points were from two Farrell penalties, the last a minute from time. Robinson, a thorn in the side of Leeds throughout the latter half, was modest about his contribution saying: 'I just kept looking for a gap and one opened up.'

Rugby League Challenge Cup Final 1995
Saturday 29 April at Wembley Stadium, London
Wigan 30
Paul (try), Robinson (2 tries), Tuigamala (try), Connolly, Offiah, Botica (5 goals), Edwards (captain), Skerrett, Hall (try), Cowie, Betts, Cassidy, Clarke. Substitutes: Atcheson, Farrell.
Leeds 10
Tait, Fallon, Iro, Innes, Cummins, Schofield, Holroyd (3 goals), Howard, Lowes (try), Faimalo, Mercer, Eyres, Hanley (captain). Substitutes: Mann, Harmon.
Half-time: 12-4. Referee: R Smith (Castleford).
Attendance: 78,550.

Super League Grand Final 1998
Saturday 24 October at Old Trafford, Manchester
Wigan Warriors 10
Radlinski, Robinson (try), Moore, Connolly, M Bell, Paul, Smith, O'Connor, McCormack, Mestrov, Gilmore, Holgate, Andrew Farrell (captain, 3 goals).
Substitutes: Cowie, Cassidy, P Johnson, Haughton.
Leeds Rhinos 4
Harris (captain), Rivett, Blackmore (try), Godden, Cummins, Powell, Sheridan, Masella, Newton, Fleary, Morley, Anthony Farrell, Glanville.
Substitutes: Mathiou, St Hilaire, Holroyd, Hay.
Half-time: 6-4. Referee: R Smith (Castleford).
Attendance: 43,553.

Graham Morris

GARRY SCHOFIELD (LEEDS)
Man of Steel Award winner 1991

Garry Schofield.

match series with Papua New Guinea during the opening leg of their trip.

Back home, he continued to impress when Great Britain won the opening Test Match 19-12 against the touring Australians at Wembley during October, watched by a British Test record attendance of 54,569, although sharing the disappointment of losing the two remaining Tests and, therefore, the series. Schofield completed his run of ten Test Matches over the year by figuring prominently in the two games

---

PROFILE

Garry Schofield was one of the most talented backs produced by the British game, a classy, ball-playing centre or stand-off, who toured the southern hemisphere with Great Britain a record four times (1984, 1988, 1990 and 1992). Born in Leeds, he was spotted by Hull, who signed him from the Hunslet-Parkside club in 1982, making his debut in 1983, eventually transferring to Leeds for £155,000 in 1987. He enjoyed a glittering international career, representing Great Britain in 46 Tests (1984-94) equalling the record of Mick Sullivan (1954-63) and being captain in the World Cup Final defeat by Australia at Wembley in 1992. He also played three times for England (1984-95) and on four occasions for Yorkshire (1985-91). He interspersed his tour commitments by journeying to Australia on four other occasions to play for Balmain (1985, 1986 and 1987) and Western Suburbs (1989).

His club honours were relatively sparse, winning the Yorkshire Cup three times; twice with Hull (1983 and 1984) and once with Leeds (1988). He was also unlucky in losing in three Challenge Cup Finals at Wembley; with Hull (1985) and Leeds (1994 and 1995). Schofield joined Huddersfield Giants in 1996, being appointed player-coach in 1997 but left during the 1998 season. In 1999, he played for both Doncaster Dragons and Bramley. He was awarded the OBE in 1994.

The 1991 Man of Steel Award went to the Leeds Player of the Year Garry Schofield after a season in which he had stood out at international level. He had preceded the 1990/91 British season by being the outstanding player on the 1990 Lions tour of New Zealand and Papua New Guinea as vice-captain to Warrington loose forward Mike Gregory. Moving to stand-off from his more accustomed role in the centre he inspired a depleted touring team – ravaged by pre-tour injury withdrawals and suffering further injury setbacks during the tour itself – to a 2-1 Test series win in New Zealand, being voted man of the match in each of them. The success over the Kiwis helped heal the shock – for Schofield and his colleagues – of unexpectedly sharing the two

against France, which were won 45-10 (Schofield scoring two tries and a drop-goal) in Perpignan during January and 60-4 (three tries in a record win over the French) at Headingley, a month later. His new aggregate of 31 Test appearances also placed him joint third (with

Man of Steel for 1991, Garry Schofield (extreme left), lines up with the evenings other category winners following the presentations at the Holiday Inn Crowne Plaza Midland in Manchester. Other recipients (from third left, going to the right) are Wigan coach John Monie, Denis Betts (Wigan), Jonathan Davies (Widnes) and referee John Holdsworth.

Billy Boston), at that time, on Great Britain's all-time list, behind Mick Sullivan and Ellery Hanley. It was hardly a surprise when he also received the Ernest Ward Memorial Trophy as Great Britain's outstanding player of the year.

Stones Bitter Man of Steel Awards 1991
Thursday 9 May at the Holiday Inn Crowne Plaza Midland, Manchester
Compered by Harry Gration
Man of Steel: Garry Schofield (Leeds).
First Division Player of the Year: Jonathan Davies (Widnes).
Second Division Player of the Year: Tawera Nikau (Ryedale-York).
Young Player of the Year: Denis Betts (Wigan).
Coach of the Year: John Monie (Wigan).
Referee of the Year: John Holdsworth (Kippax).

The Great Britain and Australia teams as printed in the official programme for the Second Test at Old Trafford on 10 November 1990, with Garry Schofield at stand-off for the host country.

PAUL SCULTHORPE (ST HELENS)
Man of Steel Award winner 2001 and 2002

St Helens loose forward and stand-off half Paul Sculthorpe is the only player, to date, to retain the Man of Steel Award, winning in 2001 and 2002, confirmation of his consistent performance in one of the toughest of all team sports.

In 2001, he was the stand-out player in a year when he was also voted the Super League Players' Player of the Year. He gave an early indication of what he had in store, dropping a

=== PROFILE ===

Paul Sculthorpe has developed into one of the most talented, ball playing loose forwards produced by British Rugby League, a born leader, who demonstrates ultimate skill in every aspect of his play. His pace and eye for an opening have also seen him utilised on many occasions at stand-off for club and country. Born in Oldham, he signed for Warrington from the Waterhead amateur club in 1994, making his debut the following year. Whilst with Warrington he was selected for the Great Britain tour of the Southern Hemisphere in 1996 whilst still only 18 years old, celebrating his 19th birthday whilst on tour. St Helens paid Warrington a reported £300,000 (plus a player-exchange) for him in December 1997. Since moving to Knowsley Road, Sculthorpe has enjoyed an honour-laden career in Saints colours, winning the Super League Grand Final (1999, 2000 and 2002), Challenge Cup (2001 and 2004, being runner-up in 2002) and World Club Challenge (2001). To date, he has appeared in 25 Test Matches (1996-2004), played for England four times (1996-2001, including one match in the 2000 World Cup) and represented Lancashire on three occasions (2001-02).

Sculthorpe was also prominent in the Test series with Australia during November, giving a superb man of the match performance at stand-off in the opener at Huddersfield's McAlpine Stadium, registering two tries – including the match-clincher – and two drop-goal in Great

Paul Sculthorpe.

crucial goal in the first competitive match of the season in January; the World Club Challenge as Brisbane Broncos were dramatically beaten 20-18 at Bolton's Reebok Stadium. During the campaign, he augmented that drop-goal with 27 tries and 82 goals (273 points) in 31 appearances for St Helens that year. The Saints went on to win the Challenge Cup in April, defeating Bradford Bulls 13-6 at Twickenham although unable to retain their Super League title, going down to Wigan Warriors in the Final Eliminator after finishing fourth in the table.

Britain's sensational 20-12 win. As so often happens, the Kangaroos took the next two legs to retain the Ashes. Sculthorpe played further representative rugby during the season, crossing the whitewash for a touchdown as Lancashire beat Yorkshire 36-24 at Headingley in June, and scoring three tries for England in defeating Wales 42-33 at Wrexham the following month. Normally associated with the loose forward berth, his combined total of 36 matches (31 for

St Helens, three for Great Britain, one each for England and Lancashire) included just 13 in that position, appearing 21 times at stand-off, plus one each at scrum half and second row.

His excellent form continued into 2002, his 297 points (17 tries, 114 goals and a drop-goal) in 33 appearances, helping the Saints reach the finals of the Challenge Cup and Super League play-offs. The former, played at Murrayfield during April, ended in disappointment with

All-action man Paul Sculthorpe tries to escape the Wigan defence.

Wigan unexpectedly winning 21-12, although better times lay ahead for the Knowsley Road fans as the season unwound. Having secured the Minor Premiership title by heading the Super League table on scoring difference over Bradford, they went on to beat their Yorkshire rivals 19-18 in a breath-taking Grand Final at Old Trafford during October.

Sculthorpe again played a major part in the autumn Test series, this time against the visiting

New Zealanders, after missing the First Test through injury, when the Kiwis won convincingly at Ewood Park, Blackburn, by 30-16. He returned to give a stupendous man of the match showing from stand-off in the second meeting at the McAlpine Stadium where, roared on by over 23,000 fans, Britain drew the match 14-14. The result represented a giant step forward for Sculthorpe and his colleagues, anxious to rebuild pride – and confidence – following the disastrous one-off 64-10 mid-season Test defeat by Australia in July (the British party having flown to Sydney and back for the occasion). Lifted by their improved showing, Britain levelled the series with New Zealand, taking the final Test 16-10 at Wigan's JJB Stadium, Sculthorpe scoring the winning try. He also represented Lancashire in the two County of Origin games against Yorkshire, played in June, winning both; 22-18 at the JJB Stadium and 36-28 at Headingley. As with the previous season, the majority of his matches were at stand-off, his 38 appearances (33 for St Helens, three for Great Britain, two for Lancashire) included 23 in the out-half role, the rest being loose forward.

Tetley's Super League Man of Steel Awards 2001
Monday 8 October at the Crowne Plaza Midland, Manchester
Compered by Eddie Hemmings and Mike Stephenson
Man of Steel: Paul Sculthorpe (St Helens).
Super League Players' Player of the Year: Paul Sculthorpe (St Helens).
Super League Young Player of the Year: Rob Burrow (Leeds Rhinos).
Super League Coach of the Year: Ian Millward (St Helens).
Super League Referee of the Year: Russell Smith (Castleford).

Tetley's Super League Man of Steel Awards 2002
Tuesday 15 October at the Palace Hotel, Manchester
Compered by Eddie Hemmings and Mike Stephenson
Man of Steel: Paul Sculthorpe (St Helens).
Super League Players' Player of the Year: Adrian Lam (Wigan Warriors).
Super League Young Player of the Year: Richard Horne (Hull).
Super League Coach of the Year: Neil Kelly (Widnes).
Super League Referee of the Year: Russell Smith (Castleford).

KEVIN SINFIELD (LEEDS RHINOS)
Lance Todd Trophy winner 2005

━━ PROFILE ━━

Kevin Sinfield signed for Leeds Rhinos in 1997 making his senior team debut the same year. Appointed captain in 2003 whilst still only 22, he has consistently demonstrated maturity and leadership beyond his years, being a gifted ball-player and motivator, equally at home as a stand-off or in his more usual loose-forward role. Born in Oldham and a product of his local Waterhead club, he has, to date, led Leeds in three major finals, winning the Super League Grand Final of 2004 but losing the Challenge Cup deciders of 2003 and 2005. He also steered Leeds to success in the 2005 World Club Challenge, against Canterbury Bulldogs at Elland Road. His representative honours, so far, include nine appearances for Great Britain (2001-03), and four each for England (2000-01 including the 2000 World Cup) and Lancashire (2001-03).

Leeds Rhinos' skipper Kevin Sinfield took the Lance Todd Trophy in 2005 after an incident packed Challenge Cup Final at Cardiff's Millennium Stadium against Hull. When the votes were collected ten minutes from time, it looked odds-on he would enjoy a double celebration by lifting the Challenge Cup as Leeds were in the ascendancy having turned a 19-12 deficit into a 24-19 lead. In one of the competitions most dramatic conclusions, however, Paul Cooke's 77th minute try, converted by Danny Brough, gave Hull a 25-24 triumph despite Sinfield's last minute attempt to draw level with a 25-yard drop-goal that was blocked by Richard Swain.

Looking like Rambo for three-quarters of the match, courtesy of a blood-stained headband that covered a gash above the eye and a cut left ear, there was no denying Sinfield's contribution to a memorable occasion, being influential in Leeds' opening two tries. The first, in the 12th minute, resulted from his high kick into the in-goal area that created uncertainty in the defense, the video referee awarding a penalty-try to Mark Calderwood after Hull's Gareth Raynor prevented the touchdown by tugging at his jersey. Leeds' second, in the 50th minute, came when Sinfield raced between two defenders to send the supporting Danny Ward crashing over. Sinfield's goal – he converted all four Leeds tries – tied the scores at 12-12.

Sinfield, whose 16 votes doubled that of the next candidate, was diplomatic in his post-match interview, saying: 'To win the Lance Todd Trophy is a huge honour. I'm sure in a few days time I'll be suitably over the moon about it.'

Rugby League Challenge Cup Final 2005
Saturday 27 August at The Millennium Stadium, Cardiff
Hull 25
Blacklock, Tony (try), Whiting (try), Yeaman, Raynor (try), R Horne, Brough (4 goals, drop-goal), Dowes, Swain (captain), Carvell, McMenemey, Kearney, Cooke (try). Substitutes: Thackray, King, Saxton, Chester.
Leeds Rhinos 24
Mathers, Calderwood (2 tries), Walker, Senior, Bai (try), Sinfield (captain, 4 goals), Burrow, Bailey, Diskin, Ward (try), Lauitiiti, McKenna, Ellis. Substitutes: McGuire, Dunemann, Poching, Jones-Buchanan.
Half-time: 6-6. Referee: S Ganson (St Helens).
Attendance: 74,213.

Kevin Sinfield – battling through the 2005 Challenge Cup final.

MICK STEPHENSON (DEWSBURY)
Harry Sunderland Trophy winner 1973

Mick Stephenson.

others, as Dewsbury set about winning the only peacetime Championship of its history.

His first touchdown, after ten minutes play, came just after Terry Clawson had put Leeds ahead with a penalty, Nigel Stephenson – no relation – adding the conversion, an Allan Agar try nine minutes before the break helping establish an encouraging 12-4 interval lead. Stephenson filled Odsal Stadium with the expectation of an upset when he got his second try four minutes after the restart, his namesake adding the extras for a surprise 17-4 lead. Leeds – down to 12 men after the sending off of skipper Alan Hardisty in the 28th minute – came back with three tries, none of which were augmented, Nigel Stephenson having better luck when converting his own try in the 58th minute for a personal haul of 13 points, establishing new seasonal Dewsbury records for goals and points in the process.

The last Championship Final held – the format changed the following season with the reintroduction of two divisions – Dewsbury finished eighth in the League table, their end of season surge thrusting several players into the

Dewsbury captain and hooker Mick (aka Mike) Stephenson deservedly won the 1973 Harry Sunderland Trophy after a scintillating display in a shock 22-13 Championship Final win over Leeds. Stephenson gave an inspirational non-stop performance, his precision passes steering his pack forward with relentless passion against the Leeds six. The talented rake also gave his team a huge psychological lift in registering the opening try of each half, as well as having a hand in the two

Mick Stephenson scores his second try of the 1973 Championship Final against Leeds, placing Dewsbury firmly in command.

spotlight. Commenting on the victory, Stephenson said: 'We didn't want to beat 12 men. I think we had shown we had the beating of Leeds in any case.' Leeds prop Clawson wrote in his acclaimed biography, *All the Wrong Moves*, that 'His (Stephenson's) play in the 1972 World Cup in France and the 1973 Championship Final for Dewsbury at Odsal was the best I've ever witnessed from a hooker.' Sadly for Dewsbury, the Championship decider was to be Stephenson's farewell appearance, accepting an offer to join Australian club Penrith two months later.

Northern Rugby League Championship Final 1973
Saturday 19 May at Odsal Stadium, Bradford
Dewsbury 22
Rushton, Ashcroft, Clark, N Stephenson (try, 5 goals), Day, Agar (try), A Bates, Beverley, M Stephenson (captain, 2 tries), Lowe, Grayshon, J Bates, Whittington. Substitute: Taylor.
Leeds 13
Holmes, A Smith, Hynes (goal), Dyl (try), Atkinson, Hardisty (captain), Hepworth, Clawson (goal), Fisher, Clarkson, Cookson (try), Eccles (try), Haigh. Substitutes: Langley, Ward.
Half-time: 12-4. Referee: HG Hunt (Prestbury).
Attendance: 18,889.

The Dewsbury team in 1973 with captain Mick Stephenson, seated, behind the ball.

JEFF STEVENSON (LEEDS)
Lance Todd Trophy winner 1957

Jeff Stevenson.

Jeff Stevenson proudly claims: 'I was the first one, in 1957, to receive the Lance Todd Trophy', referring to the fact that, from that year, the Salford Red Devils Association provided a perpetual trophy for formal presentation at the Associations annual dinner, a tradition that continues to this day. Certainly, Stevenson deserves his place in Rugby League history after his storming display in a 9-7 Challenge Cup Final win over Barrow in an exciting contest in which the Shipbuilders, who tended to make a lot of handling errors during the match, staged a second half revival.

Stevenson appeared to be involved in every attacking move in the first half, Leeds always having the upper hand. The industrious scrum-half was responsible for doubling his side's 3-0 interval lead in the opening minute of the resumption. Bringing the ball away from a scrum, he ignored his stand-off Jack Lendill in a planned move that saw Leeds' two centres, Welsh 'Golden Boy' Lewis Jones and team captain and Australian Keith McLellan running

across the back of the scrum in opposite directions. A confused Barrow defence looked on as Jones received a perfect pass from Stevenson before sending 18-year-old Del Hodgkinson flying in for an unconverted try. From that moment, however, rather than crumble as expected, Barrow fought a terrific rearguard action. Willie Horne reduced the deficit with a penalty before Leeds added a third try, ironically after Barrow's 1955 Lance Todd winner, Jack Grundy, had thrown out an untypical wild pass near his own line which was eagerly seized on by Don Robinson for an unopposed try. Despite that devastating setback, Barrow refused to capitulate, and came back with a try from Phil Jackson, goaled by Horne, but it was not enough.

Through it all, the diminutive Stevenson – whose breathtaking late 35-yard drop-goal had steered Leeds passed surprise packet Whitehaven 10-9 in the semi-final at Odsal – had been superb. One journalist, referring to his Lance Todd success, noted: 'Stevenson won it because he continued to be in every Leeds attack and at nearly every danger point in defence, as he had been from the start.'

Wembley 1957. Jeff Stevenson plays the ball back to Leeds prop Joe Anderson during the Challenge Cup Final against Barrow.

The Leeds line-up for 1957 with Jeff Stevenson, kneeling, second left.

Stevenson recalled: 'I was sat in the bus with the (players) wives waiting for all the lads to come from the dressing room. Somebody popped his head through the door and said "Stevie, you've won the Lance Todd Trophy" A great thrill!'

Rugby League Challenge Cup Final 1957
Saturday 11 May at Wembley Stadium, London
Leeds 9
Quinn (try), Hodgkinson (try), McLellan (captain), Jones, Broughton, Lendill, Stevenson, Anderson, Prior, Hopper, Poole, Robinson (try), Street.
Barrow 7
Ball, Lewthwaite, Jackson (try), Rea, Castle, Horne (captain, 2 goals), Harris, Woosey, Redhead, Parker, Grundy, Wilson, Healey.
Half-time: 3-0. Referee: CF Appleton (Warrington).
Attendance: 76,318.

A 1955 caricature of Jeff Stevenson by 'Adams' as featured in the Rugby League Gazette.

=== PROFILE ===

Former local schoolboy prodigy Jeff Stevenson joined Leeds in 1952 having represented the Royal Air Force in an inter-services Rugby Union fixture against the Royal Navy at Twickenham the same year. Standing five feet, six inches and weighing just over nine stone, he was an extremely fast and elusive scrum-half who soon rose to prominence, playing 20 times for Great Britain (1955-60), being captain on four occasions, and appearing in the 1957 World Cup in Australia. Having won the Challenge Cup (1957) and Yorkshire Cup (1958) with Leeds, he transferred to York for £7,750 in 1959, moving on to Hunslet for £6,000 in 1962 where he won the Yorkshire Cup (1962) and Second Division Championship (1962/63). He played 12 times for Yorkshire (1955-61).

BILLY STOTT (WAKEFIELD TRINITY)
Lance Todd Trophy winner 1946

Billy Stott receives the ball with which he kicked his last minute goal in the 1946 Challenge Cup Final during a presentation at Belle Vue speedway stadium during August that year. Handed over by Rugby League journalist Jimmy Breen on behalf of Stott's former club Broughton Rangers, it was autographed by both finalists and mounted on a plinth with the inscription: 'Presented to Billy Stott, the hero of the match, by his colleagues at Belle Vue Gardens, Manchester.'

Wakefield Trinity skipper Billy Stott was the difference between triumph and despair when he became the first recipient of the Lance Todd award in 1946, his 79th minute goal snatching Wembley victory from the jaws of defeat. In fact, Stott's kick – 10 yards in from the touchline and just inside the Wigan 25 yard area – was possibly not the most difficult he had ever attempted, but it was certainly a pressure kick. He had missed from a similar position minutes earlier in a Challenge Cup Final that had seen seven tries scored and none converted.

The first post-war Wembley final marked the debut of the Lance Todd Trophy.

It was not his only contribution to an exciting afternoon, a *Yorkshire Post* hack describing him as 'a rallying force when things were not going well.' Having conceded early first half tries to Wigan's Jack Blan and Brian Nordgren, it was the inspirational centre that brought Trinity back into the picture. His first chance came after he intercepted a pass but failed to beat the last man, making amends with a telling break when he was also on hand to accept a return pass from winger Ron Rylance to power through three defenders and score in the corner. He missed the conversion but his penalty goal five minutes before the break meant Trinity returned to their changing room trailing only 5-6.

Wigan drew first blood in the second half when Stan Jolley raced 70 yards after recovering Stott's dropped pass, the latter compensating for his error with his second touchdown seven minutes later, which left Wigan 9-8 ahead with just over 20 minutes remaining on the clock. A try each followed before Wigan were penalised for obstruction, setting the stage for Stott's late dramatic winner giving Trinity the verdict by 13-12.

A Wakefield official claimed the foundations for their narrow win were laid the previous day when Stott – who received six of the seven votes cast – had some brief goal-kicking practice inside the stadium, saying 'kicking can

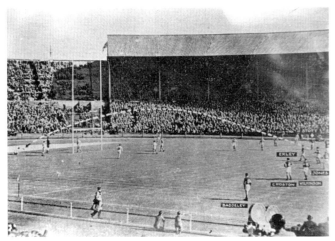

A postcard tracking Billy Stott's late Wembley winner in 1946.

PROFILE

Billy Stott began his career as a stand-off with his local team Featherstone Rovers in 1930, eventually moving into the centre. He transferred to Salford-based Broughton Rangers for a 'substantial fee' in 1933, playing one match for England (1936) and seven for Yorkshire (1933-38) during his time there. His next move was to Oldham for £800 in 1939, Wakefield Trinity picking him up for just £95 in 1944. At five feet seven inches and 13 stone, he was by then a stocky looking player who, whilst lacking the pace of earlier years, provided experience and leadership to Wakefield in the early post-war years. He won the Challenge Cup (1946) and Yorkshire Cup (1947) with Wakefield before retiring in 1948 and taking over as club coach.

be tricky at Wembley when the wind blows into the bowl in extra-ordinary fashion at times.' The 33-year-old Stott was one of six Wakefield players in their Wembley line-up on the wrong side of thirty, a legacy of the Second World War, which had made the development of young talent virtually impossible during the preceding six years.

Rugby League Challenge Cup Final 1946
Saturday 4 May at Wembley Stadium, London
Wakefield Trinity 13
Teall, Rylance, Stott (captain, 2 tries, 2 goals), Croston (try), Badderley, Jones, Goodfellow, Wilkinson, Marson, Higgins, Exley, Howes, Bratley.
Wigan 12
Cunliffe, Nordgren (try), Ratcliffe, Ashcroft, Jolley (try), Lowry, Bradshaw, Banks, J Blan (2 tries), Barton, Atkinson, Watkins (captain), B Blan.
Half-time: 5-6. Referee: A Hill (Leeds). Attendance: 54,730.

Wakefield Trinity captain Billy Stott is chaired around Wembley in triumph by his euphoric side after their last-gasp win over Wigan.

175

ALAN TAIT (WIDNES)
Harry Sunderland Trophy winner 1989 and 1990

Scottish full-back Alan Tait was the first player to win the Harry Sunderland Trophy twice, a feat he achieved in consecutive Premiership Trophy Finals as his club Widnes defeated Hull 18-10 in 1989 and Bradford Northern 28-6 in 1990. On both occasions he was a clear winner of the award, catching the attention of voters with his ability to run the ball out of defensive situations with style and pace, providing a valuable extra three-quarter when the opportunity arose.

Alan Tait.

In the 1989 decider, one such foray led to Widnes' vital third and last try, a minute into the second half, when he provided Martin Offiah – who drifted in from the wing – with the scoring pass after the Chemics' won a scrum on the Hull 25. Jonathan Davies' conversion placed Widnes two scores ahead, at 16-8, the only remaining

points of the match being a penalty each by Davies and Hull's Gary Pearce. Tait had come close to creating a try just before half-time, his dazzling break almost producing a try for Andy Currier who was held up on the line. Currier made amends a few minutes later running 95

PROFILE

Alan Tait was an established Scotland Rugby Union international centre with eight appearances (1987-88) behind him when he signed with Widnes from hometown club, Kelso, in 1988. Amazingly, having arrived towards the conclusion of the 1987/88 season, he gained a winners' medal in that campaign's Premiership Trophy Final in only his third match (coming off the bench for all three). He was to establish himself as an accomplished, classy full-back who provided dangerous attacking options when linking with his three-quarters. He added to his medal haul with two further successes in the Premiership Trophy (1989 and 1990) plus wins in the World Club Challenge (1989), Championship (1988/89), Regal Trophy (1991/92) and Lancashire Cup (1990). He transferred to Leeds in 1992 but was unable to add further honours although he did appear in two Challenge Cup Finals at Wembley (1994 and 1995), Leeds losing on both occasions. He was a tourist in 1990 and appeared in 14 Tests (1989-93) including the 1992 World Cup Final against Australia at Wembley. He also represented Scotland on one occasion, captaining his country against Ireland in Glasgow during 1996, as well as representing them in the 1995 Emerging Nations World Cup (which did not carry full international status). With Rugby Union accepting professionalism in its ranks, he left Leeds in 1996, returning to the 15-a-side code with Newcastle and, later, Edinburgh Reivers. He also played a further 19 times for Scotland (1997-99). His father Alan had previously played Rugby League as a centre with Workington Town from the late-1960s to the early-1970s.

yards down the flank after fielding a Hull miskick for a crucial score that put Widnes 10-8 up at the break. The win gave Widnes their second successive Championship-Premiership double, whilst, according to the *Widnes Weekly News*, Tait gave 'an assured defensive display and always caused problems for Hull when he elected to go forward.'

He was even more prominent in the 1990 decider, his enterprising support play leading to the first four Widnes tries, two of which he scored himself as they comfortably disposed of a below par Bradford, despite the 39th minute dismissal of Widnes scrum-half Paul Hulme. The first try came in the 3rd minute, loose forward Les Holliday making a midfield break that was eagerly continued by the alert Tait, returning the ball for Holliday to score between the posts. The Scot again linked up in spectacular fashion, racing between two defenders for the second in the 27th minute, adding the third just after the interval following a run out of defence by Tony Myler (introduced in a half-time reshuffle following Paul Hulme's departure). Widnes now led 14-0 as the trophy began to move out of Bradford's reach. Tait was credited with preventing Bradford from scoring on a half-dozen occasions during the course of the match, none more vital than when he hauled down Ian Wilkinson who had beaten seven defenders on an incredible run amidst increased second half pressure from the Yorkshire side. Bradford eventually breached the Widnes defence with a Tony Marchant try before Currier rounded off a good days work for Widnes with two further scores, the first of

which was set-up by Tait after he again surged out of defence, Widnes claiming their sixth Premiership win from seven finals.

Premiership Trophy Final 1989
Sunday 14 May at Old Trafford, Manchester
Widnes 18
Tait, Davies (3 goals), Currier (try), Wright (try), Offiah (try), D Hulme, P Hulme, Sorenson (captain), McKenzie, Grima, M O'Neill, Koloto, R Eyres. Substitutes: Myler, Pyke.
Hull 10
Fletcher, Eastwood, Blacker, Price, O'Hara (captain), Pearce (3 goals), Windley, Dannatt, Jackson, S Crooks, Welham (try), Sharp, Divorty. Substitutes: Nolan, Wilby.
Half-time: 10-8. Referee: J Holdsworth (Kippax). Attendance: 40,194.

Premiership Trophy Final 1990
Sunday 13 May at Old Trafford, Manchester
Widnes 28
Tait (2 tries), Davies (4 goals), Currier (2 tries), Wright, Offiah, D Hulme, P Hulme, Sorenson (captain), McKenzie, M O'Neill, Koloto, R Eyres, Holliday (try). Substitutes: Myler, Grima.
Bradford Northern 6
Wilkinson, Cordle, McGowan, Marchant (try), Francis, Simpson, Harkin, Skerrett, Noble, Hobbs (captain), Medley, Fairbank, Mumby (goal). Substitutes: Cooper, Richards.
Half-time: 10-0. Referee: C Morris (Huddersfield). Attendance: 40,796.

Rugby League Writers' Association annual dinner 1990. Alan Tait (with Harry Sunderland Trophy), sharing the stage with Widnes team mate Jonathan Davies, left (Jack Bentley Trophy), and Oldham's Mike Ford (Tom Bergin Trophy).

REES THOMAS (WIGAN)
Lance Todd Trophy winner 1958

Rees Thomas.

Welsh scrum-half Rees Thomas turned into the surprise hero of Wigan's star-studded outfit in their exciting 13-9 Challenge Cup Final win over Workington Town in 1958. Workington, making their third visit to Wembley in six years proved a tough nut to crack but, ably led by props John Barton and Brian McTigue, Wigan's pack gained the ascendancy allowing the tough five feet six inch Thomas to control operations in the middle of the field.

Having scored a try apiece, the industrious Thomas had a touchdown disallowed with the scores locked at 5-5 after referee Ron Gelder ruled a forward pass had taken place. Wigan's second try did eventually come, however, Thomas taking full advantage of a gap created by Terry O'Grady and Jack Cunliffe to jink passed

three defenders and send Barton crashing over, Wigan leading 10-7 at the break. Thomas continued to run the show in the second half, McTigue grabbing Wigan's third and final try, whilst Norman Cherrington pulled off a late try saving tackle on Workington's ever threatening winger Ike Southward.

The esteemed *Daily Express* writer Jack Bentley suggested that Thomas had 'served up probably the best performance of his career' whilst *The Wigan Examiner* said: 'Thomas was here, there and everywhere and, at the end of the game, he was first to go racing off the pitch because of the wonderful feeling inside that this had been his day.' An excited Thomas, who received a majority vote, said: 'I never expected the Lance Todd Trophy, an appearance at Wembley and a winners' medal all in one day. It has really shaken me!'

Rugby League Challenge Cup Final 1958
Saturday 10 May at Wembley Stadium, London
Wigan 13
Cunliffe (2 goals), O'Grady, Ashton (captain), Boston, Sullivan (try), Bolton, Thomas, Barton (try), Sayer, McTigue (try), Cherrington, Collier, McGurrin.
Workington Town 9
McAvoy, Southward (try, 3 goals), O'Neil, Leatherbarrow, Wookey, Archer, Roper (captain), Herbert, Eden, Key, Edgar, Thompson, Eve.
Half-time: 10-7. Referee: R Gelder (Wakefield).
Attendance: 66,109.

PROFILE

Originally from Maesteg, Rees Thomas signed for Swinton in 1949 from Devonport Services Rugby Union club, transferring to Wigan in 1956. Although not considered a spectacular performer, the Welsh scrum-half was certainly a powerful on-field presence and a handful for the opposition. After appearing in Wigan's Challenge Cup Final victories of 1958 and 1959, he returned, in 1959, to Swinton on a free transfer, playing his last match during 1960. He joined Swinton's coaching staff, being head coach from 1972 to 1974. In 1955, he appeared for a Wales XIII against France 'B' for his only representative honour in Rugby League.

DAVID TOPLISS (WAKEFIELD TRINITY)
Lance Todd Trophy winner 1979

=== PROFILE ===

David Topliss was a stand-off half with exceptional speed and side-stepping ability. Born in Wakefield, he signed for Wakefield Trinity in 1968 from Normanton, and having been captain of the Trinity side that lost at Wembley in 1979, joined Hull in 1981 for £15,000. With Hull, he appeared twice more in Wembley Challenge Cup Finals, both times as captain, drawing in 1982 (winning the replay against Widnes), and losing in 1983. He also won the Championship (1982/83) and Yorkshire Cup (1982, 1983). He moved to Oldham in 1985, rejoining Wakefield as player-coach in 1987, continuing as coach until 1994 (his playing career ending in 1988). A Great Britain tourist in 1979, he was also in the 1972 World Cup squad in France, although not playing. He appeared in four Tests for Britain (1973-82), played twice for England (1975) and five times for Yorkshire (1971-80). He had two spells in Australia with Penrith (1976) and Balmain (1977).

Wakefield Trinity captain and stand-off David Topliss fulfilled an ambition when he led his side out at Wembley in 1979 as Trinity's longest serving player after over ten years with the club. The experience left Topliss with mixed sentiments, his team going down 12-3 in an uninspiring final where all the points came after the interval but ending the day as Trinity's fifth Lance Todd Trophy winner. Topliss recalled: 'It was a funny emotion really. We had lost the Challenge Cup to Widnes and somebody told me as I was walking down the steps at Wembley with my losers' medal "You've won the Lance Todd" which at that time was little consolation, but now I treasure it.'

The classy Topliss was one of the few players to rise to the occasion as he fought in vain to bring the cup back to Yorkshire. Widnes had taken a 49th minute 2-0 lead through Mick Burke's penalty before Topliss came close to scoring the first try of the match after being sent on a blistering run by second-row forward Bill Ashurst. It was the quick reaction of Widnes forward Mick Adams that saved his line, producing a desperate try saving tackle on Topliss. Even after the lead extended to 8-0 Wakefield continued to move the ball, Topliss providing inspiration with his quicksilver runs. Eventually Andrew Fletcher crossed the Widnes try line in the right corner but it was merely a consolation as Widnes held on to take the glory.

Rugby League Challenge Cup Final 1979
Saturday 5 May at Wembley Stadium, London
Widnes 12
Eckersley (drop-goal), Wright (try), Aspey, George, Burke (2 goals), Hughes (try), Bowden (captain), Mills, Elwell (drop-goal), Shaw, Adams, Dearden, Laughton. Substitutes: M O'Neill, Hull.
Wakefield Trinity 3
Sheard, Fletcher (try), Smith, Diamond, Juliff, Topliss (captain), Lampkowski, Burke, McCurrie, Skerrett, Ashurst, Keith Rayne, Idle.
Half-time: 0-0. Referee: JE Jackson (Pudsey).
Attendance: 94,218.

David Topliss, right, prepares to give chase to Widnes stand-off Eric Hughes in the 1979 Challenge Cup Final.

ADRIAN VOWLES (CASTLEFORD TIGERS)
Man of Steel Award winner 1999

Castleford Tigers captain Adrian Vowles became the second Australian winner of the Man of Steel in 1999, his Yorkshire side having enjoyed a magnificent Super League season. The 28-year-old, dubbed 'Mr Indestructible' by Tigers coach Stuart Raper, motivated and enthusing his colleagues, who responded with a 'never-say-die' approach to every game.

This attitude was evident in a thrilling Challenge Cup semi-final with London Broncos in late March. Behind 21-20 in an energy-sapping contest, Castleford looked down and out with ten minutes left before a determined Vowles dragged them back with his 'over-the-shoulder' pass, seized by Michael Eager for a dramatic try, Danny Orr's goal making it 26-21.

Adrian Vowles.

Wembley loomed but, somehow, a gritty London outfit broke Castleford hearts in the closing minutes, the sides exchanging points in a climax reminiscent of an adventure comic to win 33-27.

Such an early season set-back could have seen heads drop, but with Vowles that was not an option, the team finishing a gutsy fifth in the Super League table squeezing into the play-offs behind the so-called 'Big Four' of Bradford Bulls, Leeds Rhinos, St Helens and Wigan Warriors. Despite the disadvantage of facing sudden-death eliminators away from home, Castleford travelled to Wigan and Leeds, disposing of both (24-10 and 23-16 respectively) to earn a place in the Final Eliminator. The fact that Castleford went down 36-6 to eventual Super League winners St Helens could not detract from a magnificent season for Vowles and his gallant side who had brought a 'breath of air' to the campaign.

JJB Super League Man of Steel Awards 1999
Wednesday 6 October at the Crowne Plaza Midland, Manchester
Compered by Eddie Hemmings and Mike Stephenson
Man of Steel: Adrian Vowles (Castleford).
Super League Players' Player of the Year: Sean Long (St Helens).
Super League Young Player of the Year: Leon Pryce (Bradford Bulls).
Super League Coach of the Year: Matthew Elliott (Bradford Bulls).
Super League Referee of the Year: Stuart Cummings (Widnes).

=== PROFILE ===

Australian Adrian Vowles was unknown in Britain when he signed with Castleford Tigers in 1997. Normally a centre or stand-off, he was not an instant success, being considered slow, his fortunes rising when he moved to loose forward. Although not the biggest of back-row forwards his intelligent, probing play and total commitment led to him being appointed team captain, leading the Tigers to the Super League play-offs in 1999 and 2000. Leeds Rhinos claimed his signature towards the end of 2001, Vowles making his debut in 2002, but moving to Wakefield Trinity Wildcats during August of that year as player-coach, working alongside Shane McNally. After 12 months at Wakefield he returned to Castleford on a short-term deal, playing three times for the Tigers during September 2003. Born in Cunnamulla, Queensland, he played for the Charleville club, moving to the Premiership with Gold Coast Seagulls (1993-94) and North Queensland Cowboys (1995-96). He appeared once for Queensland (1994) and, whilst in Britain, represented Scotland (via the ancestor ruling) four times (2000-01, including the 2000 World Cup). After playing with Burleigh Bears in the Queensland League he made a surprise return to Castleford at the end of 2005.

DAVID WARD (LEEDS)
Man of Steel Award winner 1977

David Ward – the first ever Man of Steel seen with his winners cheque.

Leeds hooker David Ward made Rugby League history in 1977 when he was voted Man of Steel at the climax of the inaugural awards ceremony held at the Golden Garter Theatre Club in Wythenshawe, Manchester during May. For the initial event it had been decided that the title would be bestowed on one of the evening's five category winners, Ward – who had already been crowned the Young Player of the Year – getting the verdict.

The 1976/77 season had seen Ward triumph over adversity, his position in the Leeds team looking threatened when the campaign opened as his club tried, unsuccessfully, to recruit Featherstone Rovers rake, Keith Bridges, with a £16,000 bid. Ward soon demonstrated to Leeds that they should put their cheque book away, his form being such that he soon took over as pack leader, helping Leeds lift the Yorkshire Cup by beating Featherstone 16-12 in the final during October. He was then appointed team captain after John Holmes stepped down from the role,

his greatest moment being to lift the Challenge Cup at Wembley after overcoming Widnes 16-7, having played a significant part – as the man of the match – in defeating holders St Helens 7-2 in the semi-final at Central Park, Wigan.

His excellent displays in the Leeds jersey brought representative honours thick and fast during a dream term, with debuts for Great Britain under 24s (during November as a substitute against France), Yorkshire (February – helping them lift the County Championship) and England (March – in the European Championship – ironically replacing Bridges). He was also selected for the Great Britain 1977 World Cup squad that set off for Australia and

David Ward bringing the ball out of defence.

New Zealand at the end of the domestic season, where he subsequently made his first senior appearance for Britain.

The first Man of Steel Awards evening, held in front of an 800-plus 'full house' audience, was acclaimed by officials as a highly successful venture, creating interest and valuable publicity for the sport. Sponsored by Trumann's Steel, Ward received a cheque for £250 as the Man of Steel, in addition to his Young Player of the Year prize (£100 cheque plus a set of stainless steel goblets and tray valued at £80).

Trumanns Man of Steel Awards 1977
Wednesday 25 May at the Golden Garter Theatre
Club, Wythenshawe, Manchester
Compered by Keith Macklin
Man of Steel: David Ward (Leeds).
First Division Player of the Year: Malcolm Reilly
(Castleford).
Second Division Player of the Year: Ged Marsh
(Blackpool Borough).
Young Player of the Year: David Ward (Leeds).
Coach of the Year: Eric Ashton (St Helens).
Referee of the Year: WH (Billy) Thompson
(Huddersfield).

PROFILE

David Ward was only 23-years-old when he led Leeds to their 1977 Wembley Challenge Cup triumph, being skipper again the following year when they retained their prize. Born in Morley, he was a product of the Shaw Cross Boys Club of Dewsbury, signing with Leeds in 1971. A hard-working, tenacious hooker, he had his first experience of Wembley when Leeds lost in the 1972 final, being a non-playing substitute on the day. Other successes at Headingley include wins in the finals of the Championship (1972), Premiership Trophy (1975 and 1979), Player's No.6 Trophy (1973), John Player Trophy (1984) and Yorkshire Cup (1972, 1973, 1976, 1979 and 1980). He played 12 times for Great Britain (1977-82) and travelled to the Antipodes as a member of the 1977 World Cup squad and 1979 touring party. In addition, he represented England (1977-81) and Yorkshire (1977-82) six times each. His Leeds playing career concluded in 1986, moving into coaching with Hunslet (1986-88), Leeds (1989-91), Batley (1991-94), Featherstone Rovers (1994-97) and Batley again (1997 to 2000, also having temporary charge during 2001). His son Danny is a member of the current Leeds Rhinos squad.

A kick to safety from David Ward.

182

ERNEST WARD (BRADFORD NORTHERN)
Lance Todd Trophy winner 1949

Graham Morris

Ernest Ward.

grabbed the second and final try eight minutes from time. Northern scrum-half Donald Ward (elder brother of Ernest) and loose-forward Ken Traill combined to create an opening for second-row Trevor Foster to go under posts. Ward added the goal to cap a perfect day, accepting the Challenge Cup from the Duke of Edinburgh and becoming the third Bradford player in consecutive finals to win the Lance Todd Trophy having 'received twice as many votes as any other player nominated.' In fact, Bradford fans also owed their win to former Lance Todd

---

PROFILE

Ernest Ward joined Bradford Northern as a 16-year-old from Dewsbury Boys' Club in 1936, developing into an excellent ball-handling centre, tactician and goal-kicker, who became captain for club and country. He made 21 appearances for Great Britain (1946-52) including 20 Tests, and was a tourist in 1946 and 1950, being tour captain on the latter. He played for England 20 times (1941-52) and Yorkshire eleven (1942-52). His honours with Bradford include the Championship (1940/41 and 1944/45), Challenge Cup (1944, 1947 and 1949) and Yorkshire Cup on six occasions. He joined Castleford as player-coach in 1953 for £2,500, ending his playing career with five matches for Batley in 1956.

The stage was set for skipper Ernest Ward to sparkle when he led Bradford Northern out at Wembley for the third successive year in 1949, and he did not disappoint the new world record 95,050 crowd. The 29-year-old, six feet tall, 13 stone centre inspired his team to a comfortable 12-0 victory over a Halifax thirteen that never got going, being the first to get a 'duck' at the stadium. Ward struck with a neat, perfectly placed kick into the right hand corner after just ten minutes enabling a brave Eric Batten (he fractured his shoulder in the opening minutes and played on) to dive in for the touchdown. Ward put his side five points up with a magnificent, coolly taken touchline conversion.

On a hot, sunny afternoon, Bradford's pack dominated the opposition six although there was no further scoring until Ward added a magnificent 30-yard touchline penalty after an hour of play. Despite great defence from Halifax, the match was sealed when Bradford

recipients Willie Davies, whose acceleration at stand-off opened up Halifax several times, and prop Frank Whitcombe, his 18-stone-plus, allied to that of 15 stone second-rower Barry Tyler ensuring Bradford won the scrum contest 39-18.

Rugby League Challenge Cup Final 1949
Saturday 7 May at Wembley Stadium, London
Bradford Northern 12
Leake, Batten (try), Kitching, E Ward (captain, 3 goals), Edwards, Davies, D Ward, Whitcombe, Darlison, Greaves, Tyler, Foster (try), Traill.
Halifax 0
Chalkey, Daniels, Reid, Price (captain), MacDonald, Kenny, Kielty, Condon, Ackerley, Rothwell, Healy, Pansegrouw, Mawson.
Half-time: 5-0. Referee: GS Phillips (Widnes).
Attendance: 95,050.

FRANK WHITCOMBE (BRADFORD NORTHERN)
Lance Todd Trophy winner 1948

Frank Whitcombe.

but he was better than most and in addition to some deft touch-finding kicks he drove in effectively at close quarters and tackled well.'

Watched by His Majesty King George VI, the first reigning monarch to attend a final, holders Bradford found the star studded Wigan side difficult to resist, although the atrocious weather made certain it was a closely fought affair. Wigan led just 5-3 at half-time but came out with a determined onslaught after the break, Whitcombe standing out through his leadership of a valiant defence. It was due to the unstinting efforts of the giant Welshman that Northern turned the momentum, the reporter for *The Wigan Examiner* conceding that 'Whitcombe came into prominence with some splendidly judged kicks to touch. He did this several times when Wigan had cleared dangerous situations.' It was to no avail though with Wigan prop Frank Barton eventually grabbing the only points of the second half with a try in the final minutes following a forward rush.

When Bradford Northern prop Frank Whitcombe became the third player to win the Lance Todd award at the 1948 Challenge Cup Final, he set two records that still stand today; the oldest recipient at 29 days short of his 35th birthday, and the heaviest, weighing 18 stone, six pounds. He was also the first forward to earn the honour and the first player to win with a losing team. In a final played in miserable un-Wembley-like conditions of heavy rain and strong winds, which made ball control difficult, the *Yorkshire Post's* Alf Drewry commented that 'Whitcombe's handling was not without blemish

Wembley 1948 provided a second post-war appearance for both participants.

PROFILE

One of the heaviest props of his day, packing well over 18 stone into his five feet ten inch height, Frank Whitcombe was a fearsome presence on the field and a massive influence in the scrum. He signed for Broughton Rangers in 1935, the club having bought him out of the army, who he had represented earlier that year against the Royal Air Force at Rugby Union. Born in Cardiff, he had been playing in the 15-a-side code for the Royal Engineers whilst in the services. In 1938, he transferred to Bradford Northern, where he won the Championship (1939/40, 1940/41 and 1944/45), Challenge Cup (1944, 1947 and 1949) and Yorkshire Cup four times. He was a Great Britain tourist in 1946 during which he made two Test appearances against Australia and also played 14 times for Wales (1938-48). He retired in 1949, later becoming a director at Bradford.

Frank Whitcombe, second from right, waits in line to be presented to His Majesty King George VI before the 1948 Challenge Cup Final.

The *News Chronicle* reported: 'Wigan, determined not to be deceived a second time (Bradford had defeated them 15-3 at Central Park in a Championship play-off a week earlier), cleverly devised the ways and means to prevent a repetition. One who never faltered was Whitcombe, heaviest and most prominent player on the side.' Meanwhile, the *Yorkshire Post* informs us that 'he (Whitcombe) had an emphatic majority over Ryan (Wigan) and Bradshaw (Wigan) and Northern captain Ernest Ward in the votes cast.'

Rugby League Challenge Cup Final 1948
Saturday 1 May at Wembley Stadium, London
Wigan 8
Ryan, Ratcliffe, T Ward (goal), Ashcroft, Hilton (try), Mountford, Bradshaw, Gee, Egan (captain), Barton (try), White, B Blan, Hudson.
Bradford Northern 3
Leake, Batten, Case, E Ward (captain), Edwards (try), Davies, D Ward, Whitcombe, Darlison, Smith, Tyler, Foster, Traill.
Half-time: 5-3. Referee: GS Phillips (Widnes).
Attendance: 91,465.

Frank Whitcombe (dark jersey, centre of picture) gets the ball away for Wales against England at Swinton in 1946.

DEREK WHITEHEAD (WARRINGTON)
Lance Todd Trophy winner 1974

Derek Whitehead.

The accuracy of Warrington full-back Derek Whitehead's right foot was the difference between success and failure in an unspectacular 1974 Challenge Cup Final victory over holders Featherstone Rovers. In a match littered with stoppages and regular on-field visits from the respective trainers as they patched up the wounded, only three tries – Warrington getting two of them – troubled the scoreboard in the 24-9 score-line. In fact, of Whitehead's seven goals, six were for penalty offences, the penalty count finishing 13-10 in Featherstone's favour. 'It was a hard game' recalls Whitehead, who added 'It was the forwards that had to get on top and I just kept kicking the goals. As luck happens, they went over and it kept us in the game. We had a free kick early on and I took a kick at goal and I think it went about two foot off the floor until it got more or less to the crossbar and then it went up and over and I thought from then on I can't do nothing wrong!'

With Featherstone getting on top towards half-time and scoring the opening try through their skipper John Newlove in the 40th minute, it was Whitehead, with his orthodox, straight run-up style of kicking, that pegged the deficit to a respectable 9-8 at the interval through his four goals, including a huge kick from the half-way line. Warrington fans could also be grateful to his marksmanship after the break, as his side nudged its way ahead 17-9 after 56 minutes, through his conversion of Kevin Ashcroft's try and two more penalties. It proved an unassailable lead for Rovers, Whitehead's coolness winning him the Lance Todd Trophy, although it was not an award he had anticipated, saying: 'One of the players told me he saw it flashing up on the scoreboard – I never had a clue! You don't think about it – all you think about is winning the cup for the supporters.' Ironically, having given such an immaculate display, he missed his ninth, and easiest, effort, failing to convert Mike Nicholas's late try, falling short of the eight needed to equal Cyril Kellett's one-year-old Wembley record.

Derek Whitehead propels another shot towards the goal posts during the 1974 Challenge Cup Final.

PROFILE

Derek Whitehead commenced his professional career with his local club Swinton from Folly Lane Juniors in 1961, transferring to Oldham for £4,000 in 1968, thence to Warrington for a similar fee in 1969. A wonderful attacking full-back who possessed a glorious side-step, he was an excellent fielder of the ball and outstanding goal-kicker. His final appearance for Warrington was in 1979, having won the Challenge Cup (1974, making a second Wembley appearance in 1975 as a runner-up), Club Championship (1974), Player's No.6 Trophy (1973/74) and Captain Morgan Trophy (1973/74). He represented Great Britain on three occasions (all 1971) and Lancashire six times (1968-74).

Rugby League Challenge Cup Final 1974
Saturday 11 May at Wembley Stadium, London
Warrington 24
Whitehead (7 goals), M Philbin, Noonan, Whittle, Bevan, Murphy (captain, 2 goals), Gordon, D Chisnall, Ashcroft (try), Brady, Wright, Nicholas (try), B Philbin. Substitutes: Pickup, Wanbon.
Featherstone Rovers 9
Box (3 goals), Dyas, Smith, Hartley, Bray, Newlove (captain, try), Nash, Tonks, Bridges, Harris, Thompson, Rhodes, Bell. Substitutes: Busfield, Stone.
Half-time: 8-9. Referee: S Shepherd (Oldham).
Attendance: 77,400.

Handshakes all around as a smiling Derek Whitehead stands behind the Challenge Cup following Warrington's win over holders Featherstone Rovers.

Derek Whitehead, about to kick the ball into touch during a League fixture for Warrington.

187

MICHAEL WITHERS (BRADFORD BULLS)
Harry Sunderland Trophy winner 2001

=== PROFILE ===

Hailing from the Sydney suburb of Penrith, Michael Withers began his career with the Penrith Juniors team, being Australian Junior Player of the Year in 1994. He played for Balmain Tigers (1995-98) before his acquisition by Bradford Bulls in November 1998 brought him fame in British Rugby League, following his debut in 1999. The strong running centre or full back, is nicknamed 'The Ghost' due to his ability to appear, as if from nowhere, to support a break, usually resulting in a try. He was in the team that won the World Club Challenge (2002 and 2004), and appeared in five Super League Grand Finals (winning in 2001 and 2003) and two Challenge Cup Finals (winning in 2000). He missed the 2003 Challenge Cup success in a campaign where he was mostly sidelined through injury. Due to the ancestral rule, he played four times for Ireland during the 2000 World Cup.

Bradford Bulls full-back Michael Withers (aka 'The Ghost') helped his club lay their own 'ghost' to rest in the 2001 Super League Grand Final during an emphatic 37-6 win over Wigan Warriors, the Bulls having failed to win any end of season prizes (Grand Final or Premiership Trophy) in the opening five Super League campaigns despite being a major contender.

Withers was the first player to complete a try hat-trick in the Grand Final. His triple came during a 20-minute period midway through the first half as Bradford – and Withers – ran hot in establishing an untouchable 26-0 interval lead, hooker James Lowes having dived over from dummy-half for the opener in the 9th minute. Withers' first effort came two minutes later, escaping the clutches of two defenders as he shot over from acting half-back after Henry Paul made a terrific run which covered half the length of the field. In the 27th minute, Withers went under the posts for his second, having supported another break, this time from Scott Naylor and Tevita Vaikona, completing his set four minutes later, backing up a move by Henry Paul, Robbie Paul and Stuart Fielden. Withers – originally a centre who took over as full-back earlier that season when Stuart Spruce was

injured – also stood out in saving his line three times as Wigan tried to exert pressure in the second half.

Despite an outstanding performance, earning him 15 of the 29 votes, Withers just got the verdict two ahead of Henry Paul, who landed six goals in his farewell match, prior to switching to Rugby Union.

Super League Grand Final 2001
Saturday 13 October at Old Trafford, Manchester
Bradford Bulls 37
Withers (3 tries), Vaikona, Naylor, Mackay (try, goal), Pryce, H Paul (5 goals, drop-goal), R Paul (captain), Vagana, Lowes (try), McDermott, Gartner, Peacock, Forshaw. Substitutes: Fielden (try), Anderson, Rigon, Deacon.
Wigan Warriors 6
Radlinski, Dallas, Connolly, Renouf, Carney, Johns, Lam (try), O'Connor, Newton, Howard, Cassidy, Furner (goal), Farrell (captain). Substitutes: P Johnson, Cowie, Betts, Chester.
Half-time: 26-0. Referee: S Cummings (Widnes). Attendance: 60,164.

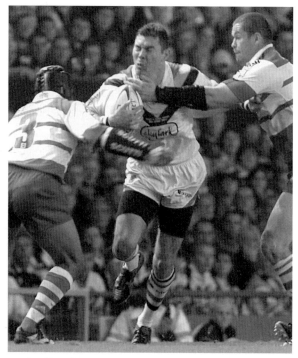

Michael Withers – giving a man of the match performance for Bradford Bulls in the 2001 Super League Grand Final against Wigan Warriors.

APPENDIX 1. THE ROLL OF HONOUR

Year	Lance Todd Trophy	Harry Sunderland Trophy	Man of Steel
1946	Billy Stott (Wakefield T)		
1947	Willie Davies (Bradford N)		
1948	Frank Whitcombe (Bradford N)		
1949	Ernest Ward (Bradford N)		
1950	Gerry Helme (Warrington)		
1951	Cec Mountford (Wigan)		
1952	Billy Ivison (Workington T)		
1953	Peter Ramsden (Huddersfield)		
1954	Gerry Helme (Warrington)		
1955	Jack Grundy (Barrow)		
1956	Alan Prescott (St Helens)		
1957	Jeff Stevenson (Leeds)		
1958	Rees Thomas (Wigan)		
1959	Brian McTigue (Wigan)		
1960	Tommy Harris (Hull)		
1961	Dick Huddart (St Helens)		
1962	Neil Fox (Wakefield T)		
1963	Harold Poynton (Wakefield T)		
1964	Frank Collier (Widnes)		
1965	Ray Ashby (Wigan) and Brian Gabbitas (Hunslet)	Terry Fogerty (Halifax)	
1966	Len Killeen (St Helens)	Albert Halsall (St Helens)	
1967	Carl Dooler (Featherstone R)	Ray Owen (Wakefield T)	
1968	Don Fox (Wakefield T)	Gary Cooper (Wakefield T)	
1969	Malcolm Reilly (Castleford)	Bev Risman (Leeds)	
1970	Bill Kirkbride (Castleford)	Frank Myler (St Helens)	
1971	Alex Murphy (Leigh)	Bill Ashurst (Wigan)	
1972	Kel Coslett (St Helens)	Terry Clawson (Leeds)	
1973	Steve Nash (Featherstone R)	Mick Stephenson (Dewsbury)	
1974	Derek Whitehead (Warrington)	Barry Philbin (Warrington)	
1975	Ray Dutton (Widnes)	Mel Mason (Leeds)	
1976	Geoff Pimblett (St Helens)	George Nicholls (St Helens)	
1977	Steve Pitchford (Leeds)	Geoff Pimblett (St Helens)	David Ward (Leeds)
1978	George Nicholls (St Helens)	Bob Haigh (Bradford N)	George Nicholls (St Helens)
1979	David Topliss (Wakefield T)	Kevin Dick (Leeds)	Doug Laughton (Widnes)
1980	Brian Lockwood (Hull KR)	Mal Aspey (Widnes)	George Fairbairn (Wigan)
1981	Mick Burke (Widnes)	Len Casey (Hull KR)	Ken Kelly (Warrington)
1982	Eddie Cunningham (Widnes)	Mick Burke (Widnes)	Mick Morgan (Carlisle)
1983	David Hobbs (Featherstone R)	Tony Myler (Widnes)	Allan Agar (Featherstone R)
1984	Joe Lydon (Widnes)	John Dorahy (Hull KR)	Joe Lydon (Widnes)
1985	Brett Kenny (Wigan)	Harry Pinner (St Helens)	Ellery Hanley (Bradford N)
1986	Bob Beardmore (Castleford)	Les Boyd (Warrington)	Gavin Miller (Hull KR)
1987	Graham Eadie (Halifax)	Joe Lydon (Wigan)	Ellery Hanley (Wigan)
1988	Andy Gregory (Wigan)	David Hulme (Widnes)	Martin Offiah (Widnes)
1989	Ellery Hanley (Wigan)	Alan Tait (Widnes)	Ellery Hanley (Wigan)
1990	Andy Gregory (Wigan)	Alan Tait (Widnes)	Shaun Edwards (Wigan)
1991	Denis Betts (Wigan)	Greg Mackey (Hull)	Garry Schofield (Leeds)
1992	Martin Offiah (Wigan)	Andy Platt (Wigan)	Dean Bell (Wigan)
1993	Dean Bell (Wigan)	Chris Joynt (St Helens)	Andy Platt (Wigan)
1994	Martin Offiah (Wigan)	Sam Panapa (Wigan)	Jonathan Davies (Warrington)
1995	Jason Robinson (Wigan)	Kris Radlinski (Wigan)	Denis Betts (Wigan)
1996	Robbie Paul (Bradford B)	Andrew Farrell (Wigan)	Andrew Farrell (Wigan)
1997	Tommy Martyn (St Helens)	Andrew Farrell (Wigan W)	James Lowes (Bradford B)
1998	Mark Aston (Sheffield E)	Jason Robinson (Wigan W)	Iestyn Harris (Leeds R)
1999	Leroy Rivett (Leeds R)	Henry Paul (Bradford B)	Adrian Vowles (Castleford T)
2000	Henry Paul (Bradford B)	Chris Joynt (St Helens)	Sean Long (St Helens)
2001	Sean Long (St Helens)	Michael Withers (Bradford B)	Paul Sculthorpe (St Helens)
2002	Kris Radlinski (Wigan W)	Paul Deacon (Bradford B)	Paul Sculthorpe (St Helens)
2003	Gary Connolly (Leeds R)	Stuart Reardon (Bradford B)	Jamie Peacock (Bradford B)
2004	Sean Long (St Helens)	Matt Diskin (Leeds R)	Andrew Farrell (Wigan W)
2005	Kevin Sinfield (Leeds R)		

APPENDIX 2. FACTS AND FIGURES
LANCE TODD TROPHY

Up to and including 2005, the Lance Todd Trophy has been won 61 times.

Four players have won the Lance Todd Trophy twice: Gerry Helme (1950, 1954), Andy Gregory (1988, 1990), Martin Offiah (1992, 1994), Sean Long (2001, 2004).

Two players have won the Lance Todd Trophy (LT), the Harry Sunderland Trophy (HS) and the Man of Steel Award (MoS): George Nicholls (HS 1976, LT 1978, MoS 1978), Joe Lydon (LT 1984, MoS 1984, HS 1987).

Five players have won the Lance Todd Trophy and the Harry Sunderland Trophy: Geoff Pimblett (LT 1976, HS 1977), Mick Burke (LT 1981, HS 1982), Jason Robinson (LT 1995, HS 1998), Henry Paul (HS 1999, LT 2000), Kris Radlinski (HS 1995, LT 2002).

Five players have won the Lance Todd Trophy and the Man of Steel Award: Ellery Hanley (MoS 1985, 1987, 1989, LT 1989), Martin Offiah (MoS 1988, LT 1992, 1994), Dean Bell (MoS 1992, LT 1993), Denis Betts (LT 1991, MoS 1995), Sean Long (MoS 2000, LT 2001, 2004).

The winners of the Lance Todd Trophy and Harry Sunderland Trophy have been provided by the same club eight times: Wigan (1992, 1994, 1995), St Helens (1966, 1976), Wakefield Trinity (1968), Warrington (1974), Widnes (1982).

The winners of the Lance Todd Trophy, Harry Sunderland Trophy and Man of Steel Award have been provided by the same club twice: Wigan (1992, 1995).

The Lance Todd Trophy has been shared once: Ray Ashby and Brian Gabbitas (1965).

The Lance Todd Trophy has been won eleven times by a team captain: Billy Stott (1946), Ernest Ward (1949), Cec Mountford (1951), Alan Prescott (1956), Alex Murphy (1971), Kel Coslett (1972), David Topliss (1979), Ellery Hanley (1989), Dean Bell (1993), Robbie Paul (1996), Kevin Sinfield (2005).

The Lance Todd Trophy has been won nine times by a player from the losing team: Frank Whitcombe (1948), Tommy Harris (1960), Brian Gabbitas (1965), Don Fox (1968), George Nicholls (1978), David Topliss (1979), Robbie Paul (1996), Gary Connolly (2003), Kevin Sinfield (2005). (Eddie Cunningham received the award following the 1982 drawn finally, subsequently losing the replay.)

The youngest player to win the Lance Todd Trophy is Peter Ramsden – aged 19 years exactly (1953).

The oldest player to win the Lance Todd Trophy is Frank Whitcombe – aged 34 years, 337 days (1948).

Breakdown of Lance Todd Trophy wins by club:
14 Wigan/Wigan Warriors
9 St Helens
5 Bradford Northern/Bradford Bulls, Leeds/Leeds Rhinos, Wakefield Trinity, Widnes
3 Castleford, Featherstone Rovers, Warrington
1 Barrow, Halifax, Huddersfield, Hull, Hull Kingston Rovers, Hunslet, Leigh, Sheffield Eagles, Workington Town.

Breakdown of Lance Todd Trophy wins by position:
14 scrum half
10 stand-off half
8 full-back
7 second-row forward
6 prop forward
5 wing three-quarter, centre three-quarter, loose forward
1 hooker.

Breakdown of Lance Todd Trophy wins by birthplace:
8 Wigan (includes two players with two wins each)
7 St Helens
5 Leeds
3 Leigh (includes one player with two wins), Sharlston, Widnes
2 Allerton-Bywater, Castleford, Featherstone, London (includes one player with two wins), Wakefield, Sydney (Australia), Tokoroa (New Zealand)
1 Aberavon, Cardiff, Crumlin, Dewsbury, Flimby, Hemsworth, Hensingham, Huddersfield, Leicester, Maesteg, Oldham, Penclawdd, Salford, Swinton, Workington, Auckland (New Zealand), Blackball (New Zealand), Port Elizabeth (South Africa).

Breakdown of Lance Todd Trophy wins by nationality:
49 England (includes four players with two wins each)
5 Wales
4 New Zealand
2 Australia
1 South Africa

APPENDIX 3. FACTS AND FIGURES
HARRY SUNDERLAND TROPHY

Up to and including 2004, the Harry Sunderland Trophy has been won 40 times.

Three players have won the Harry Sunderland Trophy twice: Alan Tait (1989, 1990), Andrew Farrell (1996, 1997), Chris Joynt (1993, 2000).

Two players have won the Harry Sunderland Trophy (HS) and the Man of Steel Award (MoS): Andy Platt (HS 1992, MoS 1993), Andrew Farrell (HS 1996, 1997, MoS 1996, 2004)

The Harry Sunderland Trophy has been won nine times by a team captain: Mick Stephenson (1973), Bob Haigh (1978), Len Casey (1981), Harry Pinner (1985), Les Boyd (1986), Greg Mackey (1991), Andrew Farrell (1996 and 1997), Chris Joynt (2000).

The Harry Sunderland Trophy has been won three times by a player from the losing team: Bill Ashurst (1971), Henry Paul (1999), Paul Deacon (2002).

The youngest player to win the Harry Sunderland Trophy is Kris Radlinski – aged 19 years, 42 days (1995).

The oldest player to win the Harry Sunderland Trophy is Bob Haigh – aged 34 years, 190 days (1978).

Breakdown of Harry Sunderland Trophy wins by club:
8 Wigan/Wigan Warriors
7 St Helens
6 Widnes
5 Bradford Northern/Bradford Bulls, Leeds/Leeds Rhinos
2 Hull Kingston Rovers, Wakefield Trinity, Warrington
1 Dewsbury, Halifax, Hull.

Breakdown of Harry Sunderland Trophy wins by position:
8 full-back
7 stand-off half
6 second-row forward
5 loose forward
4 prop forward
3 centre three-quarter, scum half
2 wing three-quarter, hooker.

Breakdown of Harry Sunderland Trophy wins by birthplace:
9 Wigan (includes two players with two wins each)
6 Widnes
4 St Helens
3 Sydney (Australia)
2 Dewsbury, Featherstone, Kelso (includes one player with two wins), Leeds
1 Billinge, Bradford, Glossop, Hull, Normanton, Salford, Wakefield, Auckland (New Zealand), Nyngan (Australia), Tokoroa (New Zealand).

Breakdown of Harry Sunderland Trophy wins by nationality:
32 England (includes two players with two wins each)
4 Australia
2 Scotland (includes one player with two wins), New Zealand.

APPENDIX 4. FACTS AND FIGURES
MAN OF STEEL AWARD

Up to and including 2004, the Man of Steel Award has been won 28 times.

One player has won the Man of Steel Award three times: Ellery Hanley (1985, 1987, 1989).

Two players have won the Man of Steel Award twice: Andrew Farrell (1996, 2004), Paul Sculthorpe (2001, 2002).

Eleven players have completed the 'double' of Man of Steel Award and First Division/Super League Player of the Year Award: George Nicholls (1978), Ken Kelly (1981), Joe Lydon (1984), Ellery Hanley (1985), Gavin Miller (1986), Jonathan Davies (1994), James Lowes (1997), Iestyn Harris (1998), Paul Sculthorpe (2001), Jamie Peacock (2003), Andrew Farrell (2004).

The youngest person to win the Man of Steel Award is Joe Lydon – aged 20 years, 165 days on the day of presentation (1984).

The oldest person to win the Man of Steel Award is Doug Laughton – aged 35 years, 3 days on the day of presentation (1979).

Breakdown of Man of Steel Award wins by club:
9 Wigan/Wigan Warriors
4 St Helens
3 Bradford Northern/Bradford Bulls, Leeds/Leeds Rhinos, Widnes/Widnes Vikings
2 Warrington
1 Carlisle, Castleford Tigers, Featherstone Rovers, Hull Kingston Rovers.

Breakdown of Man of Steel Award wins by position (based on position occupied most during the season):
6 stand-off half, loose forward
4 second-row forward
3 centre three-quarter
2 full-back, prop forward, hooker
1 wing three-quarter, scrum half.
(In addition, coach Allan Agar won in 1983).

Breakdown of Man of Steel Award wins by birthplace:
6 Leeds (includes one player with three wins)
5 Wigan (includes one player with two wins)
3 Oldham (includes one player with two wins)
2 Featherstone, Widnes
1 Billinge, Llanelli, London, Morley, Peebles, St Helens, Salford, Auckland (New Zealand), Inverell (Australia), Cunnamulla (Australia).

Breakdown of Man of Steel Award wins by nationality:
23 England (includes two players with two wins each and one player with three wins)
2 Australia
1 New Zealand, Scotland, Wales

Most wins in other award categories:
First Division/Super League (°) Player of the Year:
2 by Mick Adams (1979, 1980) and Jonathan Davies (1991, 1994).

Second Division/First Division (°) Player of the Year:
John Woods (1978, 1990).

Third Division/Second Division (°) Player of the Year:
No player has won this category more than once.

Young Player of the Year:
3 by Shaun Edwards (1986, 1987, 1988).

Coach of the Year:
4 by John Monie (1990, 1991, 1992, 1993).

Referee of the Year:
6 by Russell Smith (1995, 1997, 1998, 2000, 2001, 2002).

(° From 1996 the First Division was renamed Super League and the former Second Division became the new First Division. A Third Division operated in 1992 and 1993, a third tier being reintroduced in 1997 as the new Second Division. From 1998 onward, the awards ceremony was for Super League only, the lower (National League) divisions now having their own awards evening.)